Little
Billy Tallon
by Ty Munroe

The plot line about Timothy is imagined but most other
events and conversations are taken from real life, but are not
in chronological order and are not necessarily from the same
year. The descriptions of the working practises and the
working environment are authentic.

IN MEMORY OF MY FATHER

OUR FACE IS OUR ULTIMATE
IDENTITY.
IT'S WHAT MAKES US HUMAN.

INTRODUCTION

This book is about William Tallon. You will probably recognise him as the chap in the black tailcoat and white bow tie standing next to the Queen Mother on Her Majesty's birthday outside Clarence House in London. He worked for the Queen Mother as a page, which is like a butler and personal assistant but in the context of a royal residence. His ancient job title was 'Steward and Page of the Backstairs' but the British press invariably referred to him as, 'Backstairs Billy, a shopkeeper's son from Coventry.' Apparently, they thought the town where he grew up was relevant in some way to the fact he worked and lived in London?

In all, he worked for just over 50 years for her, but William wasn't required around her the last few weeks of her life, which must have tormented him for the rest of his days, but he probably only had himself to blame.

He didn't talk to the press. That may be why they seemed to resent him. Perhaps they thought, 'Who was this mysterious bouffant-haired, velvet-lapelled tailcoat, medal wearing courtier who swans around the Queen Mother on her birthday appearances?' He used to stage manage things somewhat by nipping outside on the morning of the birthdays several times at least before Queen Elizabeth appeared, to check on the mood of the crowd and to see who was about or who wanted to present a gift to her. It seemed to make everyone happy, staff, police, press, the crowds, even unaware passing tourists.

I really think that he started it for Queen Elizabeth's sake to begin with when a handful of people congregated and waited along Stable Yard one year (that's the road alongside Clarence House where everyone gathered. It was open to the public in those days so you could walk through). William told me he once suggested to Queen Elizabeth to perhaps go out on the balcony to be able to see some well-wishers waiting outside. She did go out and she acknowledged them, and so year on year the number of people grew and so it became a tradition and a big occasion attracting thousands of people and press and news teams from all over the world. By this time Queen Elizabeth no longer waved from the balcony but stepped outside the house to meet people in person. This brought worry for her as she became older with the enormous crowds, but she always coped very well. William seemed to enjoy his little bit of the limelight being part of the celebrations and the adulation, shaking hands and posing for photographs before Queen Elizabeth came out but he would decline to be questioned about her in any personal way. He was in attendance when the big black garden gates eventually opened and she appeared and stepped out to greet the waiting crowd, but he would return with Her Majesty behind the big black gates to the protection and privacy of Clarence House as soon as it was over, after all, he still had his job to do. Clarence House was his life.

It is true that Queen Elizabeth employed an unusual, flamboyant, maverick character in William Tallon. At the height of his career he was 'Steward & Page of the Backstairs' to Her Majesty, and he always appeared in his impressive uniform by her side on her birthday for the world's press. An occasion that has been described as 'The Billy Tallon roadshow'. Perhaps that's how most people recognise him, but there was more to him than that because he was real, he didn't just exist on t.v. or in print.

It was thought that he practically ran the place. He could certainly use his perceived closeness to the Queen Mother to manipulate a situation or to garner favours or requests. He

2

was regarded by some to be, "The Queen Mother's favourite servant and confidant" but nobody had the right to say that except for Queen Elizabeth. She must have confided in her page at times and no doubt he was discreet about it, as is expected as part of the job of being a good page or butler, and of course William was a good page. However, he had a reputation for being domineering and tricky at times with his colleagues.

As a faithful old retainer of several decades he always had the upper hand with the other staff, and it was always assumed he could secretly sweetly whisper into the ear of royalty to his own advantage.

He could be described as a charming, sophisticated, fascinating raconteur. Yet he could also be described as other things by different people but really, he was a straightforward simple man, who made the best out of what little he had in his life and someone who was determined to enjoy his life.

As the personal page to the last empress of India he enjoyed the high life, drinking Her Majesty's champagne and cavorting and joking with the guests, paying no or little attention to protocol either inside or outside palace walls. He loved it. He may have thought he was invincible but of course he was not, he was just a boy from Newcastle.

Most people in this country drink, some to excess. There is a black sheep on the farm in every household and William was the one there, he drank too much it's true. Although he gave it up for Lent sometimes, he really did. "Would you taste the wine for me, I've given it up for Lent?" he would say. Heard for the first time you would be forgiven for thinking it was his idea of a joke, but he was being completely sincere. Perhaps to preserve his liver, perhaps for religious reasons? He was a much quieter person at that time as you can imagine, and there could hardly be others behaving like him living under the same roof, as that would be ridiculous. It would cause competition and trouble. There was only enough room in the house for one William but yes, I would say that he was an alcoholic.

'Backstairs Billy' was his nickname contrived by the press and used by them in a disparaging manner. They hounded him when Queen Elizabeth died, and he retired. Not as bad as they hounded Princess Diana but same old thing. He never spoke to the press or gave anyone a proper interview, apart from a sentimental passing remark to a television crew on The Mall one day when she died, saying that he loved her. He kept his word to the end. He never gave in. He never sold out to the press despite their compelling attempts to persuade him over the years. He kept his word to the last. Due to this seemingly reluctance to co-operate with the press, 'Backstairs Billy' seems to have become a caricature of himself and has been cast out into the historic wilderness. This is what you get if you lightly court the press. You should be either in or out. Only enjoying the limelight is not allowed it would seem.

Clarence House is an important little house.

The Prince of Wales lives there today. It is attached to St. James's Palace where the Prince used to reside, (in York House) until the prince's household moved to Clarence House when Queen Elizabeth died. Apparently, the Prince intends to stay there when he becomes King, in the same way that King William IV remained there rather than moving to Buckingham Palace, so by making Clarence House the centre of Court.

When Princess Elizabeth became The Queen in 1952, she and the Duke of Edinburgh had to leave their home Clarence House, to move over the road into Buckingham Palace.

Her mother was now known as Queen Elizabeth the

Queen Mother to make it easier to distinguish between the two Queen Elizabeths.

The Queen Mother and the The Princess Margaret left Buckingham Palace and moved over the road into 'the little house on The Mall' the following year, only when some minor refurbishments had been completed. In effect they swoppped houses!

Clarence House was now the official residence of the Queen Mother where she hosted receptions, luncheons, dinners and parties for official and private guests.

They have lunch under the massive plane trees in the garden, in summer. The branches are never trimmed so have grown so they brush the ground, creating a large grotto-like space underneath that can easily accommodate a long Edwardian dining table and Chippendale chairs set up in there on the grass, served and waited on by scarlet-liveried footmen. It's like something out of Peter Pan!

William lived in a small lodge just outside the gates on The Mall.

In the headlines and reports in the press over the years, the insidious repetitive references to the words 'gin' and 'champagne' linked with the words 'The Queen Mother' resulted in Clarence House acquiring the unfortunate reputation of being a 'gin palace', as the papers called it. Where everyone there, it has to be surmised including Queen Elizabeth apparently drank copious amounts of alcohol or rather, gin. This would include the teetotallers presumably?

Even today these references are tagged in articles and books written about the Queen Mother. Proof indeed that wordplay and word of mouth goes on to produce enduring myths and fallacies through the power of language.

This was due to the same old headlines being churned

out whenever anybody happened to be holding a glass or Queen Elizabeth was presented with a bottle of champagne. So, for people in the know it all soon became a tiresome cliché. You don't see similar headlines about Formula 1 racing drivers and champagne, do you?

The point that was being missed by the headline writers was that Queen Elizabeth came from a social set. The fashionable set of the 1920s and 1930s where taking an aperitif and then a glass of wine with lunch or dinner was de rigueur. If you think of your older relatives here, you should be able to appreciate how people get set in their ways as they get older. This is the same sort of thing. There was no binge drinking going on and no one was rolling around the floor drunk. No one was drunk. Some people were having an alcoholic drink before their meal and then a different kind of alcoholic drink with their meal at the dining table, simple as that. Some people there didn't drink at all.

I'm not talking about the staff bedrooms or William's little house here of course as that's a private and separate matter, nor should anyone assume anything either as some of the staff were teetotallers. It should be understood that mostly a staff member's bedroom is their only place of habitat. It's their 'house' in effect as it's the only private accommodation they have. It's their 'world'. So, if they are going to have a drink or a friend round to join them, why on earth wouldn't they do it in their own room when off duty?

Please don't be taken in by that old adage, 'If you read it in the papers then it must be true.' Or, 'There must be some truth in it, at least.' Really? Think about that now. Some? Least? True? Do you want to live in a society where you are expected to believe everything the headline writers want to tell you, or would you prefer to find out things for yourself by reading the small print from a more reliable source?

I lived and worked in Clarence House as a footman and William was my immediate boss, so I worked with him

INTRODUCTION

closely for some years. He was a dictator but that didn't stop him from being a funny, mysterious, fascinating character.

The story of William Tallon's relationship with Queen Elizabeth seems misinterpreted to me. I feel it should not be denounced and neatly wrapped up in a tabloid package and discarded into the mists of social history, leaving William's reputation undeservedly tarnished and unresolved, and by association Her Majesty, Queen Elizabeth's too. I can offer a personal insight into the reality of William's life there and I feel it is important to do so, because there is no excuse in this digital age to not record what we know in order for it to be referenced in the future, so that it may be regarded and trusted as a more reliable source than that which may appear in a newspaper, or by historians or even by heresay.

Also, the memory of Queen Elizabeth deserves more respect, and we deserve more respect for ourselves. Unfortunately, respect lives next door to privacy these days on a remote unreachable island somewhere in the middle of the seas. It retired there when it became apparent it has no monetary value so must be considered worthless.

Her Majesty, Queen Elizabeth The Queen Mother was a very special person, an exceptional person indeed. It has to be said that by any standards the Queen Mother could be regarded as having a charmed idyllic life. By no means is this a romantic point of view in a sentimental or sycophantic way as the facts are there to see plain and simple: born into a wealthy loving family of nobility and growing up in privileged, luxurious, secure surroundings including servants and private tutors and even a dance teacher, (but perhaps that's not so significant because it was the culture for young adults to be tutored to dance up until the 1950s). Even so, this is truly exceptional having all these components of an ideal life brought together simultaneously. Some people may have the good fortune of being born into a privileged lifestyle but not necessarily lucky enough for it to be accompanied by a loving family. This sort of grounding would enable a person to flourish and to be able to become successful in life, (if they happen to be discerning and resolute enough to take advantage of such nurturing). At any rate it's certainly not considered to be a disadvantage. And such an assured yet sheltered upbringing would fill anybody with an abundance of self-confidence and contentment; despite there being a likelihood of it producing a false sense of life and enforcing a restricted point of view of the world upon that person.

This sublime existence was marred by tragedy all too soon however, when she lost a brother in the First World War and later in mid-life, she lost the King her husband. So very sadly these tragedies also befell on so many sisters and mothers and wives and loves of the same generation unfortunately.

She married a prince into the royal family and became a royal duchess then subsequently a queen and an empress. When her daughter became Queen, she became the Queen Mother.

Whether or not you believe in Darwin's theory of survival through adaptation, (The Origin Of Species) and taking into account the influence of pure chance of fate; it is inevitable some human beings on this planet will rise above the masses of other billions of human beings to be regarded as extraordinary, or to flourish and easily excel within their social spheres to go on to lead incredible, exceptional lives. These people seem to be forces of nature, having a sense of destiny. Queen Elizabeth was such a person in both regards.

Queen Elizabeth lived a remarkable life. Her image and purpose changed and transformed dramatically through it. The papers and media had no precedent for this. There was no label printed out for their pigeonholes; so, with a lack of imagination she was easily dropped into a default 'drunken granny' bracket or category of theirs. What seemed to be overlooked by the tabloids and the media was the fact that she was this country's Queen through the Second World War. The same person who so lifted the spirits of the people of Britain and the Commonwealth, when the Allied Forces were fighting Hitler and the Nazis!

Hitler is said to have called her, "The most dangerous woman in Europe", but even if this was propaganda, we are talking about Queen Elizabeth and yet, this was the same person whom the press and media ridiculed?

Queen Elizabeth was always recognisable to people all over the world. Firstly, she was recognised as a Queen and later in life by the way she dressed. Her hats became a sort of individual trademark style of her own coupled with her compact stature. I think at this point people, especially young people, regarded her as being only the mother of The Queen and they didn't realise her role in society before. Her identity had succumbed to the human trait of confining an image of somebody into a stereotype in order to define them. She was defined by her image at this stage rather than her face. We humans have the instinct to use our faces as identification, especially at close inspection, and these days it has become the preoccupation of people to take pictures of others but mostly to take pictures (selfies) of themselves. Now that we have the internet and digital photography, there is nowhere on the planet a person can be truly private, because our face will always give us away.

The singers Madonna and David Bowie were celebrated whenever they 'reinvented' themselves. Queen Elizabeth didn't ever 'reinvent herself', she just simply changed her style in accordance with the times she was living in; but some people reinvented their personas after the Second World War as it was easy to do at such a time. They did it out of necessity to cleanse their past or to make a new life somewhere else, although they had to be prepared to start over if they did so. They could just change their names or adjust their personal history, or they could even pretend to be someone else completely by taking on a dead person's identity. Electronic identities didn't exist then as information was kept on paper and so records were not so easily traced. Documents were often lost in bomb raids and fires, so they could be blamed as an excuse for lost information and so the opportunities to create false identities and to disappear were available. These days people can change their personas by changing their name or the way they speak or dress, but they can't change their I.D. that easily.

As a footnote, besides from all this I know of no one else who is regarded as being so Scottish who was actually born in England? This must show the great admiration and respect people have for her. It must also show the same respect the Queen Mother had for Scotland.

Writing down my memories within a typical account of life there over the birthdays and working with William answers the first question people always ask me with glee when finding out I worked for the Queen Mother, which is: "What was it like to work there and was Billy as bad as they say?"

It sets out to create a real life, time capsule of how it was to work there with William and others by bringing their voices alive using first-hand experience of our conversations and events that happened to me.

I hope you will find it entertaining, informative, and in some ways enlightening.

If I may be permitted to quote the sublime 'Morecambe & Wise' here, when Eric Morecambe said,

"I'm playing all the right notes, but not necessarily in the right order." In that respect the same could be said for this performance of a concerto of conversations written down. You should get a really good sense of what it was like to work there with William and the others.

The plot line about Timothy is imagined (sort of; remember the Prince Philip/The Queen's Tupperware affair?) but most other events and some conversations are taken from real life but not fully in chronological order. The descriptions of the working practices and the working environment are authentic.

Come away now, and I'll let you take at look at what's going on inside Clarence House, with William at least. Bring a drink if you wish; hopefully you won't get a reputation for it. You can be 'a fly on the wall' moving from room to room seeing what's going on at different times of the day, mostly in the pantry and equerry's office to begin with and later you will find out what happens to William in his retirement.

My narrative is set at an important time in William's life, the shining accolade of his career you might say, standing behind Queen Elizabeth on her one hundredth birthday, but it will turn out to be the hardest time of his life due to unfolding events. William has been in a tricky mood leading up to the birthday. Colleagues have been creeping around him not wanting to provoke his volatile state. His is normally cheerful and quite steady but he's been rather tense lately due to the anticipation of the big day and other things going on in his life.

Outside the house masses of crowds are gathering along The Mall. Inside, William and the staff are preparing for the big birthday celebrations. This should be the pinnacle of William's career but his life-long partner and work associate Reg Wilcock becomes very ill suddenly. All this, and having to quickly train up a handsome new footman for Scotland, deal with the crowds and gifts and flowers and the birthday celebrations and of course the most glamourous of annual occasions, when he and Reg serve dinner in the royal box at the ballet at the Royal Opera House (Reg was 'Deputy

Steward & Page of the Presence'). There are still all the usual day-to-day duties to attend to for them, including planning for the annual three-month summer trip to Scotland. William works half the Scottish trip with his team and Reg does the other half respectively. Reg can remember special times in the 1950s when he worked in Paris for the Duke and Duchess of Windsor and he seems to want to talk about it and revisit those happy memories of his youth, but William is more engrossed with the details for the dinner at the Royal Opera House on the evening of the birthday.

It's then up to Scotland where William pours out the drinks and pours out his heart.

It begins with Reg meeting William and his new millionaire friend after a theatre show. They go off to party all night. The next day we meet Jason, the head footman, who comes in with a bad hangover. The new footman is driving him crazy with his incessant stupid questions, (which is quite normal for a newbie), as he's finding it difficult to fit in to such an old-fashioned and competitively camp environment, as there is no formal training so the place is run under its own rules. They set up lunch in the garden. Then William starts playing his silly games.

LONDON, AUGUST 2000, 2 DAYS BEFORE QUEEN ELIZABETH, THE QUEEN MOTHER'S 100TH BIRTHDAY.

SUMMER NIGHTS IN THE CITY

People are spilling out of the theatre doors onto the sticky hot streets of London's West End, yet the foyer is still almost packed with bodies standing and milling around. Some of them are considering whether to go on somewhere else to prolong the evening or to begin their journey home. Others are lingering over a deliciously cold cocktail or drink, or ones like William, who are simply soaking up the charged atmosphere while observing the people around him, and savouring the soothing buzz you get just from being in the middle of a big city on a hot summer night. William is wearing lightweight smart trousers with a slightly blingy buckle, posh loafers and a snazzy long-sleeved shirt and, as ever, his rose gold signet bracelet on his left wrist. Reg is waiting next to him, but even having changed into linen trousers and shirt after finishing work at Clarence House half an hour ago, he can not seem to cool down. The sweat from his brow is constantly dripping and he wonders if it was such a good idea after all, to walk up the hill to the theatre in the centre of London on this sweltering summer evening to meet William and his new friend after the show, even though it's just a short distance from the house. He just wants to quickly meet her, have a glass of champagne and get into a taxi with William and go home, but as he is standing there regularly mopping his bald head with a handkerchief, a man on his way back from the bar bumps into him and spills his drink.

"Oh look!" the man says recognising them instantly although he is a complete stranger. "It's Billy Tallon and his little friend what's his name? Come out to the theatre for the evening, have you? Must be nice for you to get out, so to speak. Did the Queen Mum put herself to bed did she, or have you got to rush back and tuck her in?"

"Excuse me?" blurts out Reg, realising the man is obviously drunk.

"Leaving the poor old Queen Mum all alone in Clarence House on her hundredth birthday," the man says without any sense of formality.

"For your information," Reg starts, "Her Majesty's hundredth birthday is the day after tomorrow!"

Reg is a big tall man and even at the age of sixty-six he is a force to be reckoned with, especially with that deep booming Yorkshire voice of his.

"Have you tucked her up in bed already?" the man continues unabashed. "Give her a gin did you? Give her a hot water bottle and tuck her in did you?"

Reg tries to give this idiot short shrift by saying curtly,

"Do you mind?" in a very loud and grandiose manner with his deepest, richest voice, but the man is oblivious to any subtleties Reg may have to offer. Especially when waving his handkerchief towards this bloke makes Reg look like a Georgian fop trying to flick away a fly.

William seems to have not even noticed the man as his eyes continue to systematically search and scan everybody coming through to the foyer from the street, the auditorium and cloakrooms looking for the return of his friend. Unbeknown to anyone he is subtly and intensely listening to every word the man is saying, as he doesn't miss a trick. This is how he gleans a lot of information generally.

"House full of queens from what I heard," continues the man, "a den of iniquity, a house full of wicked old queens and bitches, although there are two less queens tonight of course 'cause you two are here. Got to mind yourself in that place eh? otherwise Billy might catch you unawares, and if Billy doesn't get you the booze will. You got to watch that Billy Tallon so they say, he's a right one. He runs that place. Got to watch yourself in that place eh? And all under the old Queen's nose."

Reg is incensed that he has to put up with this rude drunken man. Out of the blue, he hurls this tirade of insolent banter and nobody seems concerned at all. This sort of thing does happen occasionally, with irate members of the public berating a lowly member of the royal household staff for most of the historic woes of monarchy down the ages. In fact, sometimes, Reg quite welcomes it when he's in the mood for an altercation but not tonight, as tonight he is feeling a little unwell. It must appear as if they are having a friendly chat, amongst the condensed raucous noise of all the conversations in the foyer. He wishes he hadn't agreed to come. He really wants to go home now but he certainly isn't going to let this rude man get away with it. He intends to dismiss him ruthlessly with a verbal thrashing.

"Look you," Reg wags his finger over the man's head, but William interjects.

"Don't bother with him Reg," he says without even turning his head to look at them, not wanting to break the constant watch for his friend.

"I'm only having a laugh." The man seems more coherent now. "Thought you queens liked a joke, as well as a drink eh Billy? What is it? Free champagne? As much as you can drink is it, eh? And the poor old

Queen Mother pays the bill, or rather the taxpayer pays the bill more like? Well, I'm a taxpayer you know. Hey, tell you what, you can autograph our programme for us while you're here. Stay there and I'll fetch it. Stay there okay? My wife's over there somewhere."

The man turns away and goes to find his wife somewhere in the crowd, weaving through the strangers and stragglers on the foyer steps and around the bar, spilling some more of his drink as he goes. Reg glares after him with a venomous look, frustrated that his attempt to tell him off was thwarted by William's intervention. His gaze follows the man as he walks away and makes his way through the crowd. In a moment or two the man has disappeared.

"Who on earth was that moron?"

"No idea," replies William nonchalantly, still looking around for his friend, moving his head from left to right like a Meerkat. "Complete maniac."

"What was he going on about? What a prat!"

"He must have recognised us from one of the birthdays on the telly."

"So what? What an idiot. If that's the price you pay for appearing on television, you can keep it. God. And to think some people actually want to be a celebrity. Unbelievable?"

"Well, at least it's better than being totally ignored," says William. "Dillie darling!" he shouts, waving his arm in the air. "We're over here."

William waves frantically to his new friend Dillie, over the heads of people standing in front of him as he sees her approaching. She's been gone for ages and he's been wondering what she's been up to. He thinks she must have some dinner, or a party lined up somewhere possibly, as she always has done so far on their first few nights out together, and there are twelve of them in total in their party tonight including four of William's friends. Also, the three open-top American classic sports cars they were driven in here, have appeared again outside on the street, waiting to take them on to somewhere else, presumably. The shining, immaculate, stunningly colourful cars are also the reason for so many people hanging around. They have attracted a crowd of passers-by and admirers, and William is longing for the second the chauffeur opens the door for him to climb aboard again, to be driven away to appreciative cheers and applause from onlookers. Goodness, it's like being a film star, he thinks, Dillie is so generous, she pays for everything. William doesn't have the cash to be able to do the same, so he pays his way in another sense by supplying the gin and champagne and of course by providing the priceless cachet of a royal connection. William would love to be rich so he could play the gracious grand host, but he is far from rich. Being the Steward to Queen Elizabeth is the next best thing though, perhaps even better. William knows one of the cars is a Thunderbird, as it's the absolute classic of cars and Dillie told him the other one is a Mustang, but he's forgotten what the other one is, but it's as equally beautiful as the others. That is why he loves his new best friend so much as she is so glamourous but modest with it and so wonderfully quirky and let's face it — so rich!

A rather excited and animated Dillie approaches them. She and Reg air-kiss instinctively with a rather over dramatic "Mwah" each.

"Oh Reginald, I'm so sorry you couldn't see the show with us this evening, but I promise you and I will go out on the town one night to anything you want to see, and William can join us for dinner afterwards after his royal duties. I was telling him how I'm dying to get you both over to my place in Italy, our little estate by the sea. I can fly you there on our jet and you can have one of the villas. We have the whole hill overlooking the bay and our yacht, and you can walk to the village where there's a fabulous gelateria and bakery. I hope William's new beau will be able to come too, as there's plenty of room for him in one of the other villas on site if you like."

"New beau?" asks Reg, slightly puzzled.

Dillie gushes on, oblivious to her indiscreet revelations. She is as excited as William to have forged this new friendship for herself, especially with such a prestigious person as the Queen Mother's butler. None of her circle have ever had anything as special as that!

"I think it's wonderful of William to take him under his wing like that, such a lucky boy," she continues. "It will be such a boost to his career! I must say, that when William told me about his new footman having matinée idol looks, I didn't expect him to be so charming with it."

"I must have just said he reminded me of an actor I saw in a film once, that's all," chirps William, a little embarrassed.

"Are we talking about Timothy, at Clarence House?" asks Reg, still confused.

William quickly changes the subject as he can see Reg is surprised and intrigued.

"Now Reggie, I must show my new best friend one of my most treasured possessions."

William now has their full attention as he takes something from his trouser pocket. He moves like a professional magician performing tricks at a restaurant table. He adores having an audience to play to. He unwraps the object from a silk handkerchief.

"Now Dillie, close your eyes and hold out your hands," he says.

Dillie is already comfortable if not enamoured with William so she complies freely, closing her eyes and holding out her hands like children playing parlour games.

"Oh, what is it? It's not a mouse is it?"

"Don't be silly. Now, are you ready. Hold still and be

very careful, don't crush it. It's a precious jewel!"

"Ooh!" coos Dillie.

William carefully places the object onto Dillie's hands. "There. Now open your eyes."

"It's an egg!"

"It's a Fabergé egg," explains William.

"It's very small. Where's it from?"

"He laid it this morning!" quips Reg.

"Shush Reg, it's very precious, and the small ones must be more difficult to make."

"Where is it from?" enquires Dillie, looking up with joy into William's face.

"Well, we mustn't speak of such things," William pauses for a theatrical cough, "but let's just say that it was given to me, by a person or persons unknown for services rendered: also unknown!" He chuckles.

"Is that why it's so small then?"

"Reggie don't be silly."

William is in his element because he is the centre of attention and entertainment, and Reg is in good spirits making fun of him and Dillie seems happy too.

"Oh William. It's beautiful," as she admires the fantastic and rare tiny object she is holding so carefully. Then she says, "Is it stolen?"

"Of course not, it's mine!"

"But when Queen Elizabeth is gone and the shutters come down," says Reg "the papers will want to know why a shopkeeper's son from Coventry is keeping one of The Crown Jewels in his tiny London flat?"

"Except Reggie, that I am a Newcastle boy and my father was never a shopkeeper from Coventry, and it's got nothing to do with The Crown Jewels."

"Yes William. I know that. You know that. And now Dillie knows that, but do they?"

"Oh, you mean the backstairs Billy thing?" asks

19

Dillie.

"Sadly," says William earnestly. "The newspapers are this nation's conscience."

"Sadly," Reg concurs.

"But William, where do you keep it?" she asks him. "You mustn't walk around with it, you mustn't lose it. It must be very valuable."

"Don't worry, I keep it like all my things; very safely."

Dillie carefully hands back the egg and William deftly wraps it up again and places it back into his pocket.

"William, where does all this backstairs thing come from?" she enquires.

"The press like to have a handle on you in this country. It's their idea of keeping you down. The constant tapping of a drop of water on the forehead."

"And the mere fact that William hardly sets foot on the backstairs these days, or any stairs for that matter is irrelevant."

"Apart Reggie, from climbing the stairs to the page's room for my morning coffee with you when I've checked the flowers. It's my daily exercise you know. I have a bad leg."

"Oh, I see," says Dillie, in a somewhat sombre mood now.

"Now, enough of this nonsense," William says as he claps his hands in the air totally dispelling any signs of melancholy instantly. "Who want's a drink?"

"Hold that thought young man," says Dillie entering into the mood, "and I'll whisk us off to my hotel suite where a chef is waiting to cook us up a midnight feast. I've ordered Eggs Benedict for you William and lobster salad for me and whatever you fancy Reginald and there will be fireworks at midnight in a private garden! Excuse me a moment while I rustle up the others."

She shoots away and scouts around for her other guests

who have now seemingly completely dispersed. The cars outside have attracted an even larger crowd around them which has decanted the foyer of people, including the drunken man and his wife presumably. Reg turns to William.

"I want to go home William."

"What's the matter Reg, don't you like Dillie?"

"Yes of course I do, she's lovely."

"It's not about the new footman is it? I was only being flamboyant, you know me."

"No William. I'm tired and we've got so much to think about tomorrow."

"Oh Reg don't be a bore. Let's enjoy ourselves tonight we deserve it, and Dillie is such an angel arranging all this and inviting us on holiday."

"Oh William, why do you always do this? When will we ever get the time to go on holiday together? Don't be ridiculous. Either I'm on duty without you or you're on duty without me, or we are on duty together! It's impossible."

"I don't mean to go now. I mean sometime in the future."

"When in the future? We've been saying that for years, since I became a page in fact and it hasn't happened yet and it probably never will. We're lucky to get the weekends off when we do."

"Oh Reg don't."

"I'm just saying it's pointless making plans for something that may never happen."

William was dreading Reg would do this. He wanted them to stay out late and enjoy themselves tonight for a change, as they hardly went out together when Queen Elizabeth was in residence, but these days leading up to the centenary birthday was an exception. They were special and they should seize the opportunity

21

and indulge. William knew he would have to utilise all his little tricks to try to persuade Reg to come round, and he knew he didn't have the luxury of time to be subtle about it as they would have to leave the second Dillie had gathered everyone together, so he tries the sentimental blunt approach.

"Oh Reg, don't you realise what's happened to us? All these years at Clarence House doing endless lunches and parties and Scottish trips and everything. Look at us, we've made it! the Steward and the Page to Her Majesty, Queen Elizabeth the Queen Mother! A couple of working-class boys made good. We started from nothing but now look at us Reggie, this is it, so now we can enjoy ourselves, we've earned it."

William thinks he is winning him round so he goes in for the kill.

"Look at us, who would have thought it eh? Billy Tallon from Newcastle and Reg Wilcock from Wakefield, the toast of London! I hate to admit it you know Reg, but underneath all this grandeur, I'm still just little Billy Tallon."

"And I'm knackered old Reggie Wilcock and I'm tired and I want to go to bed!"

Reg is having none of it as he knows what William is like after all these years.

"Now don't be silly, the night is young and so are we."

Even Reg with his dry sense of humour had to raise an eyebrow to this remark. Young they were not. Yet he could always remember when they had been, and what that felt like. William was one of those people who retained the same young attitude to life he always had, despite his age.

"Billy, I'm sixty-six!"

"You're as old as you feel," William reassures him. "Look at us Reg" he went on seriously, "we're here. All those years we've been working up to this fantastic day, the pinnacle of our careers. We should take advantage of every second of it love before it's gone; not go to bed early with a cup of cocoa. Everything is organised now so there's no need to worry. Let's dance Reggie, I want to dance, everyone should dance! Come on let's dance?"

"Don't be daft," says Reg, smirking at him, now realising it will be harder than he thinks if not impossible to persuade William to go straight home, as he isn't able to put up such a good fight due to the strange way he is feeling in the heat. He knew William could be relentless in pursuing what he desired: namely, to stay out all night and party. Reg knew that as long as he could keep up the dialogue to match William's banter then he might be able to change his mind, but he doesn't have the energy tonight with the heat and the way he feels, so he bows to the inevitable. Secretly though, he admires William's inimitable style he had with charming people round, including himself.

"Come on now, dance with me," says William, taking Reg's arm in an attempt to coerce him into a dance. "Come on Reg, you know you want to. Come on? You remind me of someone, now who is it? Let me think now who could it be? … I know, could it be?"

William starts to sing his party piece 'Nina' by Noël Coward.

"♪ Nina from Argentina …♪" he sings.

Dillie returns to find William singing and becomes ecstatic.

"Oh William," she gasps, clasping her hands to her cheeks in delight, "you're singing it for us, how wonderful! Come on everyone, William is singing his Noël Coward for us!"

William prances and swaggers out of the foyer towards the exit with a theatrical dance to the utter delight of Dillie and some friends and some people who were leaving the theatre, initiating a conga dance causing

Dillie and her friends to trail along after him in a line towards the street, with William doing a few arm actions to go with the lyrics or a jaunty kick to the side as he goes. They all love being around him because they think he is so much fun and naughty. William knows perfectly well what he's doing, so is singing all the way, seemingly entranced in a party mood, as he leads them in a conga line outside to the cars to the giggles and admiring looks of the crowd, leaving a somewhat reconciled and forlorn Reg behind, standing almost alone in the room as most people have gone outside to watch.

He spots a man he knows who is about to leave with the others and approaches him as he's making his way out.

"Tom? Tom?" he shouts, "are you going home with Gill now?"

"No Reg, we're going to The Dorchester with this lot. Are you coming?"

"No love I'm going to bed. Look, will you do me a favour? Will you make sure that William gets home safely?"

"Yes all right Reg."

"No Tom, I mean, don't put him in a taxi by himself or he might tell the driver to take him to The Moulin Rouge in Paris or somewhere, you know what he's like, we don't want him wandering off into the night. Can you go with him to make sure you can see him close his front door?"

"Yes, don't worry Reg. We won't disturb you."

"No love, you don't understand. I'm going to my room at Clarence House. William is going to his little house on The Mall."

"Will do Reginald! You can leave it with me. I'll get him back as soon as I can. We are so proud of you boys you know, not that we see you on television on the birthdays these days, it's all William, so I want to see your face all over the television this year so the whole world can see you enjoying yourself. I know how much it means to you both having worked up to this all this time. Now you get yourself to bed and get an early start so you can be up bright and early to crack the whip. It's only twenty-four hours away now!"

"Oh, I don't know about cracking a whip."

"I want you to make it look like the best birthday party in the world! Such a jubilant and enduring occasion! It's going to be magnificent. I'd better go now. Night, night Reggie, sleep tight."

"If I can Tom? If I can?"

Tom gives a quick wave as he rushes outside to join the others. Reg follows on and steps out of the theatre onto the pavement, just in time to wave Dillie and William and company off as they speed away in their white-wheeled convoy of sexy chrome, cheered and whistled and waved away by the gathered crowd. The guttural growl and roar of the powerful automatic engines discharge a sickly pungent smoky metal smell of petrol fumes that hangs in the air. Reg laughs as he waves and watches them drive away as they join the heavy traffic of Theatreland. Some people rush into the road dodging taxis and bicycles just to get closer to these iconic beauties totally thrilled and enamoured by the whole thing. He longs to go along with them and have some fun, but he knows he isn't very well. He watches as the hazy red tail-lights of the last car moves away into the distance, before the convoy waits for a green light and eventually disappears around a corner. The deep rhythmic purring sound of the engines gradually fades away into the night.

He turns away and starts to walk home, still chuckling to himself. What an exciting thing to do to drive through London in those wonderful cars, he thinks. He hopes they won't be up all night drinking, but then realises that William will probably be the only one drinking alcohol all night as most millionaires in his experience seem to favour herbal tea late at night and not vintage champagne. Older millionaires do anyway. A sense of self-preservation against overindulgence on their part, he feels.

The walk home is not far back down the hill, towards Pall Mall that leads to Clarence House. He is a little annoyed with William for staying out just before the birthday, as he knows it will be a long night with the Dorchester Hotel and the fireworks and everything, but he hopes he'll be all right with Tom and Gill around. In fact, he knows William will be all right. After all, it is a special time, and he would have joined them and gone out for a drink if he wasn't feeling so strange and so hot, if only to experience a ride in one of those amazing cars.

He waits to cross the road at Piccadilly Circus. There is so much traffic still, albeit sluggish lazy traffic and so many people hanging around the streets. Mostly groups of young people laughing and stumbling about. He carries on walking back with his head down not catching anyone's eye, as he concentrates on the lovely comforting thought that in about ten or fifteen minutes, his head will lay down on the pillow in his bed, and he will fall fast asleep in the sanctuary of his bedroom in Clarence House. Safe from all the drunks and the idiots and the noise and traffic and pollution, and away from the overbearing heat and the ominous heady atmosphere of a London summer night.

LUNCH

The time is approaching 7.00am the next morning and Clarence House is almost silent as Jason tentatively makes his way along the corridor from his bedroom towards the stairwell that will lead him to his place of work. His head and ears are still thumping and throbbing from the night before well, this morning to be precise as it was only less than four hours ago he was 'giving it large' in a huge night club by the river. He walked home from the club in the early hours, so when he reached the palace he had to step over many people who were sleeping on the pavements. They had camped out in order to claim the best vantage spots for seeing the birthday procession and this year there were loads of them.

The good thing about living on the job in Clarence House means there is no commuting and you can be in work minutes after getting out the shower. On the other hand, it also means you are regularly called on duty when you should be off. And you never feel off even when you are because you physically are still at your place of work.

He is making his way from the top of the house where he lives to the ground floor in the pantry where he works. It will take the successful negotiation of several very long and very steep staircases to achieve this, and the ability not to crash into somebody who happens to rush out of a door on the way, so the landings will need extra care and so will the first steps on each set or he could slip and break his neck. It may even be necessary to open his eyes at some juncture.

He is the head pantry footman and the pantry is his little domain. He is responsible for the royal service of meals and drinks, whether they be in the dining room, on a tray or in a picnic. Basically; getting the food from the kitchen to the

27

consumer properly presented, and then cleared away and washed-up afterwards and he also looks after the royal china and glass at Clarence House.

Normally he wouldn't worry about being a few minutes late, but due to an untimely staff shortage of footmen at the moment, namely, two of them swanning off to better paid jobs within the space of a few weeks, he is on his own, apart from a new boy who just started working there.

He stumbles through the fire door onto the first landing feeling wretched because he's had quite a few free tequila shots in the club with his friends and an innumerable amount of triple vodka and Cokes. His friends were celebrating Queen Elizabeth's birthday early with a drinking competition. The tequila was free as there was a promotion going on, but it means he now has such a terrible pounding headache, as he usually doesn't drink. He hates getting drunk and likes ever to have no more than two alcoholic drinks, but now he's on his way to work with a vile hangover.

He opens his eyes a little now just to get on the first step then he can feel his way. He mustn't look down or he'll feel even more queasy, that's why he's chosen to take the stairs as the old lift makes such a racket with its heavy concertina doors. It would take all his strength at the moment in his fragile state to pull the doors open and shut.

Thank God it's a straight smooth run downstairs and straight in, as the pantry door will be wide open because George will have unlocked it by now, he thinks (George is the night-time policeman).

He manages to descend the stairs smoothly so tries to keep his rhythm and gentle speed going. His eyes are almost closed again as he slides his hands along the handrails already knowing where the hairpin bends are and where the straight runs of the landings should be. He knows this house so well he could walk around it with his eyes closed, quite literally, and that's exactly what he's doing now, almost.

He can hear voices and footsteps and kitchen noises coming up from the basement and the odd door slamming along the way turns out to be false alarms. Nobody has seen him, or so he thinks. His mouth feels dry. He just wants coffee. Lots of it. And water. Some of that too but mostly coffee, lots of lovely milky coffee.

"Oh hang on," he says to himself, "I think this is it now," as he steers himself around the last bend so onto the last set of stairs leading down to the ground floor. And it is. He clumps down the last dozen steps or so and swings around straight towards the open pantry door which is directly opposite the last step. He feels for the switches just inside the door and turns off the lights as he knows George always turns them on when he unlocks the door first thing in the morning. He enters the pantry just missing bumping into some plastic buckets of water full of cut flowers that have been left along the corridor.

"Morning!"

This explosion of noise bursts out of the corner of the room and thumps him bang on the ears with a whack! and scares the living daylights out of him.

He swings round surprised and angry.

"Jesus Timothy! What are you doing there? You made me jump?"

"Sorry," says Timothy, who is sitting in a chair in the corner with a mobile phone on his lap. The poor boy is very embarrassed as he only started work here three days ago, so now feels he's done something very wrong and upset Jason. He is sitting there already togged-up in his 'scarlet uniform' of starched-fronted shirt and wing collar, white bow tie and black gold trimmed waistcoat.

"What are you doing here anyway?" demands

Jason, annoyed that his morning coffee ritual has been disturbed. [He never goes to the staff canteen first thing in the morning]

"You told me to be down early this morning?"

"I didn't mean this early. I like to have a couple of coffees by myself and wake up gradually. How long have you been down then?" Jason snaps.

"Ages. I've been in the orderly's office talking to that policeman when he came off his night duty."

"You mean George!" Jason says with disdain, as he gropes for a cup. "I wouldn't take any notice of what he says, exaggeration doesn't come into it. I bet he told you about all the mad cocaine sex parties that we're supposed to have in our bedrooms upstairs although, I don't know where all these parties are meant to be, I mean, I've never been invited to one?"

"He hardly told me anything. We were talking about Princess Diana. He's got this expression he keeps using over and over again whenever I asked him about something. He kept saying,

Now if I told you that, I'd ..."

"Have to shoot you!" they both recite simultaneously.

"Not that old chestnut. Who would ever be that interested? And you can put that mobile phone away for a start thank you, I've told you before," says Jason as he approaches the mirror and hesitantly stares at it.

"I'm only playing snakes and ladders," says Timothy, looking down again to continue the game on his phone.

Jason doesn't know what snakes and ladders is. It must be one of those stupid games I saw on my phone, he thinks.

He has introduced himself to the mirror and is looking through it, at his hair.

"Would you say that I was losing my hair?" he asks.

After finishing his phone game Timothy casually looks up and glances at Jason's hair. "Yes, a little, but you've got

30

more hair than my dad."

"What's your dad got to do with it?"

"Well you are about the same age."

"Oh thanks a lot! That makes me feel fantastic first thing in the morning."

Jason takes an apron off the door hook and throws it onto Timothy's lap. Then he takes some milk out of the fridge for his coffee.

"But what exactly does that policeman George do around here anyway?" asks Timothy as he puts away his phone and stands up to put on the apron. His uniform doesn't fit well because he's so slim. The brass buttons on his waistcoat are so old they have 'GR' embossed on them and the thick navy trousers hang loose by the braces.

"Well, you obviously haven't asked him that yourself otherwise you would know,

It's not what I do, it's what ..."

"I might have to do!" they both say in unison.

"Oh, you did ask him then," says Jason. "What's this, silly question time again? Look do you mind, I need caffeine."

Jason walks over to a worktop where a shiny Swan aluminium kettle is placed next to a coffee machine with a full jug of freshly brewed coffee in it. He's so grateful that he won't have the bother of preparing it and waiting for it to drain through, not that he could manage to do either at the moment. He stands over it and pretends to bless it like a priest.

"Praise be the early housemaid who puts the coffee on for me. Bless you my child!"

He pours some coffee, has a good gulp, then jumps up to sit on a chest of drawers in the corner next to the small silver room door. He takes a box of long matches, ones that are just longer than a cigarette and strikes one on the box, waits for it to burn a little, then blows it out and holds it like a cigarette and pretends to smoke. He does this because it's the next best thing to smoking. The initial smell of the sulphur when it's lit reminds him of tobacco in a small way when he used to smoke. It's the only kind of hit he's going to get with an imaginary cigarette anyway, even if it's only a match, but he likes it. The real reason he does it is for the breathing. If you 'smoke a match' and breathe deeply mimicking the same actions of smoking a cigarette, then it has the effect of drawing oxygen into your bloodstream and brain thereby relieving stress and anxiety and calms you down. All this for the price of a match! and no harmful tobacco! and it really works. Reg told him about it. You can imagine to be your favourite film star if it helps. Jason is channelling Marlene Dietrich these days. It works with small matches too, but Jason has a long day ahead dealing with this new kid. Same old dumb questions they ask, all these new footmen who come and go, he thinks to himself. Get a year or two experience under their belt and they're off. To America or Saudi Arabia, or a yacht somewhere. This Timothy seems a nice enough kid but, well, let's just say, he's only been here a couple of days.

[There was no formal training like in an ordinary job. A new footman or housemaid would be thrown in at the deep end and start work with the others, who taught and trained them and told them what to do. They were shadowed until it was considered they could manage on their own, as long as they lasted the trial period and their face fitted]

"But if you ask me," said Jason to a friend in the night club, "William's only got him at the last minute to cover the Scottish trip, then he'll let him go because I don't think he likes him, and if your face don't fit round here well, you're out. He doesn't come across as a grafter. He could hardly lift the dining room chairs yesterday. And no silver cleaning went on. He's getting behind with the workload. If he was any more relaxed he'd be horizontal! No really. He's as much use as a chocolate ashtray; on a motorbike!"

After Jason has had a second cup of coffee and is now nursing a third, he is sitting on top of the chest of drawers still 'smoking', contemplating the day ahead. Timothy has sat down on a wooden stool at the oblong Formica topped table in the centre of the room. He has waited patiently for Jason to calm down and he's taken out a small notepad and pen, poised, as if he were a secretary waiting for dictation.

"Right, I'll do you a deal," says Jason after a rather dramatic exhale of his 'cigarette.' "Just so you don't bombard me with daft questions about the job all the time like yesterday, you can ask me as many questions as you like while I'm drinking this coffee, on the condition that once I finish it you don't ask me any more for the rest of the day. Deal?"

"It's a deal!" says a delighted Timothy, as he flips open his little spiral bound notebook. "Okay then. Who's Adrian?"

"A footman who's just left to work in America and left me in the lurch so I am doing two mens' work."

"How many people work here?"

"No idea. Next question."

"Do William and Reg live together?"

Blimey, thinks Jason. Hasn't he worked it out yet, bless him? I'd better go easy on him. Be diplomatic. "Next question?"

It's obvious that Timothy is set on this particular question and doesn't want to offer the next yet, but Jason is adamant.

"Next question!" demands Jason.

"Okay then," says Timothy, "do William or Reg own a house or any property of their own?"

"I really don't know. Honestly."

"Does the Queen Mother come in here and have coffee with you?"

"No of course not. Not in my time anyhow."

"Okay, can George the policeman shoot me with his gun if he wants to?"

Jason has to think about this one.

"Yes!"

"If the Queen Mother speaks to me, what do I call her, your royal highness? ma'am?"

Here we go again thinks Jason, questions, questions. "Timothy, it's always, always your majesty! Queen Elizabeth and The Queen are your majesty and all the others apart from about, fifty thousand exceptions are your royal highness."

"What about the Queen Mother? What do I call her?"

"I've just said! Our Queen is your majesty and The Queen is also your majesty."

"The Queen, what are you talking about?"

"No, there are two queens. The Queen at the palace is The Queen, and Queen Elizabeth is our Queen. So when I say the Queen, I mean our Queen."

"Well how do I know who you're talking about? Doesn't it get confusing with two Queen Elizabeths?"

"No, there's only one Queen Elizabeth! The Queen Mother is Queen Elizabeth, or the Queen or our Queen, and The Queen is 'The' Queen!"

"But that's so confusing! I don't understand?"

"Not really," says Jason.

"Anyway, next question," says Timothy.

"Oh I'm bored with this now," says Jason, jumping off the chest of drawers onto the ground, throwing the match in the bin.

"But you said you'd answer questions. Oh Jason. How am I supposed to learn anything like this? There's no work manual, nothing is written down. How do I know what to do?"

"You learn on the job like I did. Like everyone did, since Queen Elizabeth had her own household at one four five Piccadilly. That's the way it's always been around here since nineteen twenty-seven. You'll never change it, believe me I've tried."

Jason takes another apron off the door hook and puts it on, then washes his hands at the sink.

"Didn't you feel a strange force when you walked in off the street into this building Timothy? That was a time portal! And you've stepped into an Edwardian time warp! Spooky isn't it? But don't worry kid, I'll look after you."

Jason prepares the sink for washing-up. It's positioned between two large bare sash windows. Dark brown wood draining stands sit on the window sills containing some inverted crystal decanters.

"But I really want to get it right Jason. It's important to me! You don't know how hard it was for me to get this job."

"Well you're here now, and who knows, in years to come we may all move over to the palace with Prince Charles?"

"I'm only going to stay here for twelve months so I can put this job on my C.V."

"Oh thanks very much for that vote of confidence!" says Jason, twisting around to face Timothy. "So I'm suddenly a training officer all over again am I, like all the other times? You only replaced the guy before Adrian so I'm still a man down. What a kick in the teeth this day is turning out to be, thanks very much."

"Don't be like that Jason. This is a great opportunity for me, and I'm here to help. I mean it. My parents are so proud of me you know, I don't want to let them down."

"All right then, at least you're being honest about it I suppose" says Jason, calming down, after a few sulky seconds. He's annoyed that Timothy has turned out to be yet another lightweight and he's not that surprised really as he expected as much when they met.

Jason loves his job and would gladly tell anyone everything he knows, but people don't seem that interested in china and glass and silver. Not even these new footmen. They seem to think that being a footman is just a matter of putting on a fancy uniform and holding out a gin and tonic on a silver tray. And nearly all of them only ever ask about Diana and will they get their picture taken with the royals?

Jason is thinking about all the things he will have to teach Timothy, even if he is only staying for a year. About how they get given their own uniforms twice a year (not scarlet) and about the staff laundry, dry cleaning and where to get their food and expenses, and they don't even have to buy their own soap! He can tell him how easy it is to put your hands on exquisite rare and valuable items, but to put your hands on a bottle of Jif presents more of a challenge [the housekeeper]. And to warn him not to use the royal china to take leftover food from royal meals to your room, although some people do, including William. Timothy will have to be told that the Queen Mother is the Matriarch of the royal family and so this house is really run on its own rules. About the way; they always get driven to and from the airport whereas the palace staff sometimes take public transport. And how they serve in the different houses including all the quirky exceptions. How to manoeuvre the huge silver coffee tray over people's heads at the dining table, and how to 'feed the salad plates' to the footman who is taking round the salad, (but it's not easy to explain all this; I would have to show you).

"Let me try to put you in the picture," he says, as he

finishes tying up his blue heavy cotton apron up at the front and launches into his little speech about Clarence House; the one he saves for new footmen.

"This is the little house on The Mall, in royal circles anyhow. That's what Queen Elizabeth called it once when she was told it could be made available to her when the King died. Not to be confused with William's little house on The Mall which is the tiny gate lodge over there, stuffed with all his, stuff. Anyway, the Queen Mother moved here from Buckingham Palace in nineteen fifty-three, after the King died the previous year. This is the official residence of Queen Elizabeth the Queen Mother, yet it's also a home. It's where official gatherings are held, private ones too. Formal guests and friends come and go. It's where they may be coming back late from the theatre to have scrambled eggs and smoked salmon in the garden room. Not for Queen Elizabeth though, she doesn't care for smoked salmon. Or in the summer, they may be having a lunch party outside under the massive plane trees in the garden. We take out a long Edwardian dining table and use the same china and crystal as indoors. The branches cushion the noise of the traffic on The Mall, just over the garden wall. People walking past have no clue there's a hidden garden there, full of sweet peas and delphiniums and hostas. The Princess Margaret lived here before she got married. Princess Diana stayed here before her wedding and left from here to go to Saint Paul's. The inside of the house hasn't altered in about fifty years. The electric wiring is dodgy, the plumbing is fine, and the place is quirky and different, crowded with a royal life, several royal lives in fact. By the way," Jason breaks off, "don't accept an invitation for a drink from William if you can."

"Why not?" asks Timothy.

"Because he's a drinker and he'll fill your glass like his own, as drinkers always think other people want the same as they do, and there's an endless supply of booze in this house."

"What's he like to work for?"

"He's all right, but he's one of those people who is constantly on, you know? He can never switch off and just sit there and relax. And he can turn on you like that! So be careful. But, is it true that you knew him before you came here. Is he a friend of yours?"

"Friend, God no! What makes you think that?"

"Oh, nothing, just may have heard it mentioned somewhere. But didn't William recommend you for this job or something?"

"Absolutely not. I wrote up and applied for a job and was invited to apply fair and square, just like anybody else would. And I know how lucky I am, I can't tell you what it means to me to get this opportunity, believe me."

"Okay Timothy don't worry, that's fine. Just wondered that's all."

"So, who puts the table and chairs out under the trees for lunch?"

"We do. There're no porters here. We use the same chairs you moved yesterday for that meeting and an Edwardian mahogany dining table that's stored under the stairs."

"The Chippendale chairs in the library? But they're as heavy as lead. Haven't you got any garden chairs?"

"Timothy, they are the only chairs we have apart from those awful little white and red ones that must have been made for Victorian pixies. Not using those again since Sir Johnny Tiny Watson sat down on one and crushed it, look, I hope you're not going to turn out like all the other new footmen I get through here asking silly questions. Just do as I say there's nothing to worry about, I know what I'm doing,

I won't put you wrong."

At this point a housemaid walks into the room, or rather glides in. Kay is a slow but self-assured, very nosey housemaid who doesn't miss a trick and she was probably eavesdropping around the corner before she came in because she fancies Timothy. As the newbie, he is attracting a lot of attention from the other staff who have already taken the opportunity to meet him to size him up.

She had told Jason that she was certain she spotted Timothy and William coming out of a posh jeweller in Bond Street together then getting into a taxi, a few months ago, and she suggested that they were more that close friends. Jason thought she may be mistaken so was waiting until more information came forth so he could find out for himself, but thought that if it were true, then it may tamp down William's shenanigans at least, as he knew he wasn't able to himself. Then again, it may do the opposite and cause them to flare up, he wasn't sure.

Kay is wearing a white housekeeping tunic and black shoes.

"Morning campers!" she yells at the top of her voice. She already knows Jason came back in the early hours so he's likely to have a hangover.

Oh here she is, come to have a nose again at the new boy poor sod, thinks Jason.

"Good morning Katherine," he says.

"How are you getting on Timothy? Not dropped any more tea trays on the stairs have you?"

And she giggles to herself while looking at the memos on the board.

"A little police birdie tells me somebody came home late in a taxi last night from The Dorchester Hotel Mayfair?"

"What's the problem Kay? Didn't they give you your daily bowl of raw meat this morning with your cornflakes?"

Kay doesn't get the joke so carries on her investigations unawares.

"Who keeps polishing the kettle? I never do it?" she asks, noticing the gleaming metal in the corner.

"We noticed, and please don't interfere with Timothy. He's still recovering from that unpleasant encounter with you from the other day. He's barely been here forty-eight hours and I don't want you putting my new footmen off like that before they've even had the chance to serve royal lunch."

"He shouldn't get in the lift with me then, should he?" Kay thinks her remark hilarious and giggles some more.

"Excuse me Kay, but can I help you in any way? in your frantic little world of work?"

"The equerry wants William to go and see Sir Alastair as soon as he comes in this morning," she says in a serious tone. [Being so nosey and having access to a lot of the house with her cleaning duties she seems to know everything that's going on, so she's always a good source of information that Jason can rely on and trust]

"What for?"

"To discuss finalising the logistics for the Scottish trip."

"How do you know?" Jason asks, just to make sure it's not a wind-up.

"Because he's having a shower and I've ironed his shirt! And he says Sir Alastair won't want to hang about as he's got appointments at the barbers and his tailors first thing and if possible could he please have a coffee and a bacon sandwich with H.P. sauce as he cycled in this morning and didn't have time for breakfast and you're a star!"

That sounds genuine as she repeated the whole message without a pause, thinks Jason. And the equerry often cycles in and she's always ironing shirts for him.

"Yes, okay thank you," he says. "Message received and understood. Now don't let us keep you, you can go now Kay darling."

He tries to usher her out but without success. She doesn't budge an inch.

"I'll leave you to it then." She remains stationery but twists her body round to address Timothy as she appears to be about to move out the door.

"See you later then Timothy, that is if you're still here. It's amazing how many footmen Jason gets through in this pantry, none of them seem to stay for very long. Had one chap who came and went on the same day. He didn't even bother to unpack!"

"That was a servant's hall boy not a footman! And he probably couldn't wait to get out of here when he clapped eyes on you."

Kay roars with laughter.

"What-ever! I'll be going now then so you can get on with all your little one hundredth birthday preparations for tomorrow. Although the Queen Mother is going to be out for lunch and dinner so it makes me wonder what you've actually got to do?"

Jason manages to usher her out swiftly, as she was giving the impression that she was leaving and going through the open doorway but her legs and feet weren't actually moving.

"Goodbye Katherine, goodbye," he says, as he let's her go and she's somehow propelled forwards with what seems like kinetic motion.

She was gone.

"What was all that about?" asks Timothy, his eyes agog with suspicion.

"She knows everything that one, and I thought the new equerry had more sense. But he'll soon learn when she tries to grab his nuts as he steps out of the shower."

Jason goes over to the brown 1980s telephone and punches in the number for the kitchen. He waits for them to answer.

"Oh hello Cherry baby darling, is that the basement? My little joke sweetie. Usual for the equerry please? Can you get Robert to make the coffee and take it in for me please? Thank you darling, see you later." He replaces the receiver.

"So, Jason," says a somewhat troubled Timothy. "When are we going to get started? You said that I wouldn't be stuck in here all-day washing-up again, I'd be serving at table, and you were going to show me how to set the silver?"

The phone rings, that startles Jason, making him jump.

"Oh no, it's started already," he says. "It's always like this on the birthdays, phone never stops ringing. Bet that's more flowers being delivered."

He picks up the receiver, "Hello?"

He listens to the caller and says, "No I haven't got any buckets!"

He listens again, "Yes, the champagne can go in William's office but we can't put any flowers in here yet as we need to be able to move around to work. They can go in the equerry's office."

(There are flowers all over the place already.)

He listens again to what the caller is saying.

"Well my pantry is a working room as well tell him, that is if he doesn't want his four-course lunch on a tray! Listen Terry, before you go, if there're any chocolates from Ackerman's or Charbonnel et Walker or Prestat, let me know will you?"

He listens again to the caller, "Yes, put the orchids, anything in a pot don't send away okay? Thanks Terry, bye," and he replaces the receiver.

"Jason?" says Timothy, reminding Jason he is still there.

"Oh sorry you still here?" Jason says, turning to glance at him. "I thought you'd left and got another job."

"Don't be like that. A year is a long time you know."

"Not here it's not. It took me five years to even feel comfortable with this job."

"But what exactly do we do?"

Jason is fed up with Timothy's interrogation. Already so many questions, and he couldn't wake up gently and privately with his coffee and a 'cigarette', so he runs off a brief description of the job in the vain hope it will silence Timothy, for a while at least.

"We lay the tables, serve food, make tea, move furniture, take trays, nip to the shop, walk the dogs, open doors and look pretty, don't upset William and Reg and make sure the place doesn't run out of gin. Simple. Job done. Is that a good enough job description for you?"

"Look pretty?"

"Yes, well. That's what the new equerries are secretly told to do by the preceding one, in dress uniform of course. They don't think I know that. They also keep a dossier with their comments on the staff, and a little notebook for the next new guy about dos and don'ts in equerry duties and things about uniform and stuff."

Jason moves over to the sink and places some draining pads down for cushioning the china, glass and silver when it's being washed-up.

"Why don't you go down for your breakfast now Timothy? You remember where it is don't you? Just go downstairs towards the kitchen and you'll hear everyone talking in the servant's hall. They'll put you right of where to sit and everything," says Jason, while he's looking in the mirror watching Timothy scribble something in his little notebook.

"Are you coming?"

"No, I'll get some biscuits from the orderly's room. I need to sit myself down with another coffee and try to get my packing lists together." And my head, he thinks."

"Okay," says Timothy, who whizzes off like a shot downstairs for his breakfast. Jason can't believe his luck, no more questions for half an hour! Jason has no intention of joining him for breakfast, he just wants some peace for a while in order to contain his thoughts before he starts screaming. It was easier to totally abstain from alcohol in a night club, rather than pay deference to all the cries of your friends at the bar saying,

"Oh go on, have one! Just have one?" The first one is a downward slippery slope to a guaranteed hangover, hence Jason's nickname of 'a one-pot-screamer', given to him once by a transient footman.

Timothy had returned to the pantry within ten minutes, but Jason had already taken the opportunity of clearing the corridors of buckets and taken in several deliveries of flowers in that time. Timothy hadn't asked any more questions so far, probably because he thought he'd glean more information once Jason was in a better mood. They were washing some silver now. Timothy had been 'trained' by Jason how to pick up a linen tea towel and he was standing next to him doing the drying, at last.

Later on, at nine-thirty, about the time William usually comes in to work, the telltale creak and squeak of the heavy swing door from the royal hall to the pantry corridor tells Jason that William has entered the building. Not very glamourous but it works and is very useful. He can hear it even when standing around the corner at the pantry sink, and he can look in the mirror to glimpse him walk past the open pantry doorway. The sound of corresponding footsteps helps too.

Nearly everybody walked past there in the course of a day, even Queen Elizabeth had done so in the not so distant past.

The hall of Clarence House spans from the front doors where royals and guests arrive by car and where the dogs are fed every day in the porch before being let straight out into the garden; all the way past the morning room, the library and the dining room, almost the entire length of the house. Just like anywhere else in the house no one is allowed in this royal area unless they have business there.

William appears, walking briskly from the royal hall in a chirpy mood. He always comes in through the front doors (which is the royal entrance). Nobody questions him about it. He is in full regalia of his uniform consisting of; a black tailcoat with black velvet lapels, brass buttons, dress medals on his left chest, a starched-fronted and cuffed white shirt, and a starched detachable wing collar, and a soft white waistcoat. His shoes shine like glass. His wispy greying black hair is carefully teased backwards over his head and to coin a phrase: he looks the epitome of a chap who's just stepped out of a bandbox. Clean as a whistle, smart, pressed and dapper as always. He has an oversized old key in one hand that looks so large that it couldn't possibly be for any modern day working lock, but in fact, is the key to the huge metal carriage gates outside Clarence House where he lives, that lead onto The Mall, [which he unlocks every time he comes to work] and then walks straight through the main front doors. In his other hand he is carrying a bunch of elaborate long twisted branches. On the same side he wears his dangly, rose gold bracelet.

Walking past the pantry door to the flower porch, he doesn't look in as he passes, and addresses the footmen in there in the usual way.

"Morning chaps!" he says cheerfully as he marches

past the open door.

The pantry corridor continues to a porch with a flagstone floor, where a couple of tables hold beautiful pots, urns and vases and some flowers in containers in front of some large windows. This is where William prepares his flower arrangements before they are taken into the royal rooms. Beyond this is the orderlies and the steward's office and a stationery store.

"Morning William!" replies Jason without looking away from his washing-up.

"Does Billy always come through the main front door?" asks a rather bemused Timothy.

"Yes he does, and stop calling him Billy. I've told you nobody calls him Billy except his close friends. Call him William."

"Did you see that enormous key he was carrying? What's that for?"

"The big black gates on The Mall. How do you think he gets through from his little house every day? You don't expect him to walk around the block dressed like that do you? He'd get mobbed by tourists!"

William puts the branches on the flower porch table and places the huge key in his inside pocket. He walks back towards the pantry while taking out a rolled-up readymade bow tie out of a pocket. As he walks, he pinches together his wing collar and flicks the bow tie to unravel it.

[It is very unlikely that William bought fancy branches like this himself. They had most likely been given to him by a friend and he may have promised to display them in one of the rooms, to please them]

"Anyone there?" he calls, knowing full well there is someone there as he just walked past them a moment ago. He doesn't care who attends him as long as they do.

"Yes William," says Jason reassuringly.

Jason walks to the pantry entrance in the corridor

46

drying his hands quickly on his apron, where William meets him. They are watched closely by Timothy who seems to be absorbing everything about his new environment.

"Could you just help me with this collar?"

"Of course. Let's have a look." Jason bends down a little and peers under William's chin and tries to pull the two ends of the collar together.

"Is it the right size? It's very tight." Jason tries to do up the collar with no success.

"I know, I spent ages trying to do it myself in the mirror, but I couldn't see."

William flinches with pain.

"It's too small William," says Jason giving up, dropping his arms down in resignation. "You'll have to use another one."

"This is the only one I've got at the moment," William says, pinching the ends together again. "I'm still waiting for the others to come back from the laundry."

Jason has another attempt.

"Ooh!" yells William in pain.

"Sorry. I can't see very well. Stand here in the light."

Jason is determined to fasten it so beckons William to move into the pantry where there's better light. He clicks over the light switches.

"Hold on," says Jason, trying with all his strength to line up the holes in the stiff collar ends and pull them together, and then punch them over the brass swivel collar stud then adjust it to secure it all in place. He has to squeeze against William's neck so hard as it's so tight, which is causing William to yelp.

"Ooh" William flinches.

"Sorry," says Jason, really trying hard now. "I'll do it this time but it's very tight. Hold on." He manages to

47

fasten it with tremendous force, at last.

"There, that's it!"

"Oh thank you so much," says a red-faced William clutching his throat. "Awful things."

"I know," says Jason.

William turns and walks back towards the flower porch. "So uncomfortable!"

"William?" says Jason, talking to the back of his head, "there's a message for you from Sir Alastair. He says he'd like to see you in his office as soon as you come in?"

"What about?" asks William while putting on his bow tie whilst looking in a mirror.

"The logistics for the Scottish trip."

"The what?"

"Something about finalising the transport arrangements."

William's demeanour changes instantly into a spiky mood.

"Transport arrangements? For the Scottish trip? It's already organised, it's the same every year. It's been the same for the last thirty-odd years."

"He sent the message through the equerry and Kay just told me," says Jason.

"What makes the private secretary feel the need to meddle with the transport arrangements? It's nothing to do with him. They're supposedly organised by the equerry but the head chauffeur always does them, and then they are typed up by a secretary, and Sir Alastair casts a cursory glance over them just so he can emblazon his enormous initials everywhere to put his signature to it. You could set your watch by this lady by where she is and what she's doing, she's done the same thing every year since the year dot! I can't come now tell him, I'll be along shortly."

William's expression takes on an air of extreme superiority.

"I'm expecting a call from Lord Snowdon," as he lifts his nose in the air.

[He may or may not have been expecting a call from Lord Snowdon as they were indeed friends and Sir Alastair knew this so he would not question it. William used this ploy a lot if it helped him get out of any requests on his time]

"But I think he's going out in a minute for a haircut, and he's got an appointment at his tailor," says Jason.

Jason thinks to himself, that he is always playing advocate to people around here. Why can't Sir Alastair or the equerry jolly well ask William themselves?

"Oh very well, I'll have to go and see him," says William impatiently. "I say Jason, could you arrange these branches for me? Just throw them in a vase would you and put them on the desk in the garden room."

"Those?" asks Jason pointing towards the branches. "Why do you want those? we've got all these flowers, it's like a flower shop!"

"Don't question me!" snaps William.

William starts to walk towards Sir Alastair's office.

"And would you pop to Fortnum's and get a bottle of brandy for lunch? Their own brand, not the expensive one."

"Yes all right William."

"And you can set lunch on the terrace to make the most of the sun."

"Okay William," says Jason. Is that all? he thinks to himself, I know the routine, is there anything else? No?

"And could you order some sandwiches and do up a tray for the dressmakers?" William continues, as he is about to disappear. "They are popping by this afternoon."

"Yes William of course, but they said last time they

49

don't want any sandwiches as they haven't got time," replies Jason patiently.

"Well ask for them anyway, give the kitchen something to do."

"Yes all right."

"And you can you put those white lilies in some water," says William. "And make sure you send them to Scotland with the Queen. So thoughtful of someone to send them in their boxes. They can travel and I can do an arrangement with them for the hall at Castle Mey." [A lady there would have already prepared a stunning display, but the unopened lilies would keep for a while to replace it]

William still hasn't gone to see the private secretary. He's still faffing around looking at the gifts and flowers that have been sent.

It may look like he is being bossy, but Jason always does his bidding without question, unless William is being particularly and obviously problematic or childish. Jason respects his remarkable achievement of fifty years service with the same employer. He also likes the way William seems to know everything about the job and everyone associated with Queen Elizabeth. There would never be an unforeseen problem with William around, Jason thought, as William was completely cognisant with Her Majesty's routines and schedules and friends.

[It did make for harder work sometimes though as William's insistence of covering every angle on a trip could be tiresome. For instance, making preparations for possible impromptu meals that may never occur, (lunch or tea outside). And packing equipment that we didn't need. And sometimes in Scotland and when travelling, you would have to prep-up an extra table service in case a guest was delayed and arrived late, but they seldom were. And at Birkhall, he wouldn't allow the heavy swing door to the dining room to be propped open while serving and clearing each course because he said the noise from the running taps and washing-up from the pantry would disturb the diners even though the noise of their conversation was louder. Unnecessary things like these he would request, that required time and effort. Time that was precious, and effort that was unnecessary. Reg was the opposite, he did what was required, which saved time and effort, and tempers flaring.

The chef and the housekeeper used to allow their staff to leave early sometimes, if they needed to catch a train or to meet with relatives to go to a show perhaps. William never did. Not even if you'd planned something for ages.

Once, he found out I arranged to meet my folks who had travelled across the country to meet me for a theatre show on a Saturday and a meal in a restaurant, and he made me stay on duty for no reason, so I missed the show and seeing my family. He said,

"You can't go you must stay here! Your job comes first! Your job always comes first!" even though I wasn't needed.

He was unpredictable because he didn't let anybody into his confidence, so you never knew what he was thinking. I couldn't get close to him apart from a few unguarded moments when I was alone with him and he was in a reflective mood. He could be great fun and absolutely fascinating company but only on his own terms, only when he was in charge or more importantly, was seen to be in charge. This was ridiculous really because he already was in charge and nobody seemed to have an issue with that. I think it must have been his intolerance of competition perhaps. Not that anyone was in competition with him but he may have seen things differently. He must have spent his first twenty-five years climbing the staff ladder in his job at Clarence House, so maybe he never grew out of that progressive persistence. Or it may have been a need for him to be respected?

He was notorious with the established members of staff, but not everyone knew him. I went with him to Buckingham Palace once to select a dining table to borrow, to take to Walmer Castle. He forgot his pass and the security officer at the staff door couldn't find his details on the computer, so it was taking a while to get in.

"What was your name again?"

"Tallon. William Tallon."

(Still couldn't find him.)

"How long have you worked here?"

"Forty-five years!"

In the end somebody there vouched for him so we were allowed in, but he wasn't pleased, he really wasn't pleased.

At least he used the official staff entrance at Buckingham Palace. Not like some of the staff from St. James's Palace (complex) who would stroll over the road and swan through the main gates up to the Privy Purse Door, therby using a far more glamourous entrance to the building. I wouldn't mind but, the only business they were conducting was collecting a refrigerated shop made sandwich from the staff canteen, that was supplied for their lunch!

William had been around so long that he could seemingly draw upon a ledger of information in his head, of places Queen Elizabeth had gone for dinner or the last time she had opened a new hospital wing or such like, as he had probably been there to open the Daimler door to Her Majesty upon arrival, all through the years. He had been in royal service for nigh on fifty years, so it was understandable he knew the deal inside out. It was a specialist subject for him, one that he lived and breathed every day of his life.

I thought that William would never put me wrong by sabotaging my work as that may impact on the welfare of Queen Elizabeth. However, I know he did do that sort of thing occasionally, especially if he could act stealthy and with impunity unless he really didn't like you, then you were sunk, but then you wouldn't last very long there at all if your face didn't fit. You probably wouldn't even make it through the trial period]

Timothy is at the foot of the stairs just outside the pantry door putting yet another delivery of fresh flowers into buckets of water. A voice like thunder harnessed by Laurence Olivier rumbles from above. Reg is leaning over the banisters on the next floor up calling down the stairs in his best theatrical voice.

"Cof-fee Wil-li-am?"

The powerful booming voice resonates on the porch below making Timothy freeze in fright for a split second at this unfamiliar sound.

"Five minutes Reg!" William calls back straightaway.

"Very good William," Reg calls back, using his normal voice this time, then retreats back across the landing into the page's room.

William leaves the scene and heads off towards Sir Alastair's office to 'see what all this nonsense is about' with the travel arrangements. What a waste of time this will be, he thinks. So, it's see the private secretary quickly, then up for a cup of coffee with Reg upstairs.

Jason selects a huge heavy Baccarat vase from the flower porch and carefully carries the valuable heavy piece of crystalware into the pantry and plonks it on the table in the middle of the room. He places the branches in it and proceeds to arrange them as best he can. He knows it would be a mistake to outshine William's arranging abilities as that's one of William's domains. He feels confident these awful twigs won't present any competition. Timothy stands next to him closely watching his every move, as usual.

"Do you have to do his collar up for him often?" he asks.

"No, I've never done it before, but he must be using the wrong size like you did yesterday. It's like walking around wearing a starched cardboard box."

It suddenly occurs to Jason that if he told some certain ex-footmen that he has just fastened up William's starched collar and studs and had to squeeze them really tight around his neck, they would probably ask him why he never took the opportunity to strangle the bastard?

"I got Kay to do up my collar this morning. What was William saying about you going to Fortnum's?" asks Timothy.

"I sometimes have to go and get a bottle of brandy from Fortnum and Mason's whenever we have a biggish lunch. He often sends somebody up for a bottle, not that we ever serve it much."

"But why? Haven't you got any brandy in the cellars with the rest of the alcohol?"

"I don't know, I'm never in there long enough to find out, William stands guard. There's supposed to be a bottle of Hitler's cognac in there but I haven't clocked it yet."

"Really? I'd like to see that."

"I don't know what Hitler was doing with a bottle of cognac as he was a teetotal vegetarian apparently, but there it is. You'll find Timothy, that a house like this has its funny little rules and customs that don't really make much sense, but if you want to get on it's best to go along with the flow. And I wouldn't want to be the one to cross the likes of William."

Timothy stands next to Jason watching him nudging the branches and considers what that means, but decides to concentrate on his own little agenda he currently has in play.

"You know when you go to Fortnum's?" he asks.

"Hmm?"

"How do you pay for it."

"It's on account. The Queen Mother's got an account there. You show them a little card with the number on it and you just sign for it."

"Can I go with you?"

"No, you stay here! I'll only be gone for twenty minutes at the most."

"In that case you could rob her blind, they'd never know. You can even get three bottles of brandy and we can give one to William and have a bottle each."

"No I can't. Don't be daft! Why would I want to do that? I'm not a thief. What are you talking about?"

Reg can be heard singing in the background. He is walking down the hall. He sounds in a wonderfully happy mood. He walks through the swing door and just at that moment Sir Alastair appears from a side door in the corridor and they almost collide but Reg carries on singing regardless, because he finds it funny to have cornered a captive audience like this, and feels the only thing to do is present a super mini musical that Sir Alastair will definitely not appreciate. That's what makes it funny.

"♪ Oh what a beautiful mornin'
Oh what a beautiful day ... ♪"

"Is it Reginald?"

"Sir?"

"A beautiful morning?"

"Oh yes Sir Alastair! It was beautiful strolling in the park this morning. Swans on the lake, people getting coffee on the way to work, the early morning madness. It was glorious!"

"I'm glad somebody thinks so!" and Sir Alastair walks off in a huff the same way William just went.

Reg looks after him with a wry smile then enters the pantry and addresses the boys with his usual theatrical flourish.

"Morning fellas. What a wonderful morning. Here you are then," as he pins a handwritten note and a printed list on the tiniest last bit of space left on the noticeboard.

"Royal lunch for eight people. There are twelve for household tea today and forty-five for drinks tonight for the lovely handsome equerry. There's a letter for you each and a couple of memos."

Reg places the letters on the table and Timothy opens his and reads it. Reg turns to watch Jason arranging the branches while Timothy opens his letter.

"Well go on then, arrange them!" he says, coaxing Jason into creating something wonderful out of a few twigs.

"I have, that's it!"

"Is that it?" Reg sniggers.

"I'm not very good at arranging flowers. William's the expert."

"Is that the best you can do?" He turns on his heels. "Oh, you lot have got no ..." he pauses a few seconds as he tries to think of an appropriately inoffensive phrase to use as he goes out the door, "...flair!" he laughs gaily then grabs hold of the handrail and begins to climb the stairs. He starts to sing again after the first few steps.

"♪ I've got a wonderful feeling, everything's going my way ...♪"

Jason pretends to titivate the branch arrangement, while he waits until Reg has climbed to the top and disappeared. He doesn't speak until he hears the corridor door bang shut and Reg is gone.

"Flair? I wouldn't dare. Not around here anyway. There's only room for one creative artiste and that ain't me."

Timothy paws over the lists that Reg pinned to the board.

Jason carries the heavy vase out of the room around the corner to the royal hall door.

"I'll take these through. Hold the door open for me

would you please Timothy?"

Timothy holds the door open and Jason disappears into the hall. Timothy returns to the noticeboard and quickly takes a photograph of it with a small camera he produces from his pocket that he puts back sharply. He then examines all the other items pinned to it, when Jason returns.

"What's this memo about from Sir Alastair Jason?"

"Which one in particular are you talking about, he writes so many?"

"It says: issues regarding pantry footmen are not to be described in future as a staff shortage so much as a gap from the transition of one footman who is leaving, to one who is starting, when a new one can not be interviewed and work notice in their current employment before or to coincide with the departure of the footman who is leaving."

"Oh that, it's just about a complaint I made," says Jason.

"The American Ambassador is coming to lunch, I see," says Timothy. "Think I'll speak to him about getting me a job in the future. Have you seen this Jason?" He eagerly reads out another memo. "Queen Elizabeth accompanied by the lady in waiting and the equerry, leave Clarence House by car ten-forty a.m. and arrive St. Paul's Cathedral ten-fifty. Ten minutes? How can that be? How can they get all the way across London in ten minutes?"

"It's what's known as a police escort Timothy, but you're never sure what to expect, as it's split second timing or coming 'round the mountain with this lady."

Timothy hands Jason a letter.

"I've got to go for a medical and an induction day at Buckingham Palace," he says.

William storms into the pantry obviously furious about something. He is very flustered from the quick meeting he just had with Sir Alastair and has a bunch of letters in his hand.

"The man's an idiot!" he snaps as he frantically searches his pockets for his glasses.

"Who?" asks Jason.

"Captain Aird!" spits William.

"Sir Alastair, why?"

[A military title takes precedence over a civilian title so 'Captain Aird' sounds much less impressive than 'Sir Alastair'. It so happens that Sir Alastair was a Captain in the Army, so William uses his military title rather than his civilian one whenever he's upset with the private secretary. It's possible that Sir Alastair returns the favour by referring to William as 'Tallon' on occasion, when everyone else in the house only ever calls him William, except for Reg and a kitchen porter, who call him Billy occasionally]

William doesn't answer straightaway. He is too preoccupied with trying to find his glasses and turn the muddled-up pages the right way round so he can read them. He locates his glasses about his person but is so frustrated he puts them on crooked and has to hold them in place for them to stay on. He reads the first letter. He is in an absolutely manic state.

"Oh what's this? Staff meeting! We haven't had one of those for years. I'm not going to another staff meeting. The last one I went to we spent two hours stuck in the television room and the only conclusion made was that the royal laundry would have to stop putting their reference tags in Captain Aird's socks, as he could feel them with his toes when he put his socks on."

"Sir Alastair has his socks laundered?" asks an amused Jason.

William shuffles the letters in a heightened agitated state and drops one and scurries about the floor to pick it up. Meanwhile Jason has opened and read his letter. He isn't worried or concerned with William's behaviour because, quite frankly, he's seen it all before.

"God what's this?" he squeals, "I'm having an appraisal." He looks up at Timothy, "what's an appraisal?"

William is so preoccupied with his own concerns that he wouldn't have noticed if Lord Snowdon himself had been sitting in the corner on the same chair Timothy occupied first thing this morning. He is incensed that Sir Alastair is concentrating on such trivial matters.

"We didn't even get a cup of tea," he snorts.

"Did you say that he has his socks laundered? At the royal launderers?" asks Jason.

"All the heads of departments were there," continues William, "not that we said much. Our accommodation wasn't even mentioned, it was a complete travesty, a complete waste of time. They weren't interested in anything we had to say, and it was so stuffy in there listening to him droning on. This is that new equerry this is." He madly shakes the letters in the air, "I bet he's behind all this." He selects another letter looking down at it to see what it says. "Health and safety! We never had health and safety before and managed perfectly well, why do they think we need it now?"

"I've done a heath and safety course," Timothy pipes up; naively thinking this may help proceedings in some way but William is relentless.

"He still hasn't told me yet there are forty-five of his Army pals coming for drinks and canapés this evening for his special charity thing. What's going to happen when they all turn up at the door and I tell the police to send them away as we're not expecting any visitors tonight?"

"But we are expecting them," says Jason, "he told me about it last week."

"Yes but he didn't tell me! I suppose he thinks that Queen Elizabeth will feel obliged to come down specially to entertain all his friends just because she agreed to let them use the rooms. Well he's got a lot to learn."

"But you told me to prepare for it. I've told the kitchen and everything!"

"That's not the point! He has to inform me, it's his job! So don't you set out a single thing for it until I give you the word. I will not be managed and rearranged by some young buck straight out of Sandhurst who's still wet behind the ears who thinks he knows my job better than I do. I blame Sir Alastair! It's his fault for giving the daft boy a free hand."

"I can't believe that though? Sir Alastair has his socks laundered," says Jason shaking his head in disbelief. "Talk about extravagant."

"And to think he's an Army officer and we're supposed to look up to him as a leader of men. Leader of men? Huh! Follow him into war? Would you follow him into war?"

"I wouldn't follow him round Sainsbury's" Jason quips.

William opens another letter with such amazement that his voice rises to a squeak. "Oh look, here's another one! Management liaison meeting at Buckingham Palace on Wednesday at two p.m!" He scans the letter but doesn't read out everything, "All heads of departments to attend … innovate new working practices … establish line manager channels ... pah!" He tears it up in a rage. He is genuinely quite puzzled, amazed, upset and offended. "What on earth is he thinking?" His arms and shoulders fall in despair.

"Oh, why do they send me these things?" he says despondently. "Don't they know I'll be serving lunch?"

He tears up all the letters in despair and scrunches them together in a rage and throws them in the bin in disgust, then turns to grab the letters Timothy and Jason are holding and throws them away too, and slams back the bin lid. Then he storms out and marches up the stairs for his coffee with Reg, hauling his way up to the top.

[William regarded his personal attendance at lunch far more pertinent and beneficial to Queen Elizabeth than any Health & Safety or management operations memo could ever be. When he started in service in the 1950s a royal steward in Clarence House would not have served meals, that was down to the page and footmen, but William chose to do so when he became the Steward which must have suited him as he preferred to be front of house I suppose, like a lot of others]

Jason takes down one of the large wooden trays from a wall rack and opens one of the china store cupboard doors.

"That's what I like about working here. Nothing and nobody can tell Queen Elizabeth what to do. Right, come on Timothy, let's get started there's loads to do. I'll show you what we do for lunch prep. Get that out the way first as we've got to go outside in a minute to receive some flowers from the side gates from a school party, and God knows what else will crop up during the day that we'll have to help with?"

"What was all that about, will William be all right?" asks Timothy.

"Oh yes, fine. Don't worry it's fine, I've seen it all before. Come on. Now Timothy, can you please count me out eight of these plates and eight of the blue ones and cream ones and check them over and put the patterns the same way round like you did yesterday?"

"Don't William and Sir Alastair get on then?"

"Course they do, they've been working together for years haven't they? And can you polish the same amount of glasses like yesterday too. You've got it all down in your little book there haven't you."

"But why was William so angry?"

"Don't worry it was a one-off. William rarely loses his cool unless he really doesn't like somebody. Now if you don't mind we need to get on. Can you count and check the plates for me please like yesterday?"

Jason takes out a dinner plate and holds it up admiringly.

"Look Timothy, Minton! Queen Alexandra's monogrammed set, from Thomas Goode in South Audley Street. Look at that blue, you wouldn't think they were nearly a hundred years old would you? Aren't they beautiful? Made in Stoke-on-Trent in The Midlands."

Timothy couldn't care less about Stoke-on-Trent or fine china.

"You said you would show me how to set the cutlery on the table today Jason. Can we do that first please? I can do the plates easily now, it's all written down in my book."

"Oh all right then it makes no difference," says Jason. He unlocks the small silver room vault and turns on the light. He takes out a wooden cutlery carrier and puts it on the central table. Then he takes a clean linen drying towel and lays it on the table. He proceeds to arrange different pieces of silver cutlery on it. Timothy stands next to him watching intensely.

"Now then," says Jason, "imagine this is the dining table here okay? Right, so this is the table and you come along with your silver which you've already counted out ready, which we'll do in a minute. So, all you have to do is set this cutlery the way I'm going to show you now all right? See, you put everything in a row like this."

He arranges some cutlery in a row in a special order.

"So, they start from the outside," he continues, "and work inwards. This knife and fork is for the first course, here. Then this knife and fork is for the main course. Then this spoon and fork is for dessert. This silver bladed knife is for cheese and the little butter knife goes there on the left above the side plate like that. Don't worry about the side plate, I'll do that with you later. And we put the cruet there like that at the centre. Glasses here, and the napkin goes here, which I will take care of okay, have you got that?"

"That's wrong," says Timothy pointing to it. "The spoon and fork should go at the top like this," and he moves the spoon and fork to the top.

Jason moves them back straightaway.

"No. We put them in a line like this and they use them from the outside in," showing Timothy again.

"But that's not right," complains Timothy. "We always did it like this for weddings at The Royal Haven Hotel," and he moves them back.

Jason is getting agitated.

"The what? What's that?"

"The hotel where I used to work in Warwickshire."

"Oh well I'm sure you did, but we don't do that here we always do it like this, it never changes. They work from the outside in," and Jason moves them back again.

"But I've never seen it done like that before, and they don't do it like that on the Orient Express either. I know because I worked on it once."

Jason is worked up to being extremely agitated now.

"So just because you worked on a train you think you know better than me, do you? Look, I'm not saying it's right, I'm not saying it's wrong, it's just the way we do it here."

Jason is really trying hard to stay calm and not let the day get to him. He continues to be patient with Timothy and continues explaining to him, as the boy is quite sweet but seems a bit dim, but he's on the verge of screaming if Timothy continues to be so irritating and unhelpful. Jason takes a deep breath and tries again.

"It's quite a stylish way of doing it actually and this is the way Queen Elizabeth wants it, and after all, being in a private situation they can have it anyway they wish. They can have the knives and forks glued to the ceiling if they want. Don't know how they'd eat their lunch but that's their problem. Yes, you could do it your way if you were pushed for space like on a train or at a wedding or something when there are lots of people at the table, but I'm just telling you that we never do that here."

"So, what happens when you don't have enough space?"

"Well if that's the case we wouldn't set the spoon and fork down to begin with, we'd wait until dessert is about to be served and then put them down."

"Seems odd to me, and I'm sure it's not like that in my college catering book. I'll prove it to you. I'll go and get it, it's upstairs"

Timothy turns away as if about to rush upstairs to collect the book. Jason can't believe the audacity of his overconfidence.

"God this is all I need," he cries. "I'm showing you what to do and you're already answering me back. I don't believe this! Timothy, can you just do it like this please the way I've just shown you. You can draw a diagram to remind you of where everything goes if you like. I'll take you to the storeroom in a minute and you can start taking the tables out, and I'll come along and help when I've done my errands."

"What errands?"

"Stuff you needn't concern yourself with yet. Take it easy, there's plenty of time for you to learn. I've got a lot to think about over the next few days, so I'd appreciate your undivided attention if you don't mind. Draw a diagram of it in your little book, we've got to get on now."

Timothy stands over the cutlery setting, examining it. He doesn't look very convinced which you can see from the way he is pursing his lips and the fists have gone on the hips in a defiant stance.

Jason is looking for something in the drawers, getting quite bad-tempered and opens and shuts them quickly. He rifles through each one, getting very agitated.

"Have you seen a wooden bell-push on a white lead?"

"No," replies Timothy.

"Where's that gone now?"

Timothy still stares down at the cutlery and moves the spoon and fork back to the top of the setting once more, obviously completely confused about it now. He contemplates if it's correct or not.

Jason searches everywhere in the room but can't find what he's looking for and begins to get quite frustrated.

"Where is it? It should be here. I put it back yesterday," he says.

"Maybe Robert took it when he came in here this morning," says Timothy.

"When? What for?" asks Jason.

"I don't know, but it was when I was in the orderly's talking to the policeman first thing this morning."

[Robert is one of the queen's footmen. There are only two queen's footmen, one on duty and one off, but both would come on duty if William or another steward wanted them to help serve for a big lunch or something. One of them always travelled with the Queen, as did a dresser. And they were part of the staff of course. A queen's footman would be in the same team serving meals but they had extra personal duties of setting up trays throughout the day for the Queen, and serving her meals when she was alone, and moving her luggage, and collecting her newspapers and magazines and post, and sometimes popping to a shop for something, and taking and fetching the breakfast tray to the bedroom. The dresser would open the bedroom door so the footman could go in and leave the tray and the post in place, [in my time] then close the door on their way out. Her Majesty was never there when the footman went in at breakfast time. As far as I know Reg was the only man who ever went in there when the Queen was in there, when she was not very well but she still had to speak to her page about something. She spoke to the chef in her study about the menu for a special lunch or dinner and she would speak to the housekeeper to allocate rooms to guests but not every day. She spoke to the pages every day, you see that was their job, to communicate her requests. That is where the unusual old-fashioned job title comes from. The queen's footmen also help the page and take care of the dogs mainly]

Robert is a bit of a show-off who is proud of his job. He likes to joke with the people who work in the kitchen. Robert would have no use for the wooden bell.

In desperation Jason steps outside the pantry door and hollers at the top of his voice up the stairwell to the page's room on the floor above where he knows Robert should be.

"Robert? Robert? Are you there?" he shouts; and has to wait a few seconds for an answer.

"What? I'm busy," comes a wistful reply.

"Have you seen the wooden bell?" Jason shouts.

"It's in the pantry drawer!" Robert shouts back impatiently.

"No that's the Fabergé bell. I want the wooden bell for outside. Have you seen it?"

"No. It should be there. It was there yesterday."

66

"Okay. Thanks anyway!" groans Jason.

Jason returns to the pantry and has another look around, totally bemused of where the object has gone.

"Fabergé bell?" asks Timothy.

"Yes," says Jason, looking in all the drawers again as he picks up a Fabergé bell-push and holds it up to show Timothy. "This blue enamel bell-push made by Fabergé but I'm not looking for that I'm looking for the wooden one," and he puts it back in the drawer.

"Wooden one?"

"Yes! A wooden one. A round wooden bell-push we use for outside, have you seen it?"

"No. What do you mean, for outside?"

"Oh Christ! We have to put a bell on the dining table so that Queen Elizabeth can press it to let us know when to serve the next course or to summon us for something."

"How can she ring a wooden bell?"

"Timothy! You're driving me absolutely crazy! We plug in the bell to the house bell ringing system via a cable, so certain bells ring in certain servant's workrooms. It's electric! We know Queen Elizabeth's routine so we know which bells to attend and which to ignore. Does that answer your question?"

"Yes, thank you."

"Good!"

Timothy scaresly shows concern at Jason's nervous agitated state, nor at any point does he attempt to help to find the bell-push. He seems totally immersed in his own thoughts.

"Will I be setting up the table tomorrow as well for the Queen Mother's birthday lunch?" he asks.

"No, I told you. That will be at Buckingham Palace. We won't have anything to do with that," says Jason, still looking.

"What will we do tomorrow then?"

"There will still be loads of people here mostly household, so we'll be looking after them serving them meals and whatever."

"But the Queen Mother is still going outside in front of the cameras, isn't she?"

"Yes, all that will be the same. It's just that she won't be here for lunch."

"Oh good, I'm looking forward to that bit."

Jason finally gives up searching and stands over the table, gripping the edge of it, his knuckles white. He throws his head back, closes his eyes and takes a very deep breath. Timothy is really getting to him and he has no idea of where the bell-push has gone.

"You know when the Queen Mother and everybody sit at the table in the garden for lunch today Jason."

"Yes?" Jason says, sighing.

"Will I be able to take a photo of them all sitting down?"

"No, absolutely not. Cameras aren't allowed anywhere near work and you won't get the opportunity to take a picture anyway."

"But I'll be really discreet about it, I'll make sure nobody sees me taking the pictures."

"Look Timothy, if William or Reg sees you or anybody else for that matter, you'll be out on your ear straightaway."

"But you said they have lunch under the trees in the garden."

"So?"

"So I can easily stand behind a tree to take them and nobody will see me, I can do it in a matter of seconds."

"Please Timothy forget it. I've got enough to think about without having to keep an eye on you. We are not allowed to have cameras in the house and that's the end of it. I can't believe you even asked me that. Believe me, the last

68

thing you want is to be found waving a loaded camera around. You'll get yourself shot!"

"Okay I was only asking. It was just a thought."

"Yes, well, forget it!"

"But I will be able to take a photo tomorrow, when all the royal family come over here won't I?"

"For goodness sake no! They won't be coming over! Not this year I told you! The Queen Mother is going over to Buckingham Palace for lunch and is riding down The Mall in a carriage with the Prince of Wales!"

"Oh, I see."

Jason and Timothy continue with their daily chores and duties, as does everyone else in the house.

A while later, in the equerry's office, the equerry is feeling hungry while he contemplates what may be served for lunch. He pours himself a drink.

It would appear to the untrained eye that there is some form of drinks tray in every room in Clarence House. If a doctor or a dressmaker or a tailor or whomever makes a call to the house, then a small tray of ham sandwiches and a silver mustard cruet and a Joey of whisky and some water is automatically supplied to the room that has been allocated for them to wait in, before they are presented to perform their services. It would usually be accompanied with an Evening Standard if it was out. A Joey, as William calls it, is a very small glass decanter with a pouring handle and a glass stopper, (engraved with a royal cypher of course). They would appear on a bedroom side table if somebody was staying the night at Clarence House, or could be quickly administered if a guest suddenly arrived from a long drive on a chilly evening in Scotland and needed some sustenance with a cup of tea, or a wee dram against a cold.

[When William travelled on duty to Windsor Castle with Queen Elizabeth, he never went for meals in the staff canteen. He must have survived on titbits people brought him toing-and-froing throughout the day but he always made sure of his quota of a Joey of whisky from the Keeper of the Cellar when he could. Incidentally, William was Keeper of the Cellar at Clarence House. It was a fraction of the size compared with Buckingham Palace's set-up, so the job descriptions and titles and their duties condensed and overlapped.

"If they ask," he used to say, "say the hairdresser is coming again today," he would tell his footman who collected it for him. Everyone knew that wasn't the case. The hairdresser was a little peeved when he found out, thinking he'd got a reputation with the Windsor Castle staff. Nearly all the whisky that was set out for professionals on Joey trays at Clarence House went untouched as these people had work to do and some of them had driven themselves there. Yet this did not matter to him so much as the fact the trays had been provided, that was the important thing to William. He was simply using the procedures he had learned decades ago, and people had put great store by them, but these days they were becoming outdated]

The equerry's office drinks tray is actually a walk-in cupboard under the stairs, accessed by opening a false bookcase door near the fireplace. Similar thing to many modest country houses no doubt. It is quite roomy in there and so is also used for storage of a collection of Ordnance Survey maps and a collection of telephone directories of the whole of the U.K. (Another sign of harking back to a bygone age, except this bygone age was still ongoing, so to speak.) The only remarkable thing to say about this drinks cupboard is about the ice bucket, because it holds only about a litre, if that, and that it is bright red and made of polystyrene. One of the footmen calls it the Noddy ice bucket as it is quite comical looking, but it is also his favourite as it's the best insulator and keeps ice frozen for hours. He's had his eye on it for years but it belongs in there so he can't touch it.

The equerry's office is quite large and airy. It needs to be to accommodate its secondary purpose of a space for hosting some of Queen Elizabeth's lunch guests and any visitors who may have business there. Guests of

honour and prestige are afforded the privilege of arriving at
the grand front entrance, where William comes through to
work every morning from the street whereas the other staff
come in through the staff entrance (of course). Lunch guests
who are new or nervous, or a member of the family or a
regular who is familiar with the set-up can wander into the
equerry's room. Over the years the room has hosted a whole
spectrum of society. Even today, when the orderly walks in
there to replenish the ice or collect the drinks wall chart he
might come across an interesting mix of characters. An array
of anyone from Lord Linley to Maureen Lipman to an
assistant to The Dalai Lama, to the secretary to The
Grimshaw-on-Sea Pigeon Fancier's Appreciation Society or
some other obscure organisation. There are no rules as this is
also a private household as well as a public one. It could be
such an eclectic mix of designers and actors and artistes to
the completely humdrum of an ordinary [royal] household.

Queen Elizabeth chooses the officials herself, they do
not choose each other. It has to be assumed that Her
Majesty would have compatibility in mind when making
these decisions, because as with life in any office or place of
work there is no guarantee of synchronisation with the staff.
The equerry's office is also a neutral territory of common
ground for the royal household to congregate and meet up,
in time to have an informal chat over a drink before going
through to the main house to join Queen Elizabeth for
lunch, as the equerry and Sir Alastair are doing now.

It is quiet in there today, there are only the two of them
as everyone is exceptionally busy dealing with the birthday so
all the other household members around are too busy to
attend.

Sir Alastair has to walk through the equerry's office
from his own office to get through to the house to go to
lunch or to see the Queen, unless he walks around through
the orderly's and past the pantry, which he doesn't fancy

doing because he'd most likely be waylaid by a member of staff who wants to chat or moan about something. This seems to be a recent trend with the staff in these latter years.

He came to work at Clarence House in 1960 as a temporary equerry, then became assistant private secretary for a number of years then private secretary and now comptroller to Queen Elizabeth, which means he orchestrates all her official engagements and entertaining, as well as all her private homes and staff. He is sixty-nine years old, so he knows the set-up just as well as William does, and his adept and smart style of efficiency that he displays at work, effortlessly transfers to the way he dressed.

The room is typically furnished with a large desk and some paintings and military pictures and a large fireplace. It is quite a masculine looking room apart from one unusual piece of furniture. This is a glass oriental style folding room screen, lit from inside. Quite an attractive piece that was probably acquired on an official foreign trip or perhaps may be on museum loan from a previous equerry or official from their military days. Either way it creates a convenient false wall shielding the interior of the room from the gaze of the communal hall as the door is always left open. William had explained once that this was Sir Ralph Anstruther's idea, (Queen Elizabeth's treasurer) as the ground floor rooms were rooms of business so nothing untoward or secret should be going on in them, and so being able to stroll in would save people time, not having to knock and wait for a response.

Sir Alastair is faffing about in the drinks cupboard bringing together a pink gin for himself. He stalls in mid-shake of the glass to chalk up another tot of gin against his name on the wall chart. [Private drinks have to be paid for] He is being very careful not to spill anything on his immaculate clothes, especially not on his wonderfully bulled shoes which have come up to an impressive mirror shine. (All the work of the Army orderlies.)

The equerry is looking down at his glass of fizzy water with lime and is perched against the front of his desk looking somewhat crestfallen. He is a tall, blond handsome man but his sartorial elegance does not quite match that of Sir Alastair. Major Freddie Abernethy is still young enough to be in the public schoolboy phase of expensive scuffed shoes and scrunched up shirts.

Most English public schoolboys never polish their shoes or take care of their clothes, somebody else does it for them when possible. And they are probably not even aware of the existence of shoe repairers. A public schoolboy's clothes would have been pressed and neatly folded by some considerate person at some point. But, the necessity to pack a holdall of sports kit and clobber at brakeneck speed by just stuffing it all in any old how and so creasing everything in order to catch the school rugby team bus to a match at the last minute, has resulted in the trait a typical public schoolboy seems to inherit. That is, to always pack badly like that and to carry that lack of a social grace all through their life, thereby resulting in untidy creased clothes and a 'shabby' look. That is how you can generally tell if a young man has been to an English public school or not, by his scuffed worn expensive shoes and his badly ironed shirt with only the collar and the visible v-shaped patch on the chest pressed.

This usually lasts until their late twenties when they either get married or are earning enough money to hire assistance. The equerry is still in this schoolboy mode as the equerries are usually young men still in their mid to late twenties when they set out on their two-year engagement as equerry.

"I've just been on the phone to my tailor and an

assistant said to me," says Sir Alastair, (affecting a strong London accent),

"I'm sorry sir, we've got nuffink available for that day at the moment sorry, but I can fit you in next fursday."

He looks totally perplexed, staring into space.

"I find it extraordinary that some people talk like that? I mean, putting two effs in nothing … and a kay at the end!"

"Extraordinary!" concurs the equerry, not really listening.

"I don't know how some people get the jobs," went on Sir Alastair.

"Had a footman worked here who's just got himself a job in America. Not the sharpest tool in the box but certainly not the dullest but followed orders obediently which is half the battle these days. I had to explain to his new employers that we only give verbal references here, which annoyed them enormously. They are only really interested in receiving some royal crested writing paper. That opens more doors than anything."

"Especially in America I would imagine, yes," replies the equerry, as he wonders, where on earth is this conversation going?

"I don't know what's wrong with young people these days. He told me he was only leaving because there was no prospect of promotion. Very worrying. I don't know why he was so frustrated as he made it to queen's footman, and some people have taken fifteen or twenty years to get that far in the past."

"Young people do grow up fast these days Sir Alastair, and they know what they want from an early age."

"Now if National Service was brought back they would be taught how to mature properly and how to want the right things in life, everything would be better all round."

"I agree, absolutely," says a totally uninterested equerry.

"And so when I was coming out from my barber this morning on St. James's Street, a chap bumps into me on the street while he's getting out of a car. It turns out to be the very same chap I'm telling you about, the footman who's just left. The first thing he said to me was,

Oh hello Sir Alastair, I'm picking up something for work from Berry Brothers over the road.

Then he pointed to his uniform and said,

Oh, I see you're admiring my uniform Sir Alastair. This isn't my usual uniform I'm wearing now, this is my everyday uniform. I'm having my smart livery especially made in Los Angeles by a Hollywood costume designer. And this car we're using today isn't our usual car, this is the house car that the London staff can use. It's only a Mercedes. The main car is a Rolls-Royce but that's in the garage having a service at the moment.

And he was prattling on, and standing in my way, and I was in a hurry and being very polite but I couldn't get a word in edgeways, and all I really wanted to say to him was: oh balls Adrian!"

The equerry laughs nervously.

Sir Alastair has appeared from the drinks cupboard now and is standing opposite the equerry.

"So how are you getting along so far Freddie. Are you finding your feet?"

"Actually Sir Alastair, I'm finding the going a bit tricky dealing with William Tallon."

"Oh yes?" says Sir Alastair, much intrigued.

"I'm trying to reorganise the travel arrangements for the staff to go to Scotland and so I asked him for a list of people he was sending, so I could book the plane tickets."

"And he said why are you flying them up as they always

go by train?" says Sir Alastair preempting the equerry's next intended remark.

"Yes!" the equerry says astonished. "How did you know that?"

"Because he always does this with the new equerry. He's testing you out, still trying to get the measure of you. He obviously doesn't like you. Don't you remember me telling you when you first came here Freddie? He'll be as pleasant as a puppy with you to begin with I said. See the good-looking new boy, get the measure of you, test the competition with Queen Elizabeth if there is any, see how he can manipulate you. Give it a few weeks and you can bet he may not be speaking to you. Have you forgotten that already?"

The equerry does remember but had thought Sir Alastair was joking.

"But why do I have to seek his approval on such matters? He's just a slop-jockey isn't he?"

"Indeed Freddie, but a very dangerous one, so beware the venomous asp! He is one of the very few people around here who truly has the Queen's ear, and he knows it. And goodness knows what poison he chooses to whisper when it suits him. Don't forget, Tallon has been here a very long time. He's one of the longest serving members of staff in Queen Elizabeth's household. Not only will you have to deal with him and Reginald, you will encounter all sorts of people in your new job here. I have to deal with the servant's petty grievances almost on a daily basis. In fact, I feel that the staff have far too much access to me, it makes me wonder what all these heads of departments are for? Our job is to keep Queen Elizabeth happy and as Her Majesty doesn't care for change, we must do all we can to hold everything together to keep the status quo. Whatever Tallon or anyone may think, I am responsible for running this household and the welfare of the staff. The ultimate responsibility for everything that goes on in this place lies at my door. So if you come across any more difficulties with either him or Reginald in the future then please let me know."

Sir Alastair was not expecting his new equerry to flag up a grievance straightaway, but he had noticed the boy had been subdued this morning. He had put it down to the fact that he had not been getting along with William very well since he started here, recently. Queen Elizabeth seemed to have favoured the blond good-looking man by requesting he sit next to her at lunch a few times. This may have looked like favouritism, which must have annoyed William, but it was Queen Elizabeth taking the opportunity of getting to know her new equerry a bit better. Anyhow, Sir Alastair thought the boy's spirits were low and he needed cheering up. It didn't help he cycled into work this morning from South London so he must be feeling tired.

The equerry cups his hands around his empty glass and says hesitantly,

"Reginald called me love."

"What?" barks Sir Alastair. "In what context?"

"I'd been working late on the logistics for the Scottish trip, and when I asked him if he could get a chauffeur to take me home, he said,

No! You're only a Major love!"

"Oh, that's nothing to worry about," says Sir Alastair much relieved, the strain visibly falling from his shoulders as he breathes freely again.

"He's from Yorkshire and they all talk like that up there. Anyway you're not entitled to cars for that. Don't let the side down Freddie by appearing too ostentatious, or people will be justified in thinking that all you do is mix up the martini!"

Sir Alastair doesn't really mean this as he had been an equerry himself, years ago. He just wants to cheer up the boy. He had heard someone say it once as a friendly joke and thought it quite jolly.

"I'm still trying to work out who does what around here," says the equerry.

"You'll work it out soon enough. Take heart, you may well be my very last equerry, think of the kudos. It won't be long now and we can all retire at last. Mind you, we were saying that five years ago so you may find yourself pipped at the post when your two years is up. That reminds me, what's your predecessor doing? Did he get married yet?"

"Well no. He's started his own television film production company. He's just got a commission to make some films for the BBC."

"I don't know why he doesn't go back into the Army? I don't understand you chaps. You are my umpteenth equerry, yet all you fellas seem to sail through your experience here and still end up working in a bloody bank. Makes me wonder what all that Army training was for? Thought he was getting married this summer to that nice girl what's her name, works for The Royal Collection. Her family run a golfing hotel somewhere?"

"Actually, Sir Alastair her family own a very large castle in Wales."

"Quite, but you still can't build a career on that! And what's that t.v. production company business all about? He'll end up working alongside young students taking a gap year from their media studies degree. That's what my granddaughter's doing at the moment."

Suddenly Sir Alastair seems to have noticed the time.

"Have you seen the lady in waiting?" looking around the room to see if anyone is lurking about.

"Yes," says the equerry gesturing with his thumb

towards a closed door on the far side of the room.

"She went through there a few minutes ago."

"Golly!" says Sir Alastair as he gulps down the last of his gin, swoops the glass out of the equerry's hand and places it down with his, then sweeps the equerry along towards the door.

"We'd better go through and join the others, or we may end up in the Tower!"

They scurry through the doorway and dash along all the way down the royal hall towards the glaring sunshine streaming through the open front doors ahead. They scamper along all the way until they come to an abrupt halt just before the porch, and in just a few seconds they emerge outdoors and proceed gracefully and serenely, like a couple of galleons at the head of a flotilla, appearing in the garden where lunch guests usually congregate and drinks are served, but nobody is there yet, apart from Jason and Timothy who have just finished setting things up.

Royal lunchtime is almost upon us.

Jason and Timothy return to the pantry after setting up the lunch tables on the terrace. Everything is now ready, so they have half an hour or so to spare.

It's important that you know how many things they have to do so I'll quickly go through it here; They have taken the Burgess folding tables from the storeroom and all the heavy antique Chippendale chairs needed, then carried them down the hall two by two outside to the usual position on the terrace. Jason could see Timothy struggling with the effort it took him to carry everything. He had to pause to put down the chairs to rest for a second or two on the way. There were porters at Buckingham Palace to move furniture like this, but this household was much smaller so the footmen did it.

They put up a dining table on the terrace, then they fetched two service tables and put them up in the hall near the front doors along with two tray stands and one clearing tray. Then they arranged the electric bell and the tablecloths. So now they could get to work laying it all up. The silver cutlery, cruets, napkins and glasses were carried out from the pantry on trays, so were all the plates except the ones needed for the hot food which were put into a plate warmer. Then the service tables were laid out with everything they would use to serve the whole meal, so that everything they needed was to hand and no last minute counting of plates or running about or whatever went on.

Usually the items on the service table were; (for this lunch) main course plates, salad plates, dessert and cheese plates, serving spoons and forks, silver sauce boat holders and ladles, a jug of cream and a sugar castor, cheeseboard with serving knives, port and brandy with glasses, two serving salvers, a coffee service tray, an ice bucket and tongs, water, wine cooler, service napkins, some spare cutlery mirroring whatever cutlery is being used on the table in case anybody drops a knife or spoon. [It's not the done thing to bend down and pick up your dropped fork or something, best to carry on regardless with the conversation and any attendant worth their salt should notice it and subtly they can supply you with one of their 'spares' straightaway or at a convenient moment. That's the reason they prepare, as it's a long walk from the pantry to the garden just to collect a clean fork! It's twice as far if lunch is under the trees don't forget]

A space on the lawn was already set out for drinks and nibbles. All the chairs and blankets and parasols and cushions and the drinks, ice and nibbles were out. Only the dining table butters and salad dressing were needed at the last minute now.

Jason and Timothy walk into the pantry boiling hot from working in the sun wearing their woollen scarlet tailcoats and starched collars. [They have to be properly dressed in case they come across Queen Elizabeth or another royal who may happen to be around] Jason puts away his tray in the wall rack and takes off his tailcoat and hangs it up. Timothy copies him and puts away his tray too. Jason goes over to the sink and pours himself a glass of water and wipes his brow with a paper napkin. Timothy looks shattered. He takes off his tailcoat and flops onto the stool, sitting down before his sleeves are quite off, so he sits on the coat and squashes it. He manages to wrench his hands out of the sweaty sleeves and slumps in an exhausted heap. His brain isn't tired though. That was still working overtime.

"Robert said that I might be going to the ballet at the

Opera House with you tomorrow to help serve dinner in the royal box?" he says.

"I don't think so Timothy as you've only just started, and people usually have to be here for a while to do that sort of thing as it's considered to be a treat."

"But you're going?"

"I should think so as I didn't go last time, due to a technical hitch, and I've had my tits over the sink cleaning silver all-year so I think I'm due a bit of the limelight thank you very much!"

"Do you get to see the show with the royals then?"

Jason thinks he needs to explain something to Timothy about this.

"You don't go to see the show, no! You go to be a part of the glamour. Imagine it Timothy, The Queen and Queen Elizabeth and The Princess Margaret and guests, all at the theatre on the Queen Mother's one hundredth birthday. This is a first and a last. Why do you think William is so excited? Even he hasn't seen anything like this before. It's the one hundredth birthday Timothy!"

"I suppose so." Timothy isn't duly impressed at all with going to a theatre to see a show. He can't see the point of that at all. He'd much rather go to a rugby match, or to a bar.

The sound of William's voice travels down the stairs from the floor above. He is leaning over the handrail on the landing above calling to them. He must have heard them come in from the garden.

"I say is anybody there? Chaps? Jason?"

Jason takes a couple of steps out the pantry and grabs hold of the banisters straight ahead and looks up. He then shouts back up the stairwell to William. The stairs are too steep and long to be able to see William directly from this position, so he has to shout in order to be heard on the floor above.

"Yes William, I'm here!"

"Have you set the table for lunch yet?" calls William.

Jason's heart sinks. His face grimaces before William finishes the sentence as he knows what's coming next. He knows this old trick. William is going to say that Queen Elizabeth has asked for the lunch table to be moved over from the terrace to underneath the trees or vice versa, because it's too cold or windy or something and she doesn't want to risk catching a chill. William must think this is funny in some peculiar way, but Jason can't see the joke, because the joke is on him! He hopes this may just be about something else, something to do with the birthday, perhaps?

"Yes William, we've just this minute come in."

They are having this conversation without being able to see each other. They are communicating as a couple of disembodied voices bellowing up and down the stairs at each other making arrangements. If Jason had the wits to look William in the eye or just trot up the stairs to speak to him properly, then it's very likely that William would back down. Also, Jason doesn't have the wits to realise that bellowing to each other like in an episode of 'The Waltons' is part of the joke, as anyone in the vicinity can hear. Well, William must think it's funny at least.

"Well I'm terribly sorry," comes William's voice again, "but the Queen says it would be nice to make the most of the sun, but the wind has changed and she would rather have lunch under the trees after all, so would you mind awfully changing it over?"

Jason is too dim to realise he is being played like a Stradivarius, so he carries on in vain hope, that if he plays along a bit and goes through the motions humouring William, he may be able to convince him to back down. After all, it's a boiling hot summer day so no way can he use the weather as an excuse.

"But it's lovely out there William I've just been out."

"It's blowing a gale."

"No, really William it's absolutely fine. There's hardly any wind at all and the sun's blazing down."

"It could turn again any moment."

"But it's so hot today, there's not a cloud in the sky."

"It won't take you long."

"No really William, it's beautiful out there there's no wind at all."

This was Jason's best shot. It's pathetic. What a loser! William definitely knows he's got Jason on the ropes. Just one more go will put this baby to sleep.

"What about if we wait for five minutes to see if the wind dies down?" asks Jason.

This is feeble. Sometimes the best thing to say is no! Never mind clutching at straws and appealing to someone's better nature. Still, Jason doesn't actually know if Queen Elizabeth requested this or not, so this is a tricky one. Timothy is getting a free seat on a crash course at least. All good for his C.V.

"The Queen does say she's very sorry. She wouldn't want to catch a chill."

William isn't giggling as far as Jason can tell, and he did just say that with supreme sincerity, and he sounds okay so all this could be above board? There's a tumbleweed kinda pause now in order to test each other's resolve: which lasts about three and a half seconds.

"Are you still there?" asks William.

"Okay William, I'll move it," says Jason reluctantly, totally resigned to the situation now and so he turns around and goes back into the pantry.

"Thank you so much," says William and he returns

to the page's room and the corridor door swings shut after him with a thud.

In the pantry Jason takes down his tailcoat and puts it on.

"Come on," he says, "we've got to move everything we've just set out on the terrace over to the trees. The table, chairs, service tables, glass, silver, china, electric bell, the lot!"

"You're joking?" says Timothy, lifting his head out of his hands and looking up towards Jason.

"I wish I was."

"You're not serious? It's just taken us ages to do all that! I'm shattered."

"Look, William does this sometimes, he's playing a game with us. He must think it's funny to say that the Queen's asked us to move the table, when she hasn't really. I think it's his idea of a joke."

"But that's crazy! You mean that he makes you set everything up and then waits and tells you to move it somewhere else at the last minute? And you let him treat you like this? Why do you let him get away with it? Doesn't anybody tell him where to go?"

"That's nothing! I've had to set it up in three different places in the past, from the morning room to outside and everything and anyway, we don't know what Queen Elizabeth has and hasn't said do we? It's not as if anyone's going to go up to Her Majesty and ask if she really has changed her mind, is it?"

"I'll go." Timothy stands up and turns to rush off but Jason grabs him and stops him in his tracks, pulling him back.

"Don't be daft!" he says. "You can't just burst into a room and approach Queen Elizabeth like that. Look trust me. It's just one of those things William does now and again to make himself feel in charge. Just let me handle this otherwise he'll blow up and there'll be a row and you might not have a job here any longer. The best way is to get on with it and don't let him know he's getting to us. Come on get some trays. I'm not asking Robert to help, he'll be stuck in the kitchen chatting to the girls. Why don't I ever get help when I need it?"

There had been footmen in the past who tried to question William's ways and his silly games but it just made them unpopular. Some never said anything, they moaned in private but never pushed back. Sir Alastair even installed the odd military type in the hope it would shake things up, but it never did.

Timothy was bored. He had the feeling he made a mistake in coming here, so was thinking about disappearing as suddenly as he appeared, as it wasn't what he expected workwise or otherwise. But now an opportunity has presented itself which makes him decide he is going to have some fun with Jason, by stirring things up a little.

As Jason takes down a tray Timothy stops him from walking away by grabbing his arm.

"Look mate," he says, "can I say something to you? And I don't want you to take this the wrong way 'cause you're a nice guy."

"What?"

"Don't let William treat you like this."

"Like what?" says Jason stubbornly, as he has a good idea of what Timothy is about to say.

"Like you're a piece of dirt on the bottom of his shoe! He's a bully. He talks to you like you're an idiot, don't let him get away with it. You know that all bullies are cowards inside if you stand up to them."

Jason doesn't know this as he deals with things the best he can.

"He's not even man enough to tell you something eye to eye, he leans over the bannister and barks orders at you down the stairs."

Jason never saw it like this, after all, William was his boss and he couldn't or wouldn't refuse any reasonable requests regarding work.

"That's because he's busy, it gets a bit frantic round here sometimes." And this is what Jason believes to be the truth.

"Too busy to pick up the phone? He's always on the phone to other people. He must do it so everyone can hear, to make you look like an idiot."

Jason had never thought of that before. Timothy is right. William was always on the telephone, usually the pantry telephone in the morning, because if anyone wanted to get hold of him, he would either be in the pantry, the page's room or his home. It was no use ringing the steward's office as he was hardly ever in there even though he was the Steward. He was also a page so he had the use of two offices. And the page's room was next to Queen Elizabeth whereas the steward's office was downstairs at the end of the corridor past the pantry, so William wasn't going to hang around down there all day. He wanted to be right next to the Queen.

"No he doesn't," says Jason, "that's just the way he is. Come on we've got to get this table moved before our lunch."

It's obvious that Jason's not quite the pushover Timothy imagined. He jumps up to sit on the worktop next to the sink, thinking that he would have to work on Jason some more to get what he wants.

"Hey don't get me wrong," he says, "it's none of my business really as I'm the new guy in town, but I can see from miles away that he takes advantage of your good nature. I don't want him to push me around like that. I thought I'd better mention it for your sake, that's all."

"Well thanks but there's nothing to worry about really," says Jason, getting a little agitated. He knows they will have to move everything regardless of what Timothy thinks. It's certainly given him something to mull over for later. "Come on, let's move this table."

"Well if you're sure you can handle the situation?"

"Yes I can, thank you."

"All right then, if you're absolutely sure about that?"

"Yes I am thank you," says Jason.

"All right then, but let me know if ever you need any help in that department okay?"

"Okay right."

"Okay then, let's go. But you owe me a drink!"

Timothy slides off the worktop and snatches his tailcoat from the stool and then a tray, and they head out to the garden to move everything to under the trees.

The branches of the plane trees touch the ground in places but there are large gaps enough to be able to get through easily. Putting it up here is twice the distance to the terrace, which means some very long walks from the kitchen and pantry carrying wide trays of heavy silver and china down the dark hall, then out into the blinding sunlight (reflecting off the polished gleaming silver) with your arms locked in position due to the weight, always being mindful you step over the odd snoozing Corgi on the way. Navigating such an obstacle course while partially sighted and constrained inside a sweltering, tight, heavy uniform whilst carrying a heavy load is not such a walk in the park as it looks.

In A Quiet Corridor

Timothy is taking a few stolen moments to himself where nobody can see him. He is standing in an open-air area of the basement near a place that delivery drivers can use to have a smoke. It's quite a way from the kitchens so it's very quiet at this time of the day, as people are busy working. There's hardly anyone walking about.

He is talking to a friend on his mobile phone. He knows that mobile phones aren't allowed on duty and not everyone has one, so that's why he's being so clandestine about it. He already knows what he would say if he got caught. He would say that he was new, and he didn't realise having a mobile phone was forbidden. And if anyone asked what was he doing so far away from his workplace, he would say that he was looking for the staff toilets but he doesn't know his way about yet and got lost. He has it all worked out.

"Hi mate? Yes it's me" he says to the person on the other end of the line.

"No, I'm fine, don't worry there's no one around, no one can hear me."

"No, I haven't been able to find anything out yet, William's a slippery fish but I'll definitely ask him today when I can get him on his own again and he'll tell me everything."

"Yeah, he really likes me. Listen, I wanted to let you know I've come across an old disused basement area full of old official papers and receipts. They go back to at least the nineteen-fifties. They must have kept absolutely every piece of paper over the century. Are you interested?"

He listens to his friend's reply.

"Don't worry I managed to grab a handful."

"Don't worry nobody knows, they are a bunch of idiots

round here, I'm running rings round the dimwits."

He listens.

"Yeah that's right."

"Okay, later."

He switches off the phone and puts it back into his pocket and continues on his way.

OMELETTE

A luncheon party is an important occasion for Queen Elizabeth at her noble age. It means she can spend a leisurely and amicable couple of hours in the company of different people. William knows this, so he makes every effort in making each one count [even if he drives the rest of us mad in the process].

He sees himself as the master of ceremonies of a live performance at Clarence House, just like a live show at the theatre. The staff are the players and backstage hands, producers, and publicists etc. All are acting out a part, being responsible for a certain task, and like any show there is the danger of something going wrong at any second. The whole shooting match could go tits-up without warning. After all, his job is also about delivery and timing to a live audience. The activities everyone performs dovetail, so the operation runs smoothly. Even with the tremendous upheaval of the birthday celebrations going on around, the place still has to be cleaned and meals served in the usual way. For instance, today the chef has the task of overseeing the kitchen and making yet another fabulous omelette for lunch. Jason has to look after the new boy while avoiding any personalities flaring up, and William has the task of overseeing the service of it all and generally keeping Queen Elizabeth happy. This seems to be the general plan, anyway.

Chef Michael Sealey makes superb omelettes –the classic way; thumping his fist on the pan handle to nudge the eggy mix making it roll over and slide out the pan with sizzling melted butter. Then he garnishes it around the edges with a sauce or whatever, and there it is!

Everything is prepared for lunch at last. The table is set under the trees according to William's latest instructions. It's too late to move it again now anyhow. Whether or not those instructions originally came from Queen Elizabeth we shall never know. Jason and Timothy have tidied up the pantry and managed to grab a cup of coffee and some biscuits as they both had to miss lunch.

Now, William and Reg have come downstairs to the pantry to join them waiting to start serve royal lunch. Robert is in the kitchen collecting the cold stuff, such as butter, salad dressing and cheese etc. that he will take straight out and arrange before the diners sit down. (That's not his job by the way, but it gives him the opportunity to chat with the kitchen girls, so it suits Jason.)

So now, all of them have congregated in the pantry as this is where lunch is served from and where they wait to listen for the bell that tells them to start serving the first course. (This is a very efficient way of doing things and preferable to all, as they know what's what and they don't have to hover around the diners too much.) Queen Elizabeth and her lunch guests are out on the lawn talking and having drinks at the moment, so it could be any second now or up to, let's say, fifteen minutes I suppose before the first bell rings. The bell-push is on the dining table under the trees which is a few good strides across the garden from the lawn where everyone is sitting at present. (Jason had to use the Fabergé one in the end as he can't find the wooden one that was specially made for outside by the electrician. Why anyone would take it is a mystery as it's not needed anywhere else in the house, and it can't be used without connecting it to the house system via the special cable they lay out.)

As the first course is omelette today there will be two bells, not the usual one. One bell to give chef the few minutes notice he needs to start cooking it, and the second bell to indicate to the footmen that they are sitting, or just about to sit: so bring it along. Usually a footman dashes up the stairs with it as soon as it's cooked and pops it into a hot food cupboard where it will be fine for a couple of minutes if need be. Then, when the second bell goes, they take it straight out and butler-serve it. Sometimes they can take it straight to the table, which is the perfect plan hence the two bell system.

Reg is sitting on the low pantry wooden stool, leaning against a cupboard. Jason and Timothy are standing opposite him in front of the tall fridge on the other side of the central table near the door, wearing their scarlet jackets, [they refer to them as jackets even though they are tailcoats] and William is talking to somebody on the telephone. Incidentally, Jason and Timothy are only standing up because there's only one seat, and Reg has nabbed it. It does make for a more tense atmosphere with the two boys standing up in a small room like this, as they become a captive audience under a microscope in effect to William's small talk, which Jason knows off by heart by now. They have no choice as there's nowhere else to wait. They just have to grin and bear it.

(Jason hates having to huddle together in the pantry like this, waiting, and watching William perform his predictable routines. He is wishing the bell to ring, so that they can all clear out of there and the day to unfold.)

"Oh that's wonderful Dillie darling! I'm so looking forward to it," says William, gushing to his friend on the phone. "Oh and to you too!" he laughs. "Drinks at my little house usual time? I'm sure it will be, absolutely! All right Dillie darling, take care."

He replaces the receiver then turns around and takes out a tiny key from an inside pocket and moves along towards the drinks cupboard which is right next to where

94

Reg is sitting. This means that the drinks cupboard is directly behind Reg's head with just enough room for William to open the door.

William talks to the boys while he unlocks the cupboard, "I'm being taken to the theatre again this evening. That'll be three times this week, including the Opera House with Queen Elizabeth tomorrow."

"What are you going to see?" asks Jason.

"It's always a surprise. I never know until I get to Joe Allen's, then no doubt someone will let the cat out of the bag," he says, as he opens the cupboard to reveal it's absolutely packed full of alcohol in bottles and crystal decanters with silver neck labels on silver chains.

He reaches in and twists the bottles and sorts them out a little and talks to the boys without looking round at them.

"Now chaps, what do you want to drink? Gin, whisky, vodka, sherry, wine, what?"

Jason signals to Timothy discreetly by mouthing the word 'no!' silently, but he doesn't see the warning.

William looks behind him impatiently "Come on! What would you like?"

"Oh um, whisky and Coke please" mutters Timothy, fearing he is a rabbit caught in the headlights.

"Fetch yourself a glass then," says William, and he looks into the cupboard again and continues fiddling with the bottles.

It looks as if there are bottles at the back that haven't seen the light of day for years. It also seems that if you took all the bottles out and tried to put them back, they wouldn't fit back in as they are so tightly arranged.

Timothy fetches himself a glass out of a cupboard and takes it to William, who pours whisky a third of the way up the glass then tops it up with Coke [no ice], then places it on the wooden ledge of the cupboard and leaves it there for him to pick up. He then pours a drink for himself and another for Robert, that he also puts down on the ledge.

[William doles out the drinks like a nurse would administer medicine to his ward patients. The drinks cupboard being the medicine cabinet, or the poison cupboard. It's not the case that the drinks are rationed because they are absolutely not. It's more a case of 'get it quickly while I've got the cupboard door unlocked.' It makes no difference as it will be open again in a jiffy]

"I shouldn't have had so much pudding," says Reg, holding his stomach. "Wasn't it a lovely lunch? We never get chef's omelettes. I wish he'd put a bit more parmesan in it though, he does for Queen Elizabeth. Did you have some?" he asks Jason.

"I didn't have any, there was none left when I got there."

"What did you have then, some salad?"

"I didn't fancy anything. I'm fine honestly, it's too hot to eat."

"Cheers!" calls William, as he takes a sip whilst standing in front of the open cupboard.

"You'll have a drink? Go on?" he says to Jason.

"No William thank you, not in the day, I'll fall asleep if I do and I won't be able to serve lunch."

"All right then if you're sure, only need to ask. I'll leave this one here for Robert for when he comes back from doing the cold stuff," and he moves the drink he poured for Robert over to the worktop next to the sink. [It's a third full of alcohol and no ice just like all the drinks he pours]

"Thank you anyway," says Jason graciously.

"Where's Katherine, isn't she supposed to be washing-up today?" asks Reg.

"She said she'll come as soon as she can. She's helping out sort the flowers and gifts and everything," says Jason.

William locks the cupboard door and puts the tiny key back in a pocket, and folds a paper serviette in four which he carefully places under his glass and puts it down on the worktop on the opposite side of the sink to Reg. Then he grabs his tails, holds them up at his front then jumps up backwards onto the worktop and sits there. He neatly brings his tails over his legs and twiddles his bow tie, adjusting it. He picks up the drink and the serviette together and takes a sip.

(He always does this with a drink or a coffee which puts the onlooker in mind of watching Hercule Poirot do it, as he holds the drink in one hand and shields his lap against drips with the other. He always places his hand palm upwards with a drink [with a serviette] and palm downwards [if he doesn't pick up the saucer] with a coffee. He never does this sitting at a table, only on a chair or bench where his clothes are in danger of getting soiled.)

Timothy takes a sip of his drink as he stands next to Jason. He winces at the strength of it and Jason looks at him as if to say, "I told you so."

"I'd put a slice of lemon in that for you," he says discreetly, "but there's no room," and he smiles sarcastically.

Reg leans back against the cupboards and mops his brow with a large scrunched up handkerchief then stuffs it back into his inside pocket.

"I fancy going to see Burt Bacharach at the Albert Hall, I might apply for tickets," he says. [Staff can apply for cheap tickets]

"You'll be lucky to get any," says William. "I fancied going to Wimbledon this year but the tickets for that never make their way past the typists' office, and who wants tickets for the FA Cup? The only ones I get offered these days are for Ascot and I've been there a thousand times."

"Well nobody ever takes me to the theatre!" says Reg in a playfully sarcastic way.

"Don't be silly, you get taken to the theatre, you know you do," says William.

Reg smiles to himself as he recalls a memorable show he went to once.

"The best show I ever saw at the theatre was Marlene Dietrich at The Queen's in the seventies. She was marvellous!" he says, as he wafts his white handkerchief in the air with delight.

"At the end of the show we all waited for her at the stage door. We waited there for ages, but so many people crowded round that when she eventually came out, she had to climb onto the roof of a car and stand there so everyone could see her. Everyone surrounded the car and took photographs. She must have been there for hours signing autographs and everyone gave her flowers. It was magic!"

All the boys are listening. Jason is enthralled by this story but Timothy doesn't have a clue who he's talking about.

"She used to say that her performance didn't finish when the show did, nor when she left the theatre, nor when she returned via the restaurant to the hotel. It ended only when she could shut the hotel room door and stand behind it."

He thrusts his large splayed-out hand forward, as if pushing a door shut.

"Only then was it over and she could relax. I've taken on that philosophy now," he says, "I regard my whole life as a performance so I'll only go to bed when I know that the punters are satisfied." He twirls his handkerchief in the air.

William leaves no pause after Reg's little speech as if he'd been waiting for him to finish before he could ask a burning question.

"What does logistics mean?" he asks the room.

Timothy is fired-up suddenly as this a subject he knows he can contribute to, but his mind was wandering during Reg's boring story about some woman, so his brain falters a second while he collects his thoughts.

"I know!" he says enthusiastically.

Everyone looks at him waiting for the explanation but nothing comes out his mouth.

After waiting for Timothy to say something and realising his brain has frozen, Jason turns to William.

"The process of transporting people, or commodities from point a to point b, in the most efficient way."

"Very good answer!" says William as he points his finger in an appreciative manner towards Jason. William obviously doesn't know what logistics means even though the equerry has been brandishing it about all the time lately.

"Who's serving household tea today?" he asks briskly (so the boys don't have time to think).

"Timothy," says Jason.

"Me, again?" moans Timothy. "I did it yesterday."

"And Robert has been shadowing you don't forget. This is a busy time and I don't think you're quite ready to be let loose in the royal household all my yourself.

"Why don't you do it then?"

"Because I've been here longer than you that's why! And we're still a man down and anyway I call the shots in this pantry thank you, you've only done it once so far, so you have to learn how to do it," says Jason impatiently, "and I'll be busy packing all the stuff for Scotland. Nobody ever thinks of that do they? What's the matter with you? You've only been here five minutes and you already seem to want to reorganise things."

"Well it seems to me there's a lot to reorganise, and I think I'm the man to do it."

"Remind me again, where did we pluck you from? Off the streets somewhere wasn't it, out of the gutter?" says Reg, in an attempt to put this new footman in his place.

"No! From a five-star hotel and spa in Warwickshire, actually," says Timothy with a smarmy look on his face, as if the next thing he might possibly say would be: so, ner, sucks to you!

"Oh yes. Some God-forsaken noxious countryside watering hole no doubt," Reg says as he flicks his handkerchief fanning his head.

"You were a kitchen porter there?" asks Jason, who's intrigued to find out more about Timothy's past if possible.

"Kitchen-banqueting porter, yes. What's wrong with that?" says Timothy in a defensive manner, as he's afraid Jason may ask him some tricky questions.

"Absolutely nothing at all," says Jason. "I used to be a kitchen porter, but I didn't jump from being that straight into this job. I had the good taste to make some incremental stops on the job ladder and in the process, I learned how to behave!"

William thinks he'd better pitch in here for appearances sake. Normally he would cut down any little upstart straightaway with a venomous comment, but Timothy is special.

"When I started my job as a servant's hall boy at Windsor I'd never dream of answering back to my boss. I wouldn't have said boo to a goose."

Timothy is so thick skinned that he doesn't realise he's being got at.

"Well I'm the new young blood, make way 'cause I'm coming through in the fast lane."

He does an imaginary gunslinger routine in the air with

his hands and finishes it with blowing the barrels.

William and Jason roll their eyes, putting it down to the ignorance and childish bravado of youth, Reg just looks astonished and confused.

"Adrian didn't even say goodbye to me! So disrespectful," says William changing the subject completely.

"We worked together for five years and he didn't even have the decency to tell me he was leaving. He made sure he said goodbye to the Queen though, she told me, and she was very surprised to learn that he just left like that without so much as a thank you to all the other staff."

"Another young footman seduced by the promise of eternal life, lost to the great and good of Hollywood," says Reg wistfully, camping it up, because he doesn't really care.

"Who's he working for? She's supposed to be a film star but I've never even heard of the woman. I don't know who she is?" William asks.

"Well don't look at me!" says Reg. (See, he doesn't give a hoot.)

Realising he's not going to get a sensible answer from anyone, William starts to talk about his American dream.

"I would have liked to have gone abroad and worked for somebody rich. I'd be a rich man myself by now."

"Well you still can be," says Timothy.

"No," says William. "I mean I should have gone when I was in my thirties or something."

"At least that Adrian will be able to sell his story and make a film," says Timothy jealously. "William, you could go to Hollywood and make a film about the Queen Mother!"

"And betray the royals?" shouts William, totally disgusted with such a preposterous idea.

"Bite the hand that feeds you?" joins in Reg, "then regret it for the rest of your life! No thank you. There are some people in this world who should have just slipped away quietly to work in the country and not ..."

William interrupts before he can finish.

"Shh!" he says, putting his finger across his lips, "we mustn't speak of such things."

And he puts down his drink and covers his mouth with both hands and swings his feet like a child who's just said a naughty word.

"Well really!" says Reg, who's quite offended by the idea. "It gets on my wick!" and he twirls his handkerchief in the air very annoyed, and sits there like a bird ruffling its feathers.

"I'd like to be famous," says Timothy in a deadpan voice, meaning one day he most definitely will be famous.

"You? Famous? For what?" asks Jason.

"That's what young people don't understand," Reg says, who's getting worked up now, "it's no good just being famous, what happens then? You've got to be talented and have something to offer, otherwise you become yet another one of that vacuous rabble you see in the papers all the time."

"I know," agrees William, "all these so-called celebrities you see they don't actually do anything. They don't know what true star quality is."

Reg is suddenly riled again and wants to say something controversial to cut through all this posturing of Timothy's, (the handkerchief twirling is going into overdrive).

"Go and kill somebody! Be famous in prison!"

"Oh Reg," says William.

"Well, all these fanatics killing each other so that they become martyrs. I thought we were all supposed to be humble before God?"

"Oh, let's stop now," says William in an attempt to get away from this subject completely and to prevent Reg becoming too upset which could make him ill.

"Talking of talent, my party piece when I was young, was to walk into a room, put my hands in front of me on a table, kick my legs up off the ground and do a handstand," he says triumphantly.

"What? A handstand? On the table?" asks Timothy, completely confused with the mental picture forming in his head.

"Yes."

"You mean you'd go from a standing position to doing a handstand on the table?" he says, now getting very worried.

"Yes."

"Really?"

"Yes."

"How did you realise you could do that?"

"I don't know I just did it. I was only a teenager at the time."

Timothy is beginning to wish he never got to be friends with William now. He's very puzzled about this handstand thing and thinks if it's possibly some weird kind of rite of passage ritual, perhaps?

"Well did somebody have to lift your legs up?" asks Jason.

"No, I just kicked my legs up behind me."

"And then you did a handstand on the table?" asks Timothy.

"Yes!" shouts William, who was wishing he never mentioned it.

"Without any support?" asks Jason this time.

"Well, how did you first learn you could do that?" he asks, "I mean, it's not something you would happen to do my mistake is it?"

William definitely wishes he never mentioned it now. He was only trying to make some jolly conversation to ease the boredom of waiting for the bell for the three thousandth time and suddenly he feels like he's on an episode of Mastermind.

"Well, were people impressed when you did it?" asks Timothy.

"I suppose so," William sighs, "I can't really remember, it was a very long time ago. It was considered to be quite special at the time. I was very young at the time of course. People didn't take any notice once they'd seen me do it a few times and anyway, there was always somebody who'd come along and do something that people thought was more impressive. Somebody always does."

"Awesome," says Timothy, nodding his head looking troubled.

"Wow," says Jason. Who can't stop himself from wondering what the more impressive feat was all about.

"It never got me anywhere," says William, who thinks he'd better add this information just for good measure, so nobody would waste their time trying it.

All this time Reg has been watching Timothy's reactions towards William. He wants to ask the questions now.

"So, what's your talent? What can you do?" he asks Timothy in a contemptuous manner.

Timothy isn't phased in the least at the mocking way Reg just asked the question, but he isn't going to give him the first answer that comes into his head because that one is the truth. He thinks he'd better not tell them his talent is saying anything and pretending to be someone else in order to get what he wants, so he plumps for his second talent on the list.

"Er, I can swim ten laps of the pool without stopping. Did it yesterday." (Which he did, at the Queen Mother swimming baths in Victoria.)

"Well. That's not really a talent, is it?" Reg replies, very sarcastically.

"What's your talent then?" Timothy responds, whilst thinking: what's so good about you, you old fart?

But Reg doesn't get the chance to answer as William speaks for him or rather before Reg has the chance to speak for himself.

"Reg cooks a lovely Sunday roast, don't you Reg?" says William turning to look at him.

"Well, one tries one's best William one tries one's best," says Reg, acting camp and coy.

Reg smirks but then becomes serious and adds,

"I do cook a lovely Yorkshire Pudding though!"

"He doesn't have any beef," adds William, jerking his thumb towards Reg, "he just eats the pudding."

"Well I don't fancy anything else after cooking all that food all morning. A big piece of Yorkshire Pudding and some gravy does me nicely, and I might have something sweet. I sometimes get something from Marks and Spencer to save me the time."

"What do you do in the kitchen then William?" asks Timothy, in an attempt to discover what the dynamic is between these two men.

"Ask me what I do in the kitchen, go on?" William asks eagerly, just like Kenneth Williams would say it.

"I don't know. What do you do in the kitchen?" asks Timothy, who has no clue this is a joke he's travelling in.

"The same as The Princess Margaret!"

"What's that?"

"I get in the way!" William claps in the air and laughs rather too animatedly, but all this carry on never strays far from organising the job in hand.

"Now, you did show the equerry how to ring the

bell didn't you?" William asks Jason.

"Yes! Well no, I didn't show him, I mean, it's not difficult is it? You just do that," and he imitates pressing a bell-push on a table top with his finger.

"But does he know he has to press it hard and to ring it two separate times with a five minute interval?"

"Yes I told him!"

"Why is he pressing the bell and not Queen Elizabeth?" asks Reg.

William jumps down from the worktop and goes over to open the drinks cupboard again.

"Oh you know what the Queen's like with these new equerries," he says. "She wants to make him feel needed, and it's omelette today. Anyway, Queen Elizabeth doesn't press the bell she strokes the bell with a graceful touch you hardly see her do it. Now then, who wants a top-up? Jason you'll have one?"

"No really William, I can't drink in the day it'll knock me out." Jason thinks that if he puts a mental image in William's brain of a comatose head footman unable to finish serving lunch, that it might stop him asking, despite the fact he knows he doesn't really drink.

"Miss. Hailsham was another one who never drank in the day do you remember Reg?"

"What, the dresser? Miss fancy pants?"

"Yes, she was a bit of a fancy pants. She wouldn't touch a drop during the day but always knocked back a few sherries come eight o'clock when the Queen had gone through to dinner. She was very glamourous, she always wore nail varnish. She did them herself do you remember Reg? She used to come in of a morning drying them like this," (he wiggles his fingers) "and her hair was always perfect. She put so much lacquer on, it was just like candy floss."

"Dear boy, a little more whisky?" referring to Timothy.

"No thanks William, I'm fine with this one," he says,

and it's bloody awful, he thinks. "That's an impressive drinks cupboard William," he says, "you seem to have every drink imaginable."

William unlocks the cupboard and takes out the whisky.

"Many years ago the steward, who was my boss at the time, used to sit on that very stool and say,

All the wine and spirit you can see in those cupboards and in the cellars and on the table, it's all mine, mine! And I can drink as much as I want!

And he did, didn't he Reg?"

Reg attempts to answer but he's too slow.

"He never helped serve lunch though. The stewards didn't bother in those days." And this story ends here suddenly for some reason as it seems William's got bored with it.

"I did tell you the dressmakers are coming today at three o'clock didn't I? Have you ordered the special sandwiches?" [vegetarian] William asks Jason.

"Yes William, but they said they would do a separate plate of ham and chicken sandwiches just in case."

"Oh good. I wonder what wonderful creation they will come up with next. I wish I could afford to have a new outfit made just to go to the theatre."

"Princess Diana was the one for new clothes wasn't she? What was she like? Did she come here for lunch a lot?" asks Timothy rather clumsily.

"Here we go again!" cries Reg, (he is riled good and proper this time). "They all ask the same questions don't they? Why do they ask about Princess Diana? They all want to know about that poor girl, can't they leave her in peace?"

"What do you mean?" asks Timothy.

"All you new young footmen, that's all you can

think about. If I were you, I'd concentrate on learning the ropes of my new job before you start worrying about anything else. I know you dropped a tray on the stairs yesterday."

Oh no! thinks Jason. How did he find out about that? I bet it was Kay, and he apologises to Reg on Timothy's behalf.

"I'm sorry it won't happen again. Robert should have seen it and told him how to load a tray properly," he says.

"Don't blame Robert!" booms Reg. "You're responsible for the pantry not Robert, although I find it bizarre that these young people can't work it out for themselves."

There is an awkward pause while everyone tries to figure out who should speak next.

Reg is prepared to wait and is glaring at Timothy, silently commanding him to speak.

"Well?" says Reg, eventually.

Another pause, but Jason knows he's out the game as Reg isn't looking at him, but Timothy needs to show his hand.

There's another awkward pause with Reg's piercing eyes fixed on Timothy and William sits silently in the corner on the worktop looking down shyly at the glass in his hand.

Timothy is nonplussed. He has no clue of what is expected of him, so he carries on looking at Reg and then glancing at Jason in case he can enlighten him?

Jason is terribly embarrassed now as he knows Reg is furious with Timothy. He mutters under his breath to Timothy, "Say sorry to William."

Reg's patience has expired, so he puts it into plain English for the boy.

"Apologise!"

Another pause while the penny drops in Timothy's head. Jason gives Timothy a gentle kick.

"I'm sorry William," Timothy says, mortified and

embarrassed to have been made a fool of and more so, to have failed in his ability to anticipate what was expected of him.

"I should think so!" booms Reg, and resumes waving his handkerchief in the air like an irked cat flicks his tail.

William just carries on sitting there silently, not making eye contact with anyone.

Everyone feels so awkward and embarrassed that they all remain silent for a minute. Suddenly, the bell rings, piercing the scene, releasing an air of salvation from their suspended animation.

William springs into life, thankful this excruciatingly embarrassing scene has ended. He jumps off the worktop onto the floor and Jason spurts into action doing his thing.

"Here we go chaps!" he says, as pleasant as can be as though nothing has happened.

"Slave to the bell!" booms Reg, in his usual pleasant loud voice again as everything became sweet and dandy as he stood up.

"Fabergé bell Reg!" says William, correcting Reg in a playful way as he picks up a silver beastie griffin shaped claret jug.

"Fabergé bell. Sorry William," says Reg, and he stands still and pretends to sulk for being mockingly chastised by William and smirks at the others. William does not see this.

"Don't be daft!" says William, amused as he knows Reg is teasing him. "Will someone hand me a tissue?" and he fiddles with the beastie lid then stretches out his arm for someone to place a paper napkin in his hand.

Jason pushes Reg's stool under the table and prepares the sink area for washing-up.

"He means paper napkin," he says, and hands

Timothy a folded one who then passes it to William.

"Thank you so much," says William, and he takes the silver beastie and walks out the pantry to go outside to the garden where lunch is set. Reg follows him.

As Reg is walking behind he says, "The table's so far down the garden we'll be able to feed the ducks in St. James's Park. It'll take us ten minutes just to get there!"

William carries on, but can be heard to say, "Oh shut up you," in an amused way.

Jason takes a bottle of white wine from the fridge, gives it to Timothy and signals to him to follow the others.

"Here you are take this!" he says.

Timothy takes the bottle and follows them out to the garden.

Jason takes down a large tray from the wall rack and strides downstairs with it to the kitchen.

"Let's go and kick some culinary ass," he says out loud to himself.

On his way down to the kitchen, as a joke with the kitchen staff (who get fed-up waiting sometimes) he shouts really loudly like a drill sergeant with an American accent.

"Okay people wake up! I want straight and melba toast, a tomato omelette heavy on the parmesan and cream and hold the garnish, I ain't no rabbit!"

[From the moment the bell rings this routine of action happens very quickly like clockwork, as they've done it so many times before]

One minute passes. There is nobody in the pantry and nobody walking past in the corridor. It's as if the place is deserted apart from the muffled sound of marching bands on The Mall and chatter from the mingling crowds in the park.

The heavy swing door of the royal hall creaks open and Reg appears, out of breath and wheezing quite badly, he's been running down the hall. He hooks the door open.

"Are you there love?" he shouts down the stairs towards the kitchen. "That daft equerry said that was the second bell!"

Reg turns around having called down the stairs to Jason, and walks back into the hall, hoping that he will appear any second.

Next minute, he appears, carrying the large wooden tray that's holding a silver salver with an oval china insert that contains a huge omelette, some silver racks of toast and a silver container of warm melba toast and mixed crackers. He rushes up the stairs and across the landing towards the door to the hall.

"It's all right Reg it's here," he calls out, a little out of breath, "Chef sensed there was something wrong so he went ahead and made it. He was telling me he's had that omelette pan for seventeen years and he can't remember how many new handles it's had."

"Never mind that love, hurry up they're waiting."

Reg rushes along the long hall towards the open front doors and Jason follows behind carrying the tray, but first, he has to put it down for a second and grab the Queen's toast from the pantry toaster and pop it in a special toast rack, and take out the warm plates from a hot cupboard, then he carries on. "Hang on," he says, as Reg is rushing away from him.

Reg decides to have some fun and to make Jason laugh, so he puts on the Southern American accent and dialect he heard in the film 'Gone With The Wind' having been singing the song from it all morning.

"Hurry up there Arthur or you ain't gonna be an inside servant no more, you gonna be an outside servant, an you'll want plen'y!" he says, as they both trundle along, Jason about five paces behind.

Jason enters into the mood.

"I'm comin' master, I'm comin," as he trots behind

Reg.

Reg carries on as they get further down the hall coming nearer to the front doors where the sunlight is blazing outside.

In his hurry Jason feels the need to rearrange the items on the tray as the balance feels wrong, so he stops to rest it on the edge of the marble-top table for a second. Reg looks back to see where he is.

"Hurry up now child, run! That ain't no good! Billy Joe can run faster than that child, you gonna find yourself an outside servant again child, you ain't no good."

Jason starts to giggle, but finds he can't giggle and talk and run with the tray at the same time so it wobbles a bit.

"I'm comin' fast as I can master honest I am, I'm comin' master, I'm comin!"

Reg is nearly at the end of the hall now. He stops at the steps just before the porch and turns around to call to Jason who is still lagging behind. Jason's run out of steam owing to the fact he is wearing a George VI scarlet woollen overcoat in the middle of August, indoors, running down a long hallway carrying a large heavy tray laden with heavy best quality silver and china, an omelette, and some plates, and some toast (and crackers).

"Run child run, or Billy Joe gonna take your job and that's a fact!" yells Reg.

Jason tries to reply but he is laughing so much that he can't carry on any longer. "Hang on Reg, I'm coming," he says.

Reg is giggling still, but he stumbles, feeling ill. He dives into a chair by the wall and grabs a handkerchief to his mouth, sweating profusely and feeling overcome, leaning on a small round mosaic marble-top table.

Jason is laughing but still manages to hold the tray level. He keeps on walking and sees Reg sitting in the chair, but thinks he's just sitting down for a quick rest.

"Are you all right Reg?" he asks when he reaches him.

Reg gestures with his hand for him to keep on going. He's obviously unwell and suffering a lot of discomfort in some way as he can barely talk. He keeps waving his hand, not wanting Jason to make any fuss, and for him to carry on and take the omelette straight out for Robert and the others to serve.

"You go on love I'll be all right," he says, taking the handkerchief away from his mouth in order to speak, then replacing it when he finished.

Jason sees that this is serious. He stands over him, still holding the tray, wondering what's the matter? Worried and unsure what to do, he tries to get Reg to say what's wrong.

"Are you sure?" he asks, making sure that Reg will be okay if he goes outside now.

"Yes I'm fine, you go before the omelette gets cold. Go on love they're waiting."

And Reg waves his hand again to shoo him away and out the front doors.

"Okay," replies Jason, still looking very hesitant and glancing back as he walks down the steps and walks through the front doorway into the garden and then rushes out to the trees carrying the tray, but still unsure.

Young And In Love In Paris

Later that evening Reg and Jason are sitting in comfortable armchairs in the page's room, which is right next to Queen Elizabeth's private living quarters. There is no one else on duty in the house except the police as it is well past ten o' clock at night, so the place is peaceful and quiet. The small television on a side table has not been switched on for ages. In comparison, the telephone on the desk next to the window is always in constant use. It's usually William phoning up Reg, commenting on what he's watching on the television in his little gate lodge a short distance away over the garden wall on The Mall, or it's about where he's going out to or has been that evening or any silly little thing he wishes to say really.

There is a cardboard Letts desk calendar on the desk. Alongside this is a diary and a telephone directory and a pen holder. The room is long and narrow with a high ceiling. There are sturdy wooden built-in cupboards floor to ceiling. Reg's black tailcoat and Jason's scarlet tailcoat are on hangers hooked onto cupboard door keys as this is more practical and convenient than squashing them together on the coat hooks on the back of the door, which is always left open. Some magazines and newspapers are spread about the place, so are many pot plants, mostly orchids. Some boxes of chocolates lie about the place, some with their ribbons untied and some still packed as when they were delivered. There are some buckets of cut flowers along the wall waiting to be sorted, as there are in most rooms as the amount of flowers sent is enormous.

Reg has asked Jason if he wouldn't mind taking over his duties for the last hour or so in the page's room by staying up and waiting, as Robert is not available. Reg gets tired easily these days and the working day is long. In fact, the working day is all day for a page. Too much for a young man never mind a man of retirement age like Reg. It is simply a matter of Jason waiting for Queen Elizabeth to ring the bell at some point before retiring for the day, and then for Jason to switch off some lights etc.

Jason is peeling a tangerine.

"Why are you still here? I said you can go when you like you know Reg, I'm going to finish reading my book."

"I'm too settled now, I might go in a minute. Thank you for agreeing to wait up for me, I didn't like asking you myself."

"Don't mention it. I don't mind at all."

"I didn't think you would. William said you'd probably be going out somewhere."

"No, no, I had nothing planned. I'm going out later though, just for a drink."

"Tonight?" says Reg astonished, "but it's the birthday tomorrow love you can't go out tonight, you'll be shattered."

"I'm a party animal Reg I can't help it."

"A middle-aged one. You're not getting any younger love, none of us are."

"I've been invited out Reg. It's a posh bar in a posh hotel, and you're forgetting I won't get any more invitations soon as I'll be in Scotland. Don't worry, I did a few errands today and I've started to pack the silver and stuff to take to Mey, it's all under control."

"Oh that's good," says Reg sarcastically. "I just hope you know what you're doing."

Reg looks down to the floor, gathering his thoughts for a second.

"Did William tell you why I've been going home

early lately?"

"No, he didn't say a word. I do sort of know. I've heard things mentioned."

"Well, you should hear it from the horse's mouth."

Reg leaves a prominent pause in his speech, knowing that what he is about to divulge to Jason may shock him. Then he continues.

"I'm having treatment for Leukaemia at the hospital, that's where I've been going. I've been going for a while now."

Jason is taken aback at this and really doesn't know what to say but there is only one thing to say.

"I'm sorry Reg."

"The treatment's vile. Chemotherapy. It really knocks you about, I'm fed up with it. I've been making appointments and going to the outpatients. You have the treatments in blocks at a time as it's such a shock to the system I can't tell you. I mustn't complain though. They are good there you know. Everyone's helping me the best they can."

"How long will the treatment be for?"

"There's one outstanding then I'm done. Well they said that this course of treatment should do the trick for a while, we'll have to see how it goes but I'd rather not talk about it. I don't want to think about it any more. I just wanted to let you know what's going on. Don't say anything will you?"

Reg seems to want to reveal this to Jason but doesn't seem to want anyone else to know.

"No, I understand."

Jason feels he must be very privileged in some way for Reg to have told him such a personal thing, but he can't think of any reason for it.

"Thank you for telling me," he adds.

"I'm not the first. Cancer runs in the family. It's funny how life turns out. It's true what they say about life you know. You look away for what seems a second, and years have flown by when you look back again. That's when you realise you're either getting old or you're not enjoying yourself anymore, no matter who you are. I can't believe it's the Queen Mother's one hundredth birthday tomorrow. It used to be so far away, on the horizon. And now it's only minutes away. Where does the time go?"

Jason finishes peeling the tangerine, trying to play things cool.

"I know Reg. Would you like some of this?" offering him some.

"No thanks love. That reminds me, I saw you the other night going out the back door while I was having my supper. You didn't go out up town looking like that did you?"

"Like what?"

"Dressed in that bright orange tee-shirt?"

"Oh, the one with the green and red diamanté lettering?"

Reg begins to chuckle, amused by the memory of it.

"What did it say on the front?" he asks still chuckling.

"Er, rock chic, in red letters," replies Jason, as he wipes some juice away from his chin.

"And on the back it said, product failure."

"Don't you get stopped at the police barrier looking like that?"

"No. Most times depending who's on duty, they want to see what I've got on. Well, they must get bored standing there. Thing is, they also want to know where I'm going and who I'm going there with and what I'm going to do when I get there? They are ever so nosey."

This amuses Reg and makes him giggle. He has

reached up and grabbed his tailcoat off the hanger while Jason was telling him this, and draped it over his knees to keep warm. He is now leaning forward enthralled in this camp conversation.

"What's new pussycat?"

He gives out a hearty giggle and carries on the conversation, hoping to give Jason some sound advice but still amused by the mental images he is providing.

"I suppose it's part of their job to know what's going on. But you want to be careful who you make friends with, as you never know who your real friends are. Not in this job. I'd never go out looking like that though. We had more style in my day. We had a better time of it too, well, everything was more dignified then, in private, behind closed doors, not like now. No, in my day other people didn't have to know your business. My best times were during the sixties, that's when I had the most fun. But even back in the fifties I've been known to enjoy myself. I worked for the Duke and Duchess of Windsor then. I'd often roll in at seven o'clock in the morning just in time for duty, sometimes at the last minute, but I was never late!"

"Where had you been?"

"I'd been out all night, where do you think? I was in the middle of Paris! I used to come in, get changed into my uniform quickly and do the calling tray, then get washed and shaved during staff breakfast. Ooh, I could have gone out every night then if I'd have wanted to."

He amuses himself with the memory of it and attempts to suppress an involuntary laugh without any success.

"I remember the duchess had this French hairdresser who really fancied me. I had to escort him out sometimes when he'd finished doing her hair. They had this grand entrance hall and this big sweeping staircase and he used to chase me all the way down the stairs. I couldn't believe it, a middle-aged man chasing me down the stairs. What made him think he had a chance with a young thing like me? I think he wore a toupée. I never let him catch me though. I could run fast in those days and he'd be out of breath by the time he'd reached the hall."

Reg screws up his face trying desperately to recall the hairdresser's name.

"Mon-sieur Pomp-e-doope, was his name, or something?"

(This is obviously the wrong name of course but it makes no difference either way.)

"What was your job there exactly?" asks Jason.

Reg reaches over and pulls his tailcoat off the hanger and puts it over him up to his shoulders. He settles down and sits back and crosses his legs and covers himself with it up to his neck.

"I was the duke's valet. I was only there a couple of years. He kept me on my toes though as he used to change several times during the day. He had loads of clothes. He loved clothes, well they both did. Clothes were very important things to them, as you can imagine. Public image was so important for them. He never threw anything away. He used all his old clothes for gardening. I always remember, I misplaced some of his keys or something once and I couldn't find them anywhere. We looked everywhere for them. When it was apparent that they weren't going to be found, I felt so embarrassed about it that I decided the only proper thing to do was to hand in my notice, which I did. The duke wouldn't accept my resignation. He said that I looked after him so well and that losing the keys was such an unfortunate thing to happen, and that it wouldn't ever be mentioned again, and I should carry on in his service and continue being his valet. Some time after that I happened to take out one of his suits that had been pushed to the back of the wardrobe and I

119

found them in one of the pockets. He had pockets everywhere in his clothes, different pockets for different things, it took me bloody ages to check everything. I must have put this particular one away in a hurry and not checked the pockets properly."

"I saw a television programme once about the duke," says Jason. "They said he helped to design a lot of his clothes himself, asking for special pockets in different suits for different things."

"That's it, that's the sort of thing I mean. A special pocket for a certain watch in a suit, like a posh watch in a suit he wears for the theatre or one in his golf clothes for a sporty watch and so on. And you know there's a special hidden pocket for a packet of cigarettes in the tails of those old scarlet tailcoats you wear don't you? But that must have been George the sixth's idea I suppose [a heavy smoker], unless it was fashionable earlier for everyone at the time?"

"That must have been a difficult job then?"

"Not difficult as such, a lot of responsibility sometimes though, with all that luggage.

"They also said on that programme that the duke used to do embroidery and he used to monogram tablecloths and napkins and things."

"Yes that's true. He learned that skill at his mother's knee Queen Mary. She was patron of the Needlework Guild for years, she was a very skilful embroiderer. That's where he got it from, but he kept it secret for years."

"Blimey. So what happened in Paris with you after the keys thing?"

"I stayed on there after that, then eventually came back to this country. When I left, the duke wrote me a note to say that he had never been so beautifully looked after before."

"Sounds great, what was she like? Mrs. Simpson?"

"She wasn't Mrs. Simpson!" retorted Reg. "She was the Duchess of Windsor! She married the duke so she was the duchess. She should have been her royal highness as she married the prince but they never gave her the title. She was her royal highness really, and we called her that. She had these large hands, almost like a man's you know, because she was a very petite woman, and they were just out of proportion to her body. She must have known they were her worst feature so she made the most of them. She always wore a beautiful bracelet and some jewellery and you know,"

He begins to wiggle his hands in front of his face to demonstrate how she moved hers.

"Moved her hands right in front of your face like this if she was talking to somebody new, and played with a ring or something to make it look natural. So that would make whoever she was talking to HAVE to concentrate on looking at her hands, which she knew they wanted to do anyway, and they could have a really good look and get it over with, out the way, and that was it, so nobody had been embarrassed and they could move on with having a serious conversation. She knew what she was doing, she wasn't daft, and likewise she knew her limitations. She was a brilliant hostess. The house was kept beautifully, it was a show-house really which made it harder work for the staff but she ran it brilliantly as everyone knew their place and what was expected from them. The maids had to walk up the stairs with the ironed monogrammed sheets like this."

He pretends to hold one up in the air like they did.

"And then they had to re-iron them once they were on the beds."

"Carry them like what?"

"Vertically! They had to carry them vertically up the stairs like this! Not over their arms. There couldn't be a single crease! Crazy. Her tables were fabulous and the attention she paid to the food for her guests was unbelievable, although she hardly ate anything herself, to keep that lovely figure of hers. She had a little notepad in a silver case on the dining table which she would scribble in now and again during meals."

"What for?"

"To write notes to herself about the meal. The soup was too cold or too hot. The soufflé was delicious, we must use the same recipe for another special occasion, anything. You were serving the food too quickly or the tablecloth isn't quite right or something. Whatever she thought of at the time and she'd tell you or the chef about it later or the next day."

"Blimey, you've certainly had an exciting life."

"Well, I always fancied doing something a bit different."

"You certainly got it here, in royal service."

"Yes I suppose so, but still, there's no security."

"What do you mean?"

"I still had to get myself my little flat in Kennington so I could look after my dad. Without the flat I wouldn't have been able to look after him when he became ill. He made it 'til his nineties."

"But you've been all around the world with the Queen Mother, that must have been an amazing experience?"

"Ooh it was! We went to some fabulous places, fabulous tours. Queen Elizabeth was a star, everybody loved her wherever she went. It felt like being at the centre of the universe at times when we were out with her, thousands of people would crowd round, the world's eyes were upon us. It was great. Pure theatre!"

"Wow."

Jason is amazed as it's nothing like his job.

"That's one good thing about this job, it gives you a taste of the good life, but it leaves you with expensive tastes at the end which can be hard to meet. These people can afford to live that way, but it can turn your head if you come from a modest background like us."

Jason is letting Reg free fall with his memories as he loves to hear about the old days and hopes the enthusiasm will last as Reg seldom talks about his past. Jason has never heard any of this before.

"I know, but you must have enjoyed it all the same and what a unique experience. Sounds very glamourous."

Reg pauses for thought.

"It depends on how much you want people to know, I mean, anybody only knows what they think they know about you, whether it's true or not. So how can they know what you really feel inside? If you wanted to, you could create your own persona that's a complete fantasy, by telling people only the things you choose to tell them about yourself, made up or otherwise. And you could easily pull it off, if you have enough self-confidence. So how can anyone else truly know what you want from life, they can only go on appearances. Some people dream about living in a little country cottage with roses round the door but it's no good thinking like that working in this job, as you may work all your life, you may never retire. That's why there's no point making plans about it. That's a luxury to be able to plan ahead like that anyway. That's why you should make the best of things now. I wouldn't say I'd like to live in someone else's pocket, as I believe it's always good to have your own front door, but, to have someone ... to be able to go back home to somebody you love every day, and to know ... that you can just ... fall asleep in their arms."

Reg closes his eyes and rests back his head letting out a sigh, and seems to fall into a dream, in total bliss. A look of sublime happiness spreads across his whole face as he's sitting there with his legs still crossed and his tailcoat pulled up to his chin and spread over his shoulders.

Jason thinks he may doze off completely, so he stretches out his arm and taps his foot, causing him to open his eyes and blink.

"Why don't you go to bed Reg? There's no point two of us being here. I said I'd stay up for you tonight."

"It's all right love, the Queen will be ringing in a minute, it must be late by now."

Reg uncrosses his legs and pulls himself out of the chair to stand up. He wraps his tailcoat onto a coathanger again, then sits back down in the chair and so, this change of atmosphere signals to both of them that the opportunity for reminiscing is over for the evening. No more walks down memory lane tonight.

Jason is fond of Reg so he feels obliged to ask a few questions like a good friend should.

"Are you going to the hospital again this week for Chemotherapy?" he enquires.

"No love I'm not doing that any more."

"But I thought you had an appointment?"

"It was today. I should have gone this afternoon."

This is worse than Jason thought.

"You should go Reg! What happens if you miss out a treatment?"

"I don't want to do that any more, it makes you feel dreadful the next day."

"But you should go if they think you need it."

"I can't go again. It'll be all right. It doesn't matter."

Jason doesn't understand this remark.

The house bell rings and Reg instinctively gets up to put on his tailcoat.

"That's the Queen!" he says, realising the evening has just flown by while they've been talking.

"You go to bed love, go on, I'll say goodnight."

"Are you sure?" asks Jason reluctantly, not wanting to

make it look like he was rushing off and also because Reg must have forgotten he was going out.

Reg laughs.

"Yes of course!"

"All right then thanks," Jason says hesitantly. He thinks that Reg never got an early night as he planned after all. But somehow, for some peculiar reason, Reg doesn't mind that much.

"Good night Reg."

Ever jolly even when he is down, Reg does his usual impersonation of someone without a care in the world.

"Goodnight love," he says. "See you tomorrow for the one hundredth birthday! Don't be late!"

"I won't," replies Jason, trying to sound as positive as possible. He picks up his book and tailcoat and makes his way out.

Reg bursts into impromptu song whilst putting on his tailcoat.

"♪ The best of times is now ...♪" he sings. [From 'La Cage aux Folles']

"♪ La la la la la la la la la laaa ...♪"

Jason knows this is for his benefit alone and that Reg is trying to make it look as though everything is okay and perfectly normal. He leaves the room and makes his way to the lift with the sound of Reg's singing in the background. He knows full well that all this is a front and Reg is putting a brave face on things. He walks slowly up the back stairs rather than using the lift, as he wants the time it takes along that solitary route to his bedroom to analyse the implications of what Reg has just told him.

HAPPY BIRTHDAY YOUR MAJESTY!

The atmosphere is thrilling as thousands of happy faces line The Mall. Most of them are waiting for the moment the Landau pulls out of St. James's Palace carrying Queen Elizabeth and the Prince of Wales, so they can cheer as it's driven past and rolls along The Mall on through the gates of Buckingham Palace. Then, Queen Elizabeth will appear on the balcony for the crowds. This will be the culmination of 21-gun-salutes around the United Kingdom and church bells ringing for Queen Elizabeth's one hundredth birthday.

Before this happens however, the big black wooden gates of Clarence House will be opened as usual, and Queen Elizabeth will step out to make her traditional appearance outside her house on her birthday.

Today is different as Queen Elizabeth will step out to watch a procession of military bands and service men and women march by. Also, the Buckingham Palace postman will deliver a special birthday card from The Queen, a tradition afforded to British centenarians.

It has become a tradition for masses of people to gather along the strip of road named Stable Yard. It leads off The Mall from William's lodge down the side of the house and is always the first place to attract well-wishers. Today that stretch of road already filled up hours ago when the police let people come in from The Mall.

Staff inside Clarence House are franticly sorting out the flowers and gifts and cards that have been arriving for days, and there's a backlog of deliveries. The orderlies and drivers simply can't manage to move the flowers out before more and more arrive. Extra staff have been taken on to help with all the labels and thank you letters. It's as though Covent Garden flower market has transferred to this house in SW1.

Today will be the busiest day of deliveries as most people want their gifts to arrive punctually on the birthday.

The three main hubs of operation today will be in the orderly's, the lady in waiting's offices and the pantry.

William made his way out of his little house this morning to get the other side of the gates as usual, giving a wave or a word to people in the crowds but he was unable to operate in the same way by nipping in and out like he usually did because today was different as a whole procession was marching past, and the catalogue of participants was already approved and stamped with military timing.

He is not his usual self but putting a brave face on things. He just wishes that the day will go as planned. He doesn't know how it will end but it's here at last.

Everything appears normal but there is a strange atmosphere in the house because William is in a tense mood. For the first time ever, he didn't wish a good morning to Jason but just walked straight past him to go to the telephone. His eyes are red and it's obvious he's been crying as he knows Reg is ill. The kitchen staff noticed it, too, and mentioned it to Jason so he's decided to keep out of William's way if he can. He is too tired to deal with him in one of his short-tempered snappy moods, not today.

The pantry is a hive of activity. Bouquets of flowers and arrangements and pot plants are everywhere, on every available surface. There are flowers in buckets of water standing on tables and on the floor because there's nowhere else to put them. Champagne bottles of all sizes sit around the place, Fortnum & Mason hampers and Harrods basket hampers have been left in corridors. Giant birthday cards, boxes of chocolates and soft toys have been collected and left neatly on temporary trestle tables, ready to be sorted later. Staff are moving about to-and-fro. Telephones ring out regularly all over the place. There's not much space to move around. There's a constant background noise of chattering from the crowds outside and the odd squeal and spontaneous round of applause and waves of cheering when a huge teddy bear or a fantastic floral arrangement is delivered.

In the pantry, Reg is looking into the mirror, adjusting his white bow tie and checking his face. William is on the telephone about to finish a call. Timothy is examining something on the noticeboard as usual. Jason is checking and scribbling out the odd note on his lists for silver and equipment for Scotland that he needs to finish packing within the next twenty-four hours, but really, he's just trying to look busy in front of William. Timothy and Jason are wearing their scarlet tailcoat uniforms.

William replaces the receiver and walks out towards the orderly's. He checks on Reg on his way out.

"Are you all right Reg? Not long now?"

Reg doesn't answer. He looks in the mirror and lets his singing do the talking.

"♪ I'm coming out of make-up, the lights already burning, not long until the cameras will start turning, it's the early morning madness la la la la la la la la la…♪" [Lyrics from a song in 'Sunset Boulevard']

William is pleased, this is a good sign. Reg has taken in Queen Elizabeth's tea tray to the study this morning and wished her happy birthday —a delight for them both. Rumours have been going around the house that Reg was ill and so would miss Queen Elizabeth's birthday, but those rumours have been quashed now with his appearance on duty.

William and the boys will be walking in and out the pantry more than usual, checking and fetching birthday

128

presents and answering the telephone. The pantry is the centre of activities for the pages and footmen especially on a day like today.

Reg carries on humming the tune until he finishes adjusting his bow tie. Then he turns away from the mirror to talk to the boys.

"Some of the household are having a buffet lunch aren't they?"

"Yes," replies Jason. "Under the trees."

"Oh, but are you sure the table's in the right place?" butts in Timothy. "You'd better ask William."

"Look, the first time we lay the table for lunch, it's laid beautifully, the second time it's laid nicely, and the third time it's laid all right. But if we have to move it again I'm going to throw everything on top of the table in a heap and they can just help themselves," says Jason.

"Now that's not the attitude I want to hear!" shouts Reg, quite angrily, pointing his finger at Jason. "William likes everything to be right!"

This makes him jump.

"I was only joking. Have you ever known me not to do my job properly?"

Reg stares but is silent.

Jason takes his silence as a 'no', otherwise Reg would say otherwise.

"Well then?" says Jason, feeling absolved.

"Hey Jas, why don't we lay it up in both places so they've got the choice then?" Timothy looks rather pleased with himself for coming up with this super-dooper idea, as he sees it.

"Go and collect some more flowers Timothy. We've got to clear the hall a bit more before Queen Elizabeth comes down and the Prince comes through. Go on! Go and help the others, it's like a Dutch flower farm out there!"

"Don't worry Jas, I'm on the case!"

Timothy leaves the pantry to do Jason's bidding. Reg leaves, too, to see what's going on in the hall and to check there's still space for Queen Elizabeth and the Prince to walk through. Flowers are piling up so fast that they tend to just get plonked anywhere.

Jason follows Reg up to the corridor and leans against the doorframe. Reg is feeling sorry now for shouting so loudly and making Jason jump. He shakes his head at Timothy's flippant attitude.

"Where do we find them?"

"Search me?" says Jason. "William interviewed him, and if you ask me, he only employed him to cover the Scottish trip and then let him go."

(The Scottish trip was a big deal. The Queen Mother went to Scotland for three months and invited guests and family all through the length of the stay. They had to be served and looked after well so there was a lot of work to do. It wasn't a case of just poncing about in a fancy uniform.)

"Oh well, if William hired him I don't know what you're complaining about," says Reg. "He seems a charming young man. And being so young and handsome he's bound not to be very bright. You can't have everything in life you know, not all at the same time anyway."

He is joking of course. The sound of smashing china comes from the hall, ironically coinciding with Timothy's arrival in that vicinity.

"Oh no!" cries Jason, thinking there could be a beautiful Worcester plate lying in broken pieces on the floor. "What's he broken now?"

Reg waves, not duly concerned.

"Catch you later alligator," as he gives a wry laugh.

"Thanks! Leave me to pick up the pieces." Jason is pleased Reg is in good spirits.

Reg has disappeared from Jason's view around the

corner, but he comes back and leans on the doorframe.

"Listen love, I've been picking up the pieces all my life! Tell William I'm in the page's room would you? And make sure you get something to eat."

"Okay Reg."

Reg disappears into the hall. William walks into the pantry carrying a small box and a card he's reading as he walks to the telephone.

"I wish people would send flowers the rest of the year when I need them. Have you seen some of the arrangements? They're amazing! Have you cleared the hall yet?"

"Yes, Timothy's in there doing it now."

"Oh good, as the Prince will be popping through soon."

"Okay."

Jason pulls out another equipment list from a drawer and pretends to examine it. He wishes William would use his own telephone along the corridor instead of coming into the pantry all the time. He pretends to write something on the list.

William picks up the telephone and dials for the switchboard.

"Could you put me through to Spinks please?"

The house bell rings.

William covers the end of the telephone with his hand while turning round to speak to Jason.

"That's the Queen ringing, where's Reg?"

Jason is leaning against the fridge reading his lists. He answers without looking up.

"Page's," he says, pointing to the ceiling.

William keeps his hand over the receiver while he speaks, but Jason doesn't look up from concentrating on his lists.

"I can always tell when a royal hand is stroking the

Fabergé and it's not the footman or dresser testing the bell," says William. "Queen Elizabeth has always had footmen at the end of a bell since she was a little girl. She grew up to be a Lady, then she became a duchess and then she became a queen and an empress, and now she is the Queen Mother and the last empress of India."

He theatrically waves his hand.

"An empress touching the Fabergé!"

And he returns to his telephone call, nobody is looking at him, which makes no difference to him as he's loving the birthday celebration today regardless.

Now Timothy comes back from the hall carrying an enormous box of chocolates tied with a ribbon.

"What have you broken?" asks Jason, as soon as he sees him. "What was that noise just then?"

"It wasn't me!" claims Timothy. "It was Robert. He knocked a painting off the wall when he moved a big pot plant."

William may be concentrating on his telephone call but that doesn't mean to say he's not listening to things going on around him. He covers the mouthpiece again with his hand, Hercule Poirot style.

"I'm not surprised it's so dark in there," he says. "Noël Coward came round once to look at the art work, and when he finished he commented to Queen Elizabeth what a wonderful collection it was and how all the paintings were so beautifully lit, when in fact none of them were lit at all, and so she had picture lights installed over every one of them straightaway."

Having imparted this little golden nugget of knowledge he returns to his call, quite satisfied with himself.

"Have you seen the amount of people out there?" asks Timothy. "There must be thousands, all around the house and all down The Mall."

"I know," says Jason, "they wait for hours out there you

know, some of them camp overnight." Jason peers at the box Timothy is holding. "What you got there?"

"Robert told me to give you these, they were delivered to the police. It's chocolates."

Jason has a look and recognises the brand as one he doesn't like. They are decent enough chocolates although the manufacturer must have spent more on the box than the chocolates inside, but Jason has acquired expensive tastes over the years being exposed to the gifts sent to the house. He feels confident enough to reject these as he knows there will be loads of superior quality ones to choose from later.

"Oh, I don't like those! Put them in William's office for me please," he says.

"Okay," says Timothy as he takes them away.

"Bother!" William slams down the receiver in a huff. "They're engaged!"

'Who?" asks Jason.

"Spinks. I'm getting my medals re-dressed and they promised they'd have them back here by now."

"What have you got? Your gold R.V.M?"

Jason bites his tongue as soon as the words leave his mouth, but it's too late. He wasn't listening properly and thought Willliam said he'd got his fifty years of service award as it's been the talk and gossip in staff circles lately. But that's not due until next year probably, not this one, he wasn't thinking. He's tired and hungover and confused but it was too late, he'd said it now.

"What am I supposed to do with it?" asks William.

"Wear it with the others, it's a medal!"

"What do I need another medal for, I've got all these?"

"Surely you're pleased with it?"

"What do I want with medals? Anyway, it's just a piece of ribbon and a strip of metal in a cheap box! I'd much rather have a brand new Hostess Trolley," he says, as he scurries out of the pantry towards the orderly's room.

Sometimes Jason didn't know if William was being sincere or saying flippant things for effect, out of embarrassment.

Timothy comes into the pantry carrying a small knitted toy guardsman.

"Where did you get that?" asks Jason, who clocks it straightaway.

"Robert prised it from one of the dogs, they were playing with it in the hall."

"How on earth did a dog get hold of it in the hall? That's been sitting on top of an armchair in Queen Elizabeth's study for years."

"What is it?"

"It's a little knitted toy guardsman. A footman's mother made it and sent it as a gift. It's got real little regiment brass buttons and everything. It's really cute but it's been there for ages on that chair, the Queen loved it. How come the dog got hold of it all of a sudden?"

"Which footman was it?" asks Timothy, his mind already grasping the significance of it.

"Huh?"

"Which footman's mother made it?"

"Oh, er, Adrian's."

"I see," Timothy understood. Jason hasn't spotted William's spitefulness so thinks no more of it.

Jason takes the toy and puts it away in a drawer.

"Jason, will I get to meet Prince Charles today?"

"You'll get to see him Timothy, it's not your job to fraternise with him but if you play your cards right and listen to me then you may get your face in Hello! magazine, which should please your mother. We will go out later but it's not as easy as you think to get photographed out there. They always seem to chop my head off in the shot, or it's just my hand in the picture."

"I thought all the staff went out there with the Queen Mother?"

"Not today. The Prince of Wales will arrive here first, then William will go out with them a little later to have their photo taken outside the gates, so don't go out there when William's out there with them!"

"Why not?"

"Because he won't be very pleased with you and believe me he'll make you pay, maybe not today or tomorrow but perhaps in six months time, or when you least expect it."

"How do you put up with him?"

"You get used to it and anyway we can go out later, don't you ever listen? You miss so much vital information. As long as you do your job with respect you'll be fine. He knows everybody and he knows everything, and you can't expect that for nothing. I'll tell you when you can go out and where you can stand. The only thing you've got to remember today is that William comes first otherwise he won't be very pleased and we'll all suffer for it. It's our job to fetch all the flowers and gifts into the house so the ladies in waiting and officials can sort them out. You can't hang about as there are people relying on us to ferry them through the house so they can be taken on to hospices and nursing homes and hospitals. Trust me we'll be inundated so we've got to be organised. Don't forget you are here to do a job, not to enjoy yourself."

"I can't wait."

William enters the pantry carrying some small boxes tied with ribbon.

"Some people are so generous with their gifts to Queen Elizabeth you know. You should see some of this jewellery; although I'm not sure if it's quite in Her

Majesty's taste. Now I've just got to check these and then I must go."

He takes them to the telephone shelf and examines the attached messages but has difficulty reading without his glasses. He is looking to see who's sent them and if they are significant enough to warrant telling Queen Elizabeth straightaway. It also enables him to be fully informed if she happens to ask if a particular object has arrived, if she already knows about it.

Timothy hangs about and watches Jason as he admiringly takes out the menu cards and timings and seating plan for the evening, from a large brown envelope.

Reg enters and walks over towards William.

"William, that old baking couple are here who bring a cake every year and have just asked when it's convenient to present it to Queen Elizabeth?"

"Well it isn't so they can't!"

"Oh Billy?"

"The Queen doesn't want that Reg! not today. They get a thank you letter what more do they want? Just give them a glass of champagne, they'll be fine."

"But they are sweet old guys! And they come up every year all the way from Cornwall or somewhere. Why don't you let them?"

"No Reg, it's time!" William says sharply, showing his authority. He quickly packs up the gifts and leaves them on the telephone shelf.

"I'll be waiting by the lift if you go up now to the Queen."

"Very good William I know my place," says Reg, as he puckers his lips to Jason in a camp way pretending to appear suitably chastised, making fun of himself.

Reg follows William but William wants Reg to leave first.

"Well go on then!" he says, waiting.

William waits for Reg to move.

"I was waiting for you!" says Reg, who's teasing him now. William smiles and shakes his head.

"Oh for goodness sake, you get worse!"

They leave the pantry and go into the hall where William goes to wait by the royal lift on the ground floor for Queen Elizabeth, and Reg goes up the stairs to Queen Elizabeth's floor.

Jason talks to Timothy while he's putting away his lists in a drawer.

"I'll give you some good advice for today for being in front of the cameras. Beware of balloons! they get in the way of your face. And beware of people who've been here longer than you pushing you out of the way to get to the front — and that includes me!"

They pile out the pantry and cut along the hall to the open front doors towards the bright sunlight and then turn right into flashes and microphones of the world's press who are gathered there. They go along the lines of people to collect flowers and gifts.

Robert is excercising the Corgis in the garden, trying to keep them away from the open gates.

Timothy and Jason rush back into the pantry laden with flowers and calmly place them into buckets of water along the corridor. They put some birthday cards in a box on the side with some others then hurry out again.

Timothy returns by himself. He waits by the noticeboard to check no one is around then removes the lunch plans and another note and puts them into his pocket. Then he goes over to the small boxes of gifts William left on the side earlier. He opens the lids, takes out a small camera from his pocket and takes photos of them. He puts back the lids, and on his way out, glances at the noticeboard just to check if there's anything he missed and then leaves the pantry going back into the hall to go outside again.

Reg returns and sits on the stool and leans against the worktop behind him. He is feeling unwell and fans himself with a card. Marching bands and applause from the crowd can be heard coming from outside. Timothy enters with some flowers.

"The Queen was already down, she was waiting by herself in the library looking through the window!" says Reg, wiping his brow with his handkerchief.

"I've never seen so many flowers in my life!" says Timothy, who's obviously impressed. He places them in the buckets of water.

"That's right love, keep them coming," says Reg. "You can see why the royals don't much care for flowers, as they've all had bunches of them thrust into their faces from an early age. I think it's only our Lady and the Prince who still appreciate them."

"There are some roses out there that must be at least a metre long, I've never seen roses like that before in my life! Jason will love those when he sees them."

"Let them go round the back with the rest love, somebody can have the pleasure of them. Some poor soul in a hospital or nursing home. Put those boxes of chocolates there too, would you love?"

"Aren't you going out there Reg?"

"No love. It's too hot, and anyway I've already made my appearances out there. You have to leave the audience wanting more you know. It's a theatre thing," and he wafts his handkerchief around under his chin and smirks.

Timothy goes out to the hall again and Jason enters with more flowers.

"You should see the housemaids Reg, they're behaving like Red Indians now."

"What do you mean?"

"They are slowly closing in on the camera shot behind Queen Elizabeth. We can hardly get the flowers past them into the house, they are all trying to get their mugs on television."

"Everybody wants a bit of the limelight," Reg turns his nose in the air and swirls his handkerchief some more.

Jason deposits the flowers and rushes out, then Timothy comes back with some more flowers and an orchid plant in a pot. He puts them down.

"I'll have that one love," says Reg, referring to the orchid. "It can go to Scotland with the Queen. Anything nice or in a pot you can put to one side because they last."

Reg takes the orchid plant and puts it to one side whilst still sitting.

"Make sure you take all the cards and labels off love," he says.

"What, and throw them away?"

"No love, give them to the ladies in waiting so that they can send a thank you letter to anyone who's left their name and address. Tell them what they are though, or show them if you don't know."

A military band can be heard in the background playing 'Happy Birthday.' It's part of the march past the house gates.

Timothy goes out again and Jason rushes in carrying a huge teddy bear, nearly as big as himself. He runs in and plonks it down on the floor next to Reg.

"Here you are Reg," he says, "have you met the new footman? His name's Adrian. Reg, there's a cake! What shall I do with a cake? There's a great big cake!"

"Well get somebody to move it!"

Jason doesn't stand still, he rushes out again talking as he goes.

"The carriage will be leaving in a minute! One of those Toast Masters out there just offered me two hundred and fifty quid for this old tailcoat. Cheeky so and so."

Reg pulls the teddy bear close to him. It's so large that the teddy's head reaches his head and so he can lean on it and he stares at it and it makes him smile.

Timothy enters while trying to remove a card taped to some flowers and Jason is right behind him. He rushes in with an armful of bouquets he can just about see over and his eyes dart about looking for a place to put them. There's absolutely nowhere.

"Oh I dunno," he says and just throws them onto the floor. He grabs Timothy by the arm and pulls him backwards through the hall doorway.

"Leave that, do it later, come on. We're on!"

He pulls Timothy along backwards, who is still struggling with the sticky tape and the label stuck to his fingers. Timothy turns around and together they start striding down the hall and out towards the front doors.

"Now shall we do Hello! magazine first or O.K! magazine or Majesty magazine?" asks Jason. "Or shall we be like Marlene and be very mysterious and blasé and totally ignore everybody?"

They arrive outside the house and delve into the crowds again, Jason trying to look as nonchalant and demure as he finds possible. Which ain't that nonchalant or demure I can tell you!

Reg tuts and gets up to pick up all the flowers off the floor shaking his head in dismay. He sorts them out and checks the cards. He's still feeling unwell. Then he goes over to the mirror to adjust his bow tie, and tugs down his waistcoat that has a tendancy to ride up a little. He talks to himself through the mirror.

"Don't know where it's coming from for tonight kid? But you're still looking gorgeous!"

He goes back and sits on the stool and smiles at the teddy bear. The crowd can be heard from outside cheering away Queen Elizabeth and the Prince of Wales as they leave in the carriage.

The telephone rings and he gets up to answer it.

"Hello?" A pause. "Yes love put them through?" Another pause. "Oh hello Gill how are you?" he laughs. "And all the better for hearing you my dear. I know, he told me what a wonderful time you had" he chuckles. "Yes, yes I know. Yes, the Prince of Wales is with her in the carriage, are you watching on the telly? Oh good. No, I've done all that, leave it to the young ones, there must be hundreds of photos of me by now, I look better in black and white anyway," he chuckles. "For years and years now. Well I know but you know what he's like, as long as he can keep working he's happy. Well then, why don't you get him something from Penhaligon's? he would adore that. Not at all! All right darling take care. Take care Gill, bye!"

He laughs again and replaces the receiver. He tugs down his waistcoat again. The telephone rings while he's still standing next to it, he answers it straightaway.

"Hello?" He listens for a second. "Yes we've got a load here you can take now. I think they're going to Great Ormond Street next. All right then, thanks love."

He replaces the receiver and sits back down on the stool. He takes his handkerchief and mops his brow still chuckling to himself from the conversation with Gill. He cuddles the teddy bear and seems to be lost in thought. He's alone in the pantry while the boys have run in and out for the umpteenth time, but it feels peaceful in here, a haven. There are thousands of people just a room's breadth away cheering and clapping and a marching band and news teams splattered everywhere, but here in this room it's

141

tranquil, even with the muffled noises coming from outside. It feels safe in here, away from the buzz and excitement and distractions out there. He stays like this for a few minutes. Just daydreaming, surrounded by the lovely scent of all the flowers.

William, Jason and Timothy burst in returning in a triumphant mood, marching along, all clutching goodies. Jason is holding some sparkly birthday balloons, Timothy is struggling with a giant birthday card and a soft toy and William is carrying a large bottle of champagne. Jason is obviously finishing saying something to Timothy.

"Well, I don't know what they were complaining about, I mean, if they had to lug an Edwardian dining table to-and-fro across the lawn all day then they could have stood at the front as well!"

"That was amazing," says Timothy, who found the whole experience thrilling. "All those cameras clicking, it was like being at a film premiere in Leicester Square! I didn't realise it was such a big deal with the foreign press. Did you see the way the Queen Mother smiled at me when I opened the carriage door?"

"You shouldn't have been there!" says William, as he struggles to put down the huge bottle on the floor, so he's not able to give Timothy a rebuking tap on the shoulder which he really wanted to do.

He stands there and fans himself with a box of chocolates.

"Gosh it's hot out there. You should have seen The Mall Reg! There were people lining both sides several deep, all to the end! Never seen so many people for a birthday, the Queen was so worried they wouldn't cheer when she went onto The Mall, but they did. You should have heard them roar when the carriage appeared when it turned the corner, it was wonderful!"

"Really, that's wonderful!" replies Reg, trying to sound

as enthusiastic as he can. "I've told the orderlies to arrange to take this lot away in a minute," pointing to all the flowers.

William walks out towards the orderly's room.

"I'll just go and have a word before we nip over the road. Tell the chef they may be a little late for that household buffet lunch would you?"

At this point, Kay appears like a silent snake.

"Reg?" she says. "Have you got that big box of chocolates? William said I could have some."

"Come back later love and we'll sort it out," Reg says, which seems to satisfy the situation but she leaves reluctantly all the same.

William calls out from beyond the flower porch in the orderly's room.

"Jason are you there? Could you come here a minute please, I've got something to show you, I'm in the orderly's."

William has gone into the orderly's and straightaway opened a stationery cupboard and selected a very large royal crested cream envelope. He quickly seals it by licking the gum and pressing down the flap, giving the impression there is a document inside.

Jason walks from the pantry closely followed by Timothy. (Wherever Jason goes Timothy follows him like a shadow.)

Jason is getting used to him gradually but it's still annoying at times. He's got a very light head still with yet another hangover! He is annoyed that William is demanding his attention at this precise moment as he wants to talk to Reg about the crowds outside. He enters the orderly's to find William admiring a splendid gleaming gold model of some horses and a carriage about one and a half metres long, that's just been delivered and unpacked for his inspection. It must be worth a small fortune. William checks the card that came with it but he's squinting as he's mislaid his glasses again.

"What is it?" asks Jason impatiently.

"Well can't you see, it's a gold horses and carriage."

"Yes, but what's it for?"

"It's a gift! For Queen Elizabeth from prince," William squints at the card he's holding, "someone or other, I haven't got my glasses can you see?"

William offers Jason the card but he's not in the least bit interested. He totally ignores it.

"No. Where's it going? And please don't say the main vault?"

"Of course it must go into the vault, it's extremely valuable."

"Yes, I'm sure it cost the same as a small house but there's no more room in there, it's completely full and if I put this in as well there won't be any room for me to walk about."

"Yes well," says William, "I'm sure Her Majesty would have much rather have had some new Tupperware."

"What's Tupperware?" asks Timothy, who's been lurking about all this time glued to their conversation. Jason has had enough now. He turns to face him and decides to pronunciate his words in the way he thinks Noël Coward would do, but without any actually swearing.

"Plastic receptacles!" he states clearly, then turns back to face William.

"Well, couldn't we send it to a museum somewhere on loan?" he asks.

"Don't be ridiculous! It belongs to The Royal Collection now."

"But ..."

"Don't question me!" shouts William. "Why have you become so militant?"

William turns to Timothy and hands him the [empty]

144

envelope that he sealed when he came in the room.

"Now dear boy," he says. "Quickly take this along to the lady in waiting's office. It's an important message from the Queen so go this way it's quicker."

He points to a doorway leading upstairs.

Timothy takes the envelope and rushes away gleefully, looking fairly pleased with himself thinking he's got his hands on an important document, it being such an impressive official crested one.

(William set up this envelope trick just to get rid of him for five minutes, it's an old trick. The lady in waiting won't say anything to Timothy but she will ask William about it at some point, just to check.)

"Now then," William says, in a calm and serious manner. "I want to go over the arrangements quickly for tonight at the Opera House. You can go when you like once household lunch is over, I've booked the usual driver. Now, once you've set the table and everything with Robert, come back here and get the posh flowers which I'll do later, they'll be ready waiting for you and don't forget to take a couple of arrangements from the birthday flowers for the side tables and the sturdiest chairs out of the library."

"And the Queen's chair and a cushion and footstool of course."

"Well that goes without saying. Now, you'll send all the drinks and cold food with the first transport tonight as I'll already be there, but don't let chef send the hot food for the main course until you get the call. We've only got two intervals and if it was left to them they'd send everything in one go and then go home."

"Yes I know, but I think it's best to send all the salads later with the hot food."

"Why?"

"They'll go soggy otherwise, there's no fridge. I

145

checked with that woman with the clipboard yesterday. There's no air-conditioning either so it's gonna be roasting in that room later with everyone wearing ball gowns and dinner jackets."

"I'd rather you send the salads to begin with, we can cover them with tea towels."

"No, it's all right William, I'll have them sent with the main course they'll be fine, and I'll get Robert to send the dessert and coffee when we need it later."

"You won't be able to go! You'll have to stay here to see the Queen off."

"What? And stay here all night until she gets back?"

"Reg and Robert will be with me at the theatre!"

"Robert can see the Queen off. He hates the theatre," says Jason, quickly becoming exasperated at the thought of missing out on yet another birthday at the theatre.

"Look, I don't need to tell you, you know the Queen inside out. You know she always likes to see a familiar friendly face so I can't ask the new boy and anyway, I need you here to hold the fort in case anything goes wrong."

"What could go wrong?" cries Jason. "I'm going to organise everything and once the food has been sent and gone that's it!"

William is very calm. He never gave Jason a clue he wasn't letting him go to the Opera House to help serve dinner with the others. He wanted him to prepare the table and check and send the right plates and food and everything but to wait at Clarence House all night. He knew he would be angry about it but he's making the mistake of telling him too soon because Jason can sabotage the evening by refusing to co-operate. And Jason is so wound up at the moment that he possibly might just blow a gasket.

"I can't rely on the others. You know all about the food and the silver."

William thought a bit of flattery would go down well,

146

but it backfires on him.

"Oh thanks! So I miss out for being good at my job do I? Or rather, because others are no good at theirs?"

"I knew you'd understand."

William turns and starts to walk away. He's playing the 'ignorance is bliss' card. That is, baffle Jason with extreme politeness and pretend they agree on the issue then walk away and just hope for the best. It hasn't worked this time, Jason is furious and this time he's not taking things lying down. He's going to take Timothy's advice and stand up for himself.

"William, this happened last year. If I don't get to go to the theatre tonight then you can find someone else to send the food for you and do your little outing, because if I can't go then I'm having nothing to do with it."

He storms off past the pantry and down the hall, bumping into Reg as he goes. He is furious. He goes outside to talk to the people in the crowds to calm his nerves.

Reg has heard the argument and come to see what the fuss is about. He can't believe Jason is so angry and thinks it must be Timothy getting on his nerves, but when he sees that Timothy isn't there, he realises it was William's fault, but he doesn't care either way as he just wants to go to sleep.

"What have you said to Jason? He just pushed straight past me?"

William never expected Jason to react in this way. He can usually manipulate him quite easily. He's trying to think of the reason for it.

"What's wrong with the boy lately? When did he become so militant?"

"Militant? He's always been fine with me. Do you

want me to speak to him about it?"

"No, no, not today of all days."

Reg had been waiting for the appropriate moment to tell William he simply wasn't able to carry on for the rest of the day. He wanted to hold out as long as possible to soften the blow but there was no way he could hold out any longer. Talk about the worst possible timing but he had no choice. He knew he was ill and he knew something was going very wrong with the blood flowing through his veins. He needed the salvation of his bed, he wanted to go to sleep. He wanted to go to sleep and then everything would be all right.

"William, I think I'm going to go to my room for a while."

"What's wrong Reg? Don't you feel well?"

"No I don't feel up to it. I need to go and lie down."

"But what about the palace, and standing behind Queen Elizabeth's chair? we should leave now, we should go?"

William doesn't give himself the chance to think what Reg is saying. He understood what he meant but he wouldn't let the idea fully form in his head. He thought they could nip in a chauffeur driven car straightaway and get to the palace quickly straight down The Mall and then go straight in and find a place for Reg to rest a while. They could both still stand behind Queen Elizabeth's chair at luncheon. Tonight at the ballet is hours away and that problem could be sorted out later. No, William was thinking in tiny steps. Get Reg to the car, then get inside the palace then take things from there. There was no way Reg could miss today, not to come this far to lose grasp of it now.

"No I must go and lie down," says Reg, hoping that William will understand the implications of what he's saying.

"But it's the one hundredth birthday lunch!"

"You go William, I'm really not feeling well at all." Reg knew there was no point in pretending but he still wanted William to enjoy the day. There was no point both of them missing everything.

"But Reg what about tonight at the ballet?"

"I don't know if I'll make it William. What's the matter? you've got Robert and Jason and the boy to help you."

"Oh Reggie!" William could see in Reg's face he meant it, yet there may still be a chance, if he could reassure Reg somehow.

"Don't worry Billy, I'll be all right."

"But I wanted to do today with you!"

"I know, but I'm only going to be upstairs."

"That's not the same though is it?"

"Billy I really need to go and rest."

"But Reggie, you are going to miss everything!"

"I know William, I'm sorry."

"Why don't you sit in the garden for a while and get some fresh air?"

"No Billy, I can't!" Reg yells, finally saying those inevitable words. "Will you help me please Billy? I just need to go to bed and stay there until I feel better."

William had tried to fend off him saying that as long as possible, as long as there was a chance. Now it's gone.

"All right Reg, I understand. I'm sorry. Come on love, let's get you to the lift. Everything is going to be all right."

William holds on to Reg who can barely walk by himself now. They slowly climb the couple of steps out of the orderly's and into the corridor to the lift. William takes him upstairs to his room where he lies down. William asks a couple of staff members to keep and eye on him and they call a doctor.

IN A STATIONERY STOREROOM

Timothy is standing in-between some high metal storage shelves in a walk-in stationery storeroom. It's the only convenient place he can find to make his secret call as there are so many people about, and it's too far to go to his bedroom or the place in the basement near the deliveries door, as he has to make this call as soon as possible. He dials the number on his mobile phone and has one more look to check the coast is clear before he presses the call button. He waits a few seconds, and it connects.

"Hi it's me, can you hear me?"

"Good, listen, I've got to be quick. I'm going to the Opera House tonight to help serve dinner in the royal box. The Queen, the Queen Mother and Princess Margaret and some others will all be there. Listen, I need a tape recorder. This is harder than I thought. It's really difficult for me to get a word in the conversations. If I had a recorder I could leave it somewhere switched on and get them revved up and maybe they'll start talking about it when I'm not there."

He listens for a second to the reply.

"I don't know, you'll have to think of something."

He listens again.

"Well, send me some flowers and put a tiny tape recorder in the wrapping paper or hide it inside a box of chocolates or something. Nobody will take any notice with all the other flowers being sent today. Bike it over and make sure it's addressed to me in the butler's pantry."

He listens.

"I never thought I'd be spending the night at the ballet with the royal family! I'm going to crack this thing open tonight!"

He listens.

"Okay, later."

He slips the phone into his pocket and gets out of there sharpish.

A NIGHT AT THE BALLET

The police cordoned off the streets in Covent Garden outside the Royal Opera House, so everyone knew something glamourous and exciting was about to happen.

There has been an air of expectation for the last hour, for the arrival of the royal party and the show to begin.

A few moments before their arrival in front of the theatre William appears from within which causes a few camera flashes to go off. He patiently hovers near the doors and the people waiting behind the barriers then knew the arrival was imminent. The expectation of the crowd added to the atmosphere as everyone waited. The last time the Queen Mother and The Queen and The Princess Margaret came here together for a show was in 1999 for the gala opening after the refurbishment, when they sat in the auditorium, and now they are coming here together tonight to watch a show of ballet.

Suddenly, the line of royal cars comes into view driving up Bow Street towards the entrance, to the delight of the crowd and the flash of the world's photographers.

William walks forward and waits on the red carpet and so he too, is photographed as he opens and holds the car door steady for Queen Elizabeth, who emerges first and gracefully steps out, fully bejewelled with a set of stunning diamonds and wearing a new pale green gown with shimmering patterned detail, silver shoes and a silver handbag. The waiting crowd proceeds to sing 'Happy Birthday' to her. The Princess Margaret steps out of the same car, and they both stand there on the red carpet listening to this spontaneous little tribute while Queen Elizabeth is smiling and waving to them and William holds open the door. Then the gathered mass of people breakout into applause. Then, The Queen steps out the car onto the red carpet, and so, the Queen Mother and her two daughters enter the Royal Opera House together for the evening to watch a performance by The Kirov Ballet.

The anteroom behind the royal box has no windows, a single door on one side and double doors to the royal box on the other.

The dining table is set with a luxurious white Irish linen tablecloth, candelabra with candle shades, the flower arrangement is in the centre with four beautiful silver-gilt epergnes in the form of trochus shells, [the Karibas]. Eight chairs surround the table including the Queen Mother's own carver chair and a small cushion. A service table stands along a wall with a white cloth reaching the floor. It holds sparkling silver trays with coffee cups and saucers and silver spoons, silver sugar bowls and cream jugs. There are two oval silver salvers, some silver coffee pots, chocolates, some folded white service napkins. A silver champagne holder ready for a bottle of champagne. A silver champagne bucket. An ice bucket and silver ice tongs. A crystal stand of fruit. A crystal stand of strawberries. Some small plates, glass water bowls on plates [with a pad] for dessert [the fruit], gold dessert forks, knives and spoons. Brandy and port in crystal decanters, liqueurs in their own bottles. Some bottles of water and soft drinks. Some bottles of wine. Champagne glasses, wine, water, brandy, port and liqueur glasses also. A flower arrangement is on the service table and there is a small table standing against the other wall which also has flowers on it and some glossy ballet brochures.

The evening has past by and the show is nearly coming to an end. Timothy and Jason are sitting on a couple of dining chairs with their jackets off, relaxing trying to keep cool, their cuffs folded up. Jason is flicking through some glossy ballet brochures. Timothy is wishing he was in a Covent Garden sports bar just over the cobbled courtyard there with an ice-cold pint of lager in his hand, rather than being bored to death in this room with these two flunkies.

William is standing wearing his black tailcoat uniform despite the room being extremely hot and uncomfortable because there's no air-conditioning back here, only in the auditorium. He hasn't taken off his coat or sat down all evening and never will. He's been like a frisky alley cat all night during the performance, sneaking through the double doors that lead to the space behind the royal box where The Queen and Queen Elizabeth are sitting with their guests. All evening he's been trying to catch a glanced snippet of the ballet now and then, only coming back into the room to check on Jason and Timothy, saying always: "Is everything all right," even when nothing was happening. The table was set and ready for the next course and the royal party were watching the show, so everything was all right. Nothing else was happening, Jason and Timothy were just waiting, killing time. There was nothing else they could do. There was only one way they could come and go anyway because they were stuck in the room under police armed guard. The only singular exit at the moment was the double doors leading to behind the royal box, so whenever they happened to see the door tentatively opening a little, they knew it could only be William coming back through. He had returned a while ago now when his latest escapade had been curtailed by a strategically placed cough from the royal party when his behaviour became too disruptive. At one point however, he was gone so long that Jason thought he must have found a vacant seat somewhere in the theatre and sat down with the rest of the audience.

They have used the two intervals to serve dinner and are going to serve champagne and strawberries and chocolates at the end of the performance. William asked Jason to bring a good selection of chocolates from the birthday gifts, which he did. It is just after ten o'clock now, so the performance is approaching the scheduled ending time of ten minutes past ten. Then it should be a good few more minutes while the dancers of The Kirov Ballet take their bows and the royal party comes back in for some refreshments.

Royal boxes were invented to be seen in rather than to see a show, as the almost perpendicular aspect of their positioning in the auditorium doesn't contribute anything to a comfortable viewing point. That's why some of the royal party are sitting in the main auditorium with the public tonight, in order to save a cricked neck.

Jason is quite surprised to be sitting here in this room. It's been touch and go all afternoon not knowing if William would let him come and serve dinner behind the royal box. When early evening had come around the kitchen staff indicated everything for the first course was going to be ready to take on time, but he refused to pack anything, saying that the service of this particular dinner had nothing at all to do with him. He pointed out that nobody else was around who could chill the champagne and then organise the transfer of all the food and drink over to the theatre. And so he pranced out the kitchen as he declared he was not in the least interested. Secretly though, he had everything in hand. The word got around and reached William, so eventually, at the last minute William sent a message casually stating that: "You can tell Jason to come with the champagne anytime you like now," which gave Jason the green light to go and for the food to be dispatched in his way. Jason had won, for now. It never occurred to him that William would bear a grudge from this or the little tiff they had had earlier in the day, or some other day, as William seemed to be fine.

Jason had got a driver to sneak him over to the Opera House earlier in the afternoon to set the table by himself, just in case he wasn't going to be allowed to come and serve dinner. He didn't trouble Robert or Timothy to help him but asked the kitchen porter instead. He was quite proud how smart it looked. William's flowers looked stunning, much more conservative than his usual style.

It's hot and humid. Music from the orchestra can be heard playing in the background. Jason and William are tired but in high spirits. William is tipsy. Jason has worked hard for this event to get here and so he intends to relax and enjoy himself, but William and he are still competing with each other. Jason doesn't realise it yet, but he's extremely worn out and dehydrated from the last few nights and from having nothing to eat all day but some coffee and chocolates. He's been too occupied with doubt and worry about tonight and packing all the pantry service stuff for Scotland and too busy rushing around all day to notice.

He has read all the brochures cover to cover. He is sitting cross-legged with a brochure on his lap fanning himself with another one while pretending to 'smoke' a large match. His scarlet tailcoat is on the back of a chair.

"There's an article in here about Anthony Dowell and the English National Ballet, but there doesn't seem to be any English dancers in here?" he says. "There's not one English sounding name. So why would they call it the English National Ballet?"

William is prancing in a ballet style by himself to the music. Mostly twirling his arms and hands, not moving much from the same spot, but he is rather good.

"Tony says it's because the best dancers come from all over the world," he says,

"I love coming to the ballet," as he makes arm swirls in

the air.

Jason looks up to watch William, but he doesn't bat an eyelid. He's seen it all before. William always does this kind of prancing to any ballet music, especially when he's waiting in the hall at Clarence House for Queen Elizabeth to come downstairs for lunch, or if there's a dinner on. Jason is quite impressed with his impressions of the movements tonight, but some of them are just a little camp, even for Jason. This is the first opportunity for a chat they've had all evening as William has been absent for most of it.

"Do you think some people got wind of the royals coming tonight?" asks Jason, "I don't think there's a spare seat in the house?"

"I suppose some people would have guessed, but the majority of them would be ballet lovers," says William, still prancing.

Jason takes no more notice now as he looks down and flicks through his brochure again, but Timothy doesn't know what to make of it at all. This is so out of his comfort zone but he's giving it his best shot. Still, he's extremely puzzled. He too, is relaxing on a chair, on the other side of the room from Jason. His scarlet tailcoat is also on the back of a chair but carelessly thrown over it, not hung over it like Jason's is. Timothy isn't so affected by the heat and humidity as much as Jason, but he'd still much rather be somewhere else all the same, and he still has some business to attend to with William. Whenever he gets the urge to bolt out of the door and flee to the nearest sports bar for an ice-cold pint he tells himself: (now those of you of a sensitive disposition should stick your fingers in your ears while you read this next bit as it's a bit dodgy), "Think of the money Timmy just think of the money. I just need to nail this sucker tonight." He talks himself through his tactics, "Just play it cool Timmy, play it cool. Wait 'til everyone's gone later and it's just me and him with all that champagne."

Neither of the other two have a clue what Timothy is thinking. Jason thinks he's a bit of a plonker and William thinks he should possibly go into acting, or at least become a model with his matinée idol looks, as he calls it. An expression he embraced from someone else in the same way he's imitated the way he speaks and behaves over the years from the people he serves.

[William hardly ever talked about Coventry where he grew up. He spoke with no accent. When he spoke he emulated the people he worked for. He sort of reinvented himself, or at least, evolved his own character in the way he spoke and the expressions he used]

"I spotted a couple of celebrities, a racing driver and a weather girl," says Timothy enthusiastically. "The police said they were expecting Elton John to be here."

"I heard that to come down after doing a show, he plonks himself in front of the television and eats whole gherkins straight out of the jar?" says Jason.

"Oh, that's nonsense surely?" says William, still prancing as his gold bracelet appears from under his sleeve whilst doing a port de bras. "Anyway, if he did eat gherkins straight out of a jar, I'm sure he'd use a silver pickle fork!"

"I dare say that he does," says Jason, "that's my point. He's just being who he is, he doesn't need to prove anything. I like a gherkin meself. Not fattening," and he takes an imaginary puff of his imaginary cigarette then returns to his brochure.

All the while William is twirling and dancing gently, lost in a dream.

"It says here," says Jason, "that they spent over two hundred million pounds when they refurbished the Royal Opera House," he looks up. "And they couldn't afford to put air-conditioning in this room? They put it out there but not in here where the royals wait. I wonder what they do if they rent it out to the corporate sector? I bet they get an air-conditioning unit, and a fridge. We could have put a fridge on the landing if those policemen weren't standing there with machine guns," and he gestures towards the single door with his hand.

"And policewomen," adds Timothy, who smiles to himself at the thought of a woman in uniform. He had tried to drum up a conversation with the police outside, but they weren't in the mood for a chat, unsurprisingly.

Jason stops skimming through his brochure for a second as he's just remembered something funny that happened to him while the theatre was filling up before the show.

"When I was out there before the show standing against the wall trying to cool down, a woman came up to me with her ticket. She wanted me to show her to her seat. She thought I was an usher because I was wearing my scarlet tails, she thought I worked here. Nice woman," he says in a matter of fact way. "She sounded Canadian to me."

William suddenly stops dancing. This is news to him — stunned that his instructions weren't being carried out to the letter, and that Jason was taking it upon himself to do whatever he liked. This is a serious matter. Coming to the ballet was his gig and he wasn't going to have anybody spoiling it with their wanton ways.

"You mean you went out there in the auditorium when you were supposed to stay in this room for the royal party and to receive them? I asked you to wait in here!" he yells, and he slaps Jason across the shoulder [but quite forcefully].

Jason sits up in his chair and barks back at him.

"Oh, in order to guard the silver as you put it, yes. You disappeared! We didn't know where you'd gone having told us to wait in here while you pop out for a minute. I thought you'd gone to the loo, we were waiting for you to come back. Little did we know you'd stolen away down the stairs to the red carpet outside, just in time for the cars to arrive to bag a photo opportunity with the world's press; opening the Daimler doors to two queens and a princess while we were stuck up here like a couple of lemons."

William has been found out and exposed. He thought he'd got away with it, as it usually worked that old trick, but he doesn't care as Jason was too slow on the uptake; he should have taken more notice of the time rather than concentrating on being too hot.

"I only meant one of you to stay, to guard against souvenir pickers. You were too slow."

"Tell me! We were suffocating in here as there's no air-conditioning we needed some air, so we stood out there for five minutes watching people coming in and finding their seats. It's only when we were talking to the detective that we found out where you'd sneaked off to. It was too late then."

(This was when Jason and Timothy were in the air-conditioned auditorium where it was cooler. They'd nipped out of the anteroom for two minutes through the security, who knew them, and they were minding their own business standing against the wall cooling down watching the audience settling into their seats when that lady came up to them and asked about her ticket. She was on the wrong level. Jason directed her to the right place, as far as he could tell.)

"Actually," says Jason easing back into his chair now and becoming quite smarmy, about to deliver some information that he knows will infuriate William in revenge for missing the photo opportunity, "I was scanning the stalls circle for my friends Katie and Michael in the audience as I knew where they were sitting and the seat numbers. So when

160

they waved at me I instinctively waved back," (and he just realises something this instant) "which was a bit silly really, as I was standing in the royal box at the time."

This does infuriate William once he learns that Jason has been standing in the royal box waiting, preening himself and hamming it up and attracting the attention of a packed house while the royal party was just pulling up to the Opera House outside. William tuts and smacks him across the shoulder again. Jason grabs his shoulder in pain.

"Well I got carried away with the moment of actually seeing them didn't I?" he moans. "I didn't realise it would look like I was waving to every single person in the audience," (and that's what he just realised) "too late now."

"Did you see how Princess Margaret changed direction and came to my seats when she saw me standing there?" says Timothy. "I love the way she walked past you. You got all the old fogeys."

God how rude, thinks Jason, at this young upstart's uncouthness. Who does he think he is? Well if he wants to join in the banter he'd better put his crash helmet on now. Jason is getting very annoyed again with Timothy, as he seems to act with such disdain about everything but still expects to be treated with respect himself. This self-importance can only mean one thing: He must still be a virgin. Or he's a complete wally.

"The Princess Margaret didn't go to your seats because you were looking after them," he says. "She went there to get a better view of the stage, as she must know this theatre like the back of her hand owing to the amount of times she's been here before."

"I overheard her say to one of her friends that the new footman has got matinée idol looks," says Timothy, as he smirks in a self-satisfied manner. He really fancies himself.

"Yes, as in silent films," snaps Jason. "As in no dialogue, as in: I wish?" getting quite tetchy with him now.

"Touché!" agrees William, who is dancing again, and who Jason forgot was there for a moment when he was telling Timothy off. Even William is finding Timothy irritating now, thinks Jason. There were rumours floating around that Timothy had been round to William's gate lodge for drinks. Jason had a standing invitation to go there but he only took up the offer once. The experience was as he expected; people calling each other darling and actors and actresses he'd admired in the past popping by and playing up to William. Not Jason's scene at all. He had personal bad experience of theatricals, and drinkers.

Jason thought that William must like having Timothy around because he was young and good-looking. There was no question about it, he did have handsome features, although it pained Jason to admit it. And he had to admit to himself that Timothy could be a fashion model like William said because he was also tall, but he pacified this admission in his head by telling himself that the latest trend for models at the moment was the scraggy alien look. So that made him feel a bit better about it.

Apart from all this it was obvious that neither William or Jason wanted Timothy to join in the conversation, as they felt he had nothing to offer on the subject of ballet or theatre, or respect, it would seem. In the unlikely event the conversation ever came around to the subject of football or rugby they would gladly consult him. As it stood at the moment it was purely camp talk, so he'd better butt out as far as they were concerned.

After this harmless little sparring match was over things settled down. It was the heat that was making everyone irritable. And being stuck in that room.

What was really happening here was that some friction was flaring up between William and Jason. They worked well together as their working styles were suited. Jason knew the little different ways and styles William served and the routines he preferred, and the labourious lengths he went to; so Jason could just get on with it without interference. William would come along at the last minute and say things such as; "Have you done this? Have you done that? You did remember so-and-so didn't you? Oh good!"

You see, William had done Jason's job for ages, years ago. He had worked his way up. He spent years getting up early and working all day until the wee hours. Queen Elizabeth entertained more in those days so there was more work to do for the staff. In those days there was scope for William to develop and progress, as the steward at the time was also a drinker. That meant that William would be running around all day helping others, filling in but getting his face around and earning a reputation as a good worker and a grafter. The household was on wind-down these days. Timothy, for instance, didn't have to start work until 8:30am and he could have a thirty minute tea break at 10am and lunch at 12pm.

Jason knew all William's anecdotes off-by-heart so he got bored sometimes with the same old stories he told, because they were all centred about his time in royal service as he had no other experience to draw from. What William was doing in effect was always talking about work.

The performance is nearly coming to an end, but the boys are still relaxing. They won't need to move and think about pouring the champagne until they hear the sound of applause.

Earlier in the evening Jason had opened the single

door to go to the loo and jumped out his skin when a great
big police rifle was nearly shoved up his nose. Well, not
literally, it just felt like that to him as even seeing the guns is
quite alarming, as they are so large. Since then the police
were keeping full control of the door. So the boys were told
to knock if they wanted it opened again. Jason had asked if
he could store some boxes of champagne out there and they
agreed.

William has started turning on the spot now and
swirling his arms in the air in a most dramatic, disturbing
way.

"Did you know that Bow Street is the only police
station in London that doesn't have a blue light outside?" he
asks from the other side of the room now, as he has begun
to travel. "It's so, that the light wouldn't offend Queen
Victoria's eye when she came out of the theatre. All these
policemen with guns! All Queen Elizabeth's got for
protection is a bit of chiffon."

Jason is not really listening but thinking aloud about the
refrigerated beverage situation.

"I could have put a fridge in that corner after all, there's
enough space. I could have covered it with a tablecloth or
something."

William is still prancing.

"I'll mention it to Tony when I see him," (so he's still
listening then, and not exactly dreaming).

"I know!" says Jason, "I could put that folding screen
around it that's in my room at Clarence House couldn't I?
The one that Queen Mary embroidered, it's all green silk and
swirls. The silk's fallen off the back now but the front's
absolutely fine. I could use that next time."

William ceases dancing and drops his arms and looks at
Jason.

"But of course, you have my old room at Clarence
House don't you? Isn't it a huge magnificent room,

overlooking The Mall and St. James's Park and what a commanding view? I loved the way you could see Big Ben lit up through the trees at night. Is that enormous Victorian triple wardrobe still in there? The one with the cracked mirror? I put that note on it to say it was already damaged when I moved in, I didn't break it! Is the note still there?"

Jason is frustrated that his line of thought is being broken and that they are talking about a stupid note taped to a wardrobe mirror. He wants to discuss the pitiful catering resources available in private hospitality rooms in international venues. He thinks he had better give William an answer though, to keep him sweet.

"No, I took it off ages ago," he says.

"The staff rooms are filled with old royal furniture they can't be bothered to mend," says William. "You should have seen the parties I had in that room. I've had prima ballerinas sitting on the floor in front of the fire drinking champagne. So many people used to come and visit me I didn't have enough chairs for them all to sit. The room used to be filled with beautiful young talented people. Everybody used to come and see me after their shows. Dancers, actors and artists have all been entertained 'til the early hours."

[William is right, the staff rooms are filled with old furniture they can't be bothered to mend. All of them had an impressive old wardrobe in them. Some were silk lined with dust covers inside. They may have been rejected for only having a scratch or a cracked mirror like William's had in his old room. There may have been a mahogany breakfast table with a wonky caster, or an embroidered silk screen like Jason's. If you looked underneath a lot of the wooden furniture you may have found a little paper label printed 'The King', denoting it was The King's private property]

William continues dancing. "I love the theatre."

"I know, I've seen the photos," Jason replies, as if to remind him that he's heard all this before, many times over.

"Doesn't everyone look marvellous this evening. I must say Her Majesty looks wonderful in that beautiful new dress," William says.

"I know," says Jason, "and that jewellery is unbelievable. I don't think I've ever seen that set before. Wonder where it's from?"

"Probably a gift from an admiring Maharaja."

"Princess Diana had some wonderful jewellery didn't she?" says Timothy. "She must have loved coming here with Queen Elizabeth and showing off her fashion sense?"

William completely ignores Timothy's question about Diana and grabs a bottle of champagne. Jason also feels no urge to answer the stupid boy either.

"Dear boy, more champagne?" asks William, approaching Timothy with a bottle.

"Oh go on then," he replies, picking up his glass from the side to let William pour some champagne. "How long does this show last Billy? It's going on forever."

"I feel sorry for Lady Snaresbrook," says William, "she hates the ballet. Fancy having to sit through it all if you'd much rather be at home watching the telly."

"Does anyone know how Reg is getting on?" asks Timothy sharply.

William is shocked. He isn't expecting this.

"What do you mean, how is Reg getting on what do you mean?"

"At the hospital. Is he all right, as I saw two people walking him out to a car to take him to hospital this afternoon?"

Jason interjects quickly.

"I'm sure everything's fine, nothing to worry about."

"But he looked so ill, I saw them taking him out, he

could hardly walk by himself. What's he gone into hospital for?"

"He was just tired," says Jason, "he's got that thing that makes you tired, you know that sugar thing, what's it called?" Jason snaps his fingers trying to recall the word in his head, "Diabetes."

"But you don't go to hospital for that," Timothy says, "you have to take insulin shots or something."

"Oh no it's nothing," Jason assures him. "It's happened before, he'll be all right."

William interrupts. He is quite drunk now and his eyes have glazed over, giving out the look that hard drinkers get when they've reached their limit. (It's a gormless sickly fixed grin, making them appear to look mesmerised, as if listening to a brilliantly funny joke that's perpetually playing on a tape loop inside their head.)

"Jason! I need you to tell me something. How much champagne is left?"

"I don't know, why?"

"I just need to know how much champagne there is?"

Also, Jason recognises straightaway the certain infliction in William's voice that indicates he's reached the stage where he could easily become very difficult and tricky if not handled carefully. Jason's heart sinks, as if to say, "Why does he want to know how much champagne there is, he knows I always bring enough?" I don't want to play your controlling games, I'm hot and uncomfortable, he thinks, but when Jason checks, he sees the look on William's face that tells him this is something more than William wanting to be in control or the centre of attention. William is truly angry about something and the champagne question is a hint. A big, fat hint. So Jason acts on it.

"I put loads in the cool boxes to chill earlier. Timothy, can you go and check how many bottles are outside on the landing for me please?"

"Okay," says Timothy, unawares of the venomous looks being exchanged on the other side of the room between William and Jason, and pleased at the thought of being able to stretch his legs in the corridor where the armed policewoman is, and he knew there was a window there at least, if it was open. He moves over to the door and knocks on it and it swings open immediately, allowing him to exit as it closes after him disappearing like a Chameleon catching a fly.

Jason gets up and dives underneath the tablecloth of the service table and reaches for the cool boxes he put under there. He pretends to be counting the bottles but he's really just playing for time, trying to work out why William is so angry. He feels unwell suddenly and has no desire and no stomach for a scene with William now, but there is literally nowhere to hide. He's looking underneath the table to only gather his thoughts. He's buying precious time to get his head together and to think what on earth is it that William is doing? His head is pounding again and there are sharp pangs in his stomach.

"Did you tell Timothy about Reg going into hospital?" demands William.

"No," says Jason, still crouching on the floor next to the service table, putting the cool boxes back and straightening them up again.

"Well how did he know then?"

"I don't know I didn't tell him. I didn't know myself until one of the drivers mentioned it this afternoon."

"It's nothing to do with you."

"I never asked him about it, he just happened to mention it to me."

"They've no right. It's nothing to do with them. It's

168

nothing to do with anyone, and anyway Reg doesn't have Diabetes."

"I know."

"Then why did you just say that he does?"

"To put Timothy off the trail of finding out the truth."

"What truth?"

"That Reg has got Leukaemia."

"That's none of your business! That's private. That's nobody's business. Who told you?"

"I don't know."

"What do you mean you don't know? Of course you do! Was it the driver?"

"No."

"Then who? Somebody told you who was it?"

"I, I can't remember William. I must have heard it on the grapevine."

Jason wonders why he feels so lightheaded. Perhaps it was rushing off his seat as he did. His head is hurting, and he has pangs in his stomach that are becoming painful, and he suddenly realised he had had nothing to eat all day. And not that much yesterday either that he remembers. The heat was getting to him in a big way and he remembers now missing lunch and dinner because he ordered sandwiches from the kitchen but forgot to collect them. Also, he realised now that he'd been sitting down all evening. Usually he would have been in and out the royal box like William. Not to watch the show, but to get some fresh air or to nip up to the restaurant where he knew a couple of people who worked there.

William is relentless in his interrogation and begins to shout.

"There's no such thing as the grapevine! Think back of the exact time you learned that particular piece of information and the last place you heard it, and that was the person who told you," he claps his hands hard and smart once and points straight into Jason's face, " — now who was it?"

"It was Reg," admits Jason.

William is stunned and bewildered by this answer. He thinks: why would have Reg told Jason that? And, has Reg told him anything else? And if so, what?

Jason would often have a chat with Reg when they were sitting together in the page's room. It was never personal stuff, not even about what they did at the weekend or who they had lunch with or whatever. It was as though work and home were kept separate for Reg. The chats were more to do with how they felt about life and love, and what their dreams were, if they had any, or ever had any. Jason later realised that this kind of talk tends to come about when someone knows they don't have much time left. He had seen it before, it was sad, but a part of life.

"Reg? Reg? He told you that?" demands William, who still can't believe it.

"Yes," replies Jason in a matter of fact way. He can't see the significance of Reg telling him that and after all, Reg may have told other people, he doesn't know? But Jason never told anyone else that's for sure. Because he said he wouldn't.

"Why would Reg tell you a thing like that?"

"But why shouldn't he? He tells me lots of things." Jason still can't see the significance of this. People get ill, he thinks, they go to hospital, what's the problem? That's the sensible thing to do for goodness sake, that's what I would do if I were ill. Why is William making such a big deal of it? Jason can't think straight.

Timothy re-enters the room and interrupts them. They break apart from standing together but Timothy doesn't look at them as he walks in. There was no warning sound of the door opening as a police officer was holding down the door handle at all times, so it opened silently and Timothy appeared as suddenly as he had left. Without really looking at them, he goes straight back to the place he was sitting. William and Jason try to act naturally. William turns away in order to compose and calm himself.

"Most of the boxes had empties in, so I had to go through them all and put the full bottles to one side," Timothy says, totally unaware of the scene that just took place. "I was talking to that policewoman out there. She said the show will be finishing in a minute and she'll be able to go off duty soon." He smiles at the thought of it. Jason finds his narcissism unbelievable, unless it really is a form of innocence?

William has composed himself now so he turns to face the others.

"So, how many bottles are left?" he asks in his normal speaking tone.

"Twelve," states Timothy.

"And I need one of you to stay and help, and I don't mind who," says William.

Timothy suddenly becomes very enthusiastic at the thought of staying behind and starts behaving like a child on his way to a birthday party.

"Oh I'll stay William, I'll stay and help."

"What do you mean?" says Jason. "We'll both stay. We've got all this to clear up at the end."

Jason thinks William must be forgetting where he is, and about all the chairs and cloths that needed to be packed away, as well as everything else. Everything was brought here from Clarence House, apart from the table. William would have insisted they bring one from there or a borrowed one from the palace if the stairwell had been wide enough. It would take a while carrying everything down the stairs to the transport which was waiting in the street outside.

"The principal dancers and some others are coming up here after the show to meet the Queen," says William. "And to have a glass of champagne so I need only one of you, as the room is so tiny and it's so humid in here."

"I'll stay then William," says Jason. Ooh goody, he thinks, that will be nice. That will be compensation for the lousy way I'm feeling tonight.

Timothy sees an opportunity here. There is no way he is letting the other guy stay over him, no way, he thinks. This is my best chance, so I'll do whatever it takes. The things I do for money? he tells himself.

"You're all right Jason you can go," he says very casually, as if this was a perfectly acceptable proposition and Jason would just say, "Okay bye!"

"Excuse me, but I'll say who stays," says Jason, in an attempt to establish his authority with this kid never mind confirm it.

"Well whatever I'm staying as well."

"Excuse me but I've arranged all this," says Jason, gesturing around the room at all his handywork. "All you've done is turn up here to help serve," (which is true, more or less).

Jason can't believe the confidence of this kid. Not only does he think himself irresistible to women, he thinks he can do everybody else's job better than they can.

William is getting exasperated because of the booze he's consumed and because any minute now the royal party will come through that door, but he won't be there to open it because he's standing here having a row.

"Look, I just want to know how much champagne is left and one of you to stay, now which one is it going to be?"

"You may as well go back Timothy. You're not going to miss anything," says Jason, without thinking about it. He is really tired now and there are only the drinks and petit fours to serve, so he thinks he can manage clearing up at the end when everyone has gone, with the kitchen porter's help who was coming back later. He never imagined Timothy would be interested in hanging back to see some ballet dancers as that didn't seem to be his bag at all.

"Why do you want to stay then?" asks Timothy.

What a daft question that is, thinks Jason. The principal dancers and some others are coming up here and you think I don't want to be part of that? There is no other reason. What other reason could there be, God, you really don't get me at all do you?

(Jason loves that kind of thing and he wants to be close to the dancers and he wants to hear their voices and accents and how they speak and what they say, even if it was in a foreign language he couldn't understand. And because it would be the only time he would see them as he saw absolutely nothing of the ballet being stuck back here all night and it was such a glamourous thing to do.)

"Because I like the theatre, you know I like the theatre, everyone knows I like the theatre. You don't even know the difference between an opera and a ballet," he says.

Timothy sniggers but says nothing as he's confused, so Jason is right about that then, which makes it even more confusing as to why he wants to stay?

Applause can now be heard in the background which means that the performance must have already ended, and they should start to wet the champagne glasses.

"I need to know?" William says very earnestly, as if it's such a crucial issue that his life depends on it.

"I'm staying," says Timothy as forcefully as he could, stamping one foot forwards towards William and throwing his shoulders and head back presenting himself as if to say, "here I am, I'm the best candidate for the job, I'm the one you need!"

"No, I'm the one who's arranged all this, I'm staying," says Jason for the second time, as he can't think of another reason. He is so tired and hungry and stressed out that his brain isn't functioning properly. On top of this he'd foolishly had a glass of champagne earlier because William had said,

"Oh, you simply must, it's Queen Elizabeth's one hundredth birthday."

Jason thinks that organising the food with the kitchen and packing up everything and laying the table single-handedly is a good enough reason to stay in itself, which it is, but it doesn't seem to be working, and why are we arguing about this anyway, what difference is one more body in the room going to make?

All through this William is glancing behind towards the doors of the box, praying that they won't come in, as he knows they must do, or will do any second.

"Look, they could walk in any second," he says desperately, looking behind again checking, like he's refereeing an illegal bare-knuckle fight and wants a knockout either way before anyone bursts in and discovers them.

Timothy stamps the floor to each line like a precocious child, "I want to stay, I want to stay, I want to stay, I want to stay."

Jason is shocked. His head implodes with theories. He cannot believe what he just saw! A grown man stamping his foot in a tantrum like a little girl. Unbelievable? And it suddenly occurrs to him what they are all arguing about. Three grown men are arguing about who wants to stay and meet the ballet dancers, and he is one of those men! This is ridiculous, he thinks, and Timothy only wants to stay as he thinks he might miss something. No, this is crazy, this is not happening, there must be a gigolo thing going on here between William and Timothy. Funny, because William doesn't do that sort of thing anymore, must not have done it for years now, and anyway, he never used to get anywhere much apart from getting everyone drunk, but the rumours must be true. Cheryl in the kitchen was right, otherwise why are they both laughing at me, why are they both attacking me like this. I know they are, I can see it in their eyes. It all makes sense now how the daft kid appeared from nowhere and why he's so useless and why William never tells him off. This is stupid. I don't want to stay if I'm not wanted either. They can get on with it without me thank you very much, I'm off. See what a mess that daft skinny kid makes of clearing everything up at the end of the night and lugging everything downstairs to the street.

"Oh well if you're going to do your Shirley Temple routine I'm off!" he shouts. "You can stay if it means that much to you. My God! I thought I was supposed to be the camp one."

He grabs his tailcoat and heads straight for the door.

"I thought this evening was going to turn out to be enjoyable with all the hard work I've done but that's too much to ask with you obviously," he says to William. "I'm going back to the house, you two deserve each other," he says wagging his finger at them from one to the other.

"If you're going back to the house then take this," says William.

He produces an object and is thrusting it into Jason's chest compelling him to take it, but Jason is more concerned with saying his piece before he leaves.

(It is a very small, velvet covered footstool only a few inches high, but big enough to rest upon two royal feet in order to repose in comfort in a favoured large carver chair.)

"No, I'm not taking that!" says Jason, with such a facial expression of disgust it would appear he'd been asked to take back a sack of putrid rotting slime or something.

"But people will see it."

"So what?"

"Don't be ridiculous, no one should see it. Queen Elizabeth doesn't want anyone to know she uses a footstool."

"Why not? What's the big deal? Everyone knows she's not very tall. She hardly uses it anyway, we only bring it in case it's asked for."

"Just take it with you."

"No."

"She doesn't want anyone to see it."

"No."

"There's nowhere to put it."

"No, there's no need to take it back. Hide it underneath the service table or somewhere or ask the police to take it."

"Don't be ridiculous. There's absolutely nowhere to put it. We must take away the possibility of anyone seeing it. Take it back to the house."

They frantically jostle it between each other pushing it to-and-fro, one willing the other to dispel the foreign object completely.

"Don't be ridiculous Jason, just take it with you! They'll be here in a second."

"No."

"Just get rid of it!"

"No!"

"For Queen Elizabeth's sake! Just take it, please."

Jason is desperate now to get out of the room away from these two idiots so he gallantly concedes.

"Oh for goodness sake!"

And Jason grabs it and swishes round in anticipation of his venomous parting remark to William that he's about to spit out.

He knocks on the door and the police standing the other side open it instantly. As it opens, he can see his exit route revealed before him that will lead him away from this nuthouse. He turns on his heels and delivers his parting punchline.

The audience can now be heard in the background singing 'God Save The Queen' so that means there are only moments before the royal party start coming through.

"And there are twenty-seven bottles left!" he declares, and swishes out the door slamming it behind him. Not such a pithy punchline after all, but at least he knows how many bottles there are. He was gone.

William claps his hands and jumps in the air and skips with a squeal of delight and does a ballet type twirl. It was all a wheeze to get rid of Jason, and it worked!

"Hee-hee! That's got rid of him!" he squeals with joy. "If he makes it across Trafalgar Square in one piece dressed like that? Now then Timmy dear boy."

William now turns his attention back to the evening in hand. "You start pouring the champagne while I go and escort the royal party through."

Not only did William suddenly remember Timothy's name and he had not used the phrase 'dear boy' but he had been promoted to the pet name of 'Timmy'. William heads straight over to the other side of the room to open the double doors leading to the royal box.

"William don't go I must ask you something?"

William is in his element. He's got rid of boring old Jason and can now have his photograph taken with

Queen Elizabeth and company, the principal dancers of The Kirov Ballet and his handsome young friend Timmy who really should be a top model, without podgy old baldy Jason spoiling the shot. He can hear mutterings of the royal party approaching the double doors now, so he springs to them in one swoop and pounces on the handles and is about to turn them when Timothy grabs his hands and stops him.

"No Billy don't open the door! I've got to ask you something!"

"What is it?"

At this moment they couldn't have been any closer to each other. Timothy's hands are squeezed over William's hands and they are standing face to face, toe to toe, their bodies pressed against the doors obstructing access to the room. Timothy says what he has to say without delay.

"Billy, my friends are always talking about Princess Diana since I started this job. They say her death was a huge cover-up to protect the royal family in order to keep the peace, but what do you think Billy? you must know. What happened in Paris? Was Diana assassinated?"

"What? What are you talking about you chuntering idiot?" and William shoves him aside and turns his attention back to the doors.

"I've got to go. Jesus-Aitch-Corbett! what's the matter with you?"

Timothy's question never even registered in William's head. Timothy could have just said anything at all, and William would not have computed the words in his brain. He is so excited. So ecstatic. He can only think about the royals possibly being stuck on the other side of the doors trying to get in, and he wants to serve champagne to everyone, EVERYONE, on the one hundredth birthday. He gestures violently like a madman to Timothy indicating that he should be pouring champagne NOW!

"Champagne," he shouts, his whole face contorted into

a crazy mangle, gesticulating violently towards the glasses, "CHAMPAGNE!"

William turns his attention back to the doors. He turns the door handles and nips out through the double doors and pulls them to behind him, but doesn't click the locks, so they can be easily pushed open within a second. Now Timothy is alone in the room. He takes out a camera from his pocket and takes a picture of the room with flash, then retrieves his tiny recorder from the flower arrangement, checks the recording indicator is still on then puts it back. He has one last look at the room to check everything and rushes around the dining table to join William, but, just as he is about to leap towards the doors, they burst open and a glimpse of a pale green gown and lots of diamonds shimmer against the candlelight. Queen Elizabeth and The Queen are stepping into the room. Timothy quickly reacts by pulling out Queen Elizabeth's chair while he bows his head, stands still, and waits for the royal party to come in and sit down. Nothing seems out of place or untoward. The evening carries on as normal.

The next thing Jason knew he was walking across the southern side of Trafalgar Square still marching like a possessed madman. All he could see was red mist. (He was still carrying the footstool.) He was swerving and weaving round obstacles and people, never bumping into anything and never slowing down or stopping. He wanted to return to home base the quickest and shortest route possible. Nothing else, not slowing down or getting impaired by tourists or red stop signs at traffic lights or cars or anything. He couldn't think of anything else to do. He was in a rage. He was livid. Some tourists saw him coming and deliberately moved their children out his way well before he reached them. He could see their worried expressions and he knew he must have looked scary but he didn't care, because there was steam coming out of his ears, he was absolutely seething. He wanted to reach Clarence House as soon as humanly possible and rip off his heavy sweaty uniform and quickly shower and go out for a drink in a bar somewhere, but it never even occurred to him to run or get a taxi. The summer evening heat didn't bother him at all, as he'd been melting all night anyway in the anteroom in his swelteringly hot woollen tailcoat and trousers. He had no wallet on him anyhow so he couldn't get a taxi, not that he realised, just his security tab. He wanted to march back every inch of the way pounding his anger into the ground with every step, cursing William as he went.

He had avoided the colossal crowds in Covent Garden by going around the back and side of the theatre, then he stomped straight down Bow Street and turned into Exeter Street past Joe Allen restaurant onto The Strand that led him to where he is now. There were people milling around everywhere in the jam-packed streets on this hot summer night. He couldn't remember coming out of the Opera House, the police must have heard everything and just let him leave. He can go in any direction and never get lost because he knows all these streets so well, this is his home territory, but he is constantly looking ahead to avoid any crowds that might slow him down so he can change route if necessary. He wants a totally clear run home without missing a beat to analyse everything in his head. He came aware at some point that some passers-by were laughing at him and making jibes like, "Hey mate, looking for your lion? The circus is that way!" He had put on his scarlet red tailcoat for some reason when he came out the Opera House, and so with the footstool, looked like a lion tamer from the circus to some people. He didn't remember putting it on. He must have put it on instinctively despite the heat and the panic [but he may have been able to stride quicker with it on]. He is carrying his coat now and has taken off his white bow tie and unbuttoned his starched collar and rolled up his sleeves and unbuttoned his waistcoat, so now he just looks like a very angry theatre musician on his way home.

Jason is thinking what just happened why did I storm off like that, what's the big deal? Did that just really happen? Oh no, what am I going to tell all my friends? Oh God, they will ask me a thousand questions. He knew his friends well and the sort of questions they would ask, like; What were the dancers like? Was she too tall and he too short? Did the principal dancers hate each other's guts so could hardly stand to be in the same room together, or were they lovers? Did the ballerina gracefully collapse to the floor in front of Queen Elizabeth in a stunning curtsy, then rise like a Phoenix about to evaporate or was she too knackered after a performance of The Ballets of Fokine to even hold her own glass of water? Did they still have their stage make-up on? Did you have your picture taken with them? Did they invite you backstage? What cologne were they wearing? Did he have buns of steel? What did they say to you? Can you get me tickets for next week's performance, and more of these sorts of questions he knew they would be aching to know the answers to. The answer to them all unfortunately would have to be a resounding: "I don't know!"

All these thoughts were shouting at him at point-blank range inside his head, but the loudest, nagging one was why? Why was William so mean as it's obvious he just wanted to get rid of me to be with that daft Timothy. But why can't William be nice, he thinks. Why can't he be like me and offer a small kindness by bringing someone forward who's stuck at the back, or to save a crested menu card from the bin for someone.

Hardly official secrets is it? And these small silly kindnesses can be absolutely thrilling for the recipient, but they are so easy to do. So why didn't William let me stay as he knows I love all that camp stuff. He knows I love the theatre. But hang on, he thinks, why shouldn't I stay, because this is my job!

It must be true then, he thinks, what Cheryl the cook says, that William and Timothy are having an affair or at least there's a gigolo thing going on there. Timothy's not satisfied with being introduced to the restaurants and theatres and actors William knows, now he must want William to introduce him to ballet stars. No way, Timothy's not into all that stuff I can tell. William is an old man now. He can't keep the younger staff in check at work the way he used to never mind play gigolo with someone a third his age. No, there's something funny going on here, unless it's me, they hate me. They must do with the way they were looking at me, they wanted me to clear off. Either way that chinless wonder gets to stay on. What if he went backstage and met the cast and crew, oh my God, I would have loved to have done that!

He didn't calm down one bit on his way back. It wasn't the fact he didn't get to see the dancers so much as he'd met ballet dancers before, it was the thought of being taken for granted and the lack of respect that William showed him. He just couldn't see why William behaved like that sometimes.

Now William's spoilt everything again, he thinks. Why does he do that. Why can't he be nice? I respect my job, I'm quick and efficient, and I also think for him a lot of the time. I pack all the silver and stuff for all the trips and I always pack everything we might need. His meal service sometimes would look like a chimpanzees bun fight without me because of his drinking. He takes me for granted. Why does William always feel the need to emphasise the fact he is top dog and exert his authority? Everybody already knows he is. I don't understand. Why can't William just be nice. I really don't understand. Why can't he just be NICE?

The big summer trip to Scotland started just after the birthday and lasted for about twelve weeks. Domestic staff from Clarence House and Royal Lodge would make up two teams consisting of chefs and kitchen staff, housemaids, footmen and chauffeurs, and a dresser, and they worked six weeks each, either the first six weeks or the last six weeks. William headed one group and Reg the other. They worked every day bar one weekend and the odd early finish. After about ten days you'd forget what day it was but that didn't matter because there was always some work to do and it was a nice break being up there in the fresh air. The latter team was unlucky in that they went straight back into work when they returned to London in October. Both teams got six weeks holiday. You changed your half every year. This was the simplest way of doing it, avoiding numerous two week staff changeovers that was the norm at Buckingham Palace, and avoiding travelling up and down the country too much. Most of us preferred to work the first half.

The first three weeks were always at Castle Mey in Caithness in Scotland, a homely castle which Queen Elizabeth bought in 1952 but it was too cold to stay there in autumn and winter, it's the most northerly part of the British mainland, but Caithness in the summer months is a restorative place to be with its clean unspoilt quiet beaches and coastline and amazing sunsets. Mey stands next to the sea between Thurso and John o' Groats looking out towards the Orkneys.

William used to say that, "It's only Castle of Mey that the Queen can feel truly private."

In the countryside around there, all the unsuspecting tourist would see of Queen Elizabeth would be a flash of a sky-blue raincoat and hat with a little sprig of heather tucked into the band of it, before they managed to pluck themselves out of the hedgerow they were obliged to dive into, in order to avoid her blue Range Rover as it sped past along the country lanes.

After three weeks there, then Queen Elizabeth usually travelled south to Balmoral Castle to stay with her family for a weekend before going on to her own house Birkhall, which is a country house that stands in its own grounds a good few miles away from Balmoral Castle on the edge of the estate.

The staff had the weekend free in order to de-camp from Mey, then drive the one hundred and seventy miles south to set-up shop again in Birkhall and the whole thing started again for another three weeks. The other team would then come up from London to take over, and the first team would go back home and have six weeks off.

The royal holiday homes are not absolutely fully equipped, so Queen Elizabeth's kitchen staff packed a good deal of their own equipment in two enormous laundry baskets. Most cooks and chefs need their own familiar knives, pans and gadgets to work with whenever they have to travel.

The far reaches of the countryside is a long way to get to before you realise you haven't brought along any of your unusual breakfast cereal or exotic dried fruits, or your favourite special blend of extra fine fragrant leaf tea or whatever. Some things just can't be bought in a supermarket even if the supermarket is the size of an aircraft hangar. The shelves may be packed absolutely full but not packed with things you want. So, if you definitely want something in the line of comestibles and other supplies that's not widely available then it's only sensible to take it with you when you travel and be done with it. This completely avoids any possibility of disappointment, especially if you travel a lot and stay in several places en route.

Queen Elizabeth must have known this all her life especially having lived through two World Wars. Even after the Second World War rationing went on until 1954 and included everyone, though not necessarily the royal family who had their own dairies and farms. There wouldn't have been tins of expensive fine tea hanging about in every pantry in every royal house during this time though, surely?

So it just makes good sense to carry your own supplies with the rest of the luggage, if only to create a home from home for yourself. It was practical and sensible for Queen Elizabeth's staff to pack up tins of fragrant leaf tea, a certain type of candle needed for use with followers and shades, breakfast food supplements in the form of a selection of seeds, and all sorts of things not easily available in Scotland and especially never available in rural areas anywhere. That's where the odd Tupperware container comes in handy, which everyone has. Even Prince Philip took some for his favourite breakfast cereal on his travels, (see!), and dashing across Europe when Carriage Driving. He makes no fuss nor hangs about, so it was whisked off the breakfast table straight into his car as he left.

Queen Elizabeth stayed at Castle Mey for three weeks as usual.

William's team flew from London to Inverness (without him), then drove the rest of the way to Mey and some flew with the Queen to Wick.

Now, it is four weeks after the birthday and William is in Scotland at Birkhall. He didn't fly up to Castle Mey on the royal flight as usual with Queen Elizabeth because Reg became very ill on the evening of the birthday, [as Timothy rightly mentioned at the ballet]. Another steward took over for him temporarily for three weeks at Mey while he stayed in London to be with Reg, but exactly one week after Queen Elizabeth's one hundredth birthday, Reg died.

Queen Elizabeth and the staff heard the bad news when they were at Castle Mey, so it made for quite a solemn trip.

William answered the many letters and messages of condolence during the days he was arranging the funeral in London. Any donations were to be made to a Leukaemia charity in memory of Reg. The funeral was held with special permission at the Queen's Chapel, St. James's.

Birkhall is a lovely Highland holiday home for the summer but it was the busiest time for Queen Elizabeth's domestic staff. Imagine an exquisite country hotel in the Scottish Highlands that's fully booked for weeks, with up to sixteen regularly changing guests. Every day for the staff is a relentless treadmill of preparation then execution of tasks, with a constant flow of trays and drinks and cooking and laying tables and serving sumptuous meals, and washing-up and shifting of luggage and heavy furniture, and housekeeping and polishing brass and making beds, and driving and shopping and cleaning cars, and gardeners bringing in flowers, vegetables and logs. [With certain guests, William would arrange for garden produce to be put into their cars as they left. Sometimes jam, sandwiches and a flask of soup or coffee and a tot of something if they were going a long way]

Guests would go walking, fishing, deer stalking and shooting and a picnic lunch somewhere every day bar Sunday. It's an informal relaxed atmosphere. The Queen might pop by fleetingly, driving herself unannounced to show a friend or relative the garden or something. The Prince of Wales stayed there with his sons and some of his friends during the last few weeks of the trip.

It's been a couple of days now and William has managed to slip back into the routine of work again. Everyone is trying to run things as normally as possible out of respect for Reg and he. For some people this means keeping a low profile as much as possible. William hasn't mentioned anything so it's difficult for people to gauge the situation as nobody seems to want to broach the subject of Reg's death. Naturally, William is not his usual self in the circumstances. He is quite subdued but has quickly taken charge of things since he came up from London.

He is in the basement of Birkhall, pottering about wrapping boxes in brown paper and string. He's standing at a large, old work table against the wall which is mostly used for sorting out the post. He is wearing a smart Jermyn Street double-cuffed shirt with the cuffs turned back once so they won't show when he puts on his uniform jacket but you can still see his rose gold bracelet on his left wrist. His dark blue battledress jacket is wrapped around the back of one of the Victorian chairs there standing either side of a small table.

[Battledress is the same uniform you'll see on 'Dad's Army', the standard everyday British uniform of the Second World War. It's basically a brass buttoned jacket with a collar, a buckled waist strap and two breast pockets. It's a less formal uniform than the scarlet tails, which were only worn in London (during the week) by the queen's footmen and any other footmen serving the Queen, otherwise they would wear their battledress]

This space in Birkhall is where William usually sits and waits in case the bell rings so he can easily nip up the stairs to the Queen. He has a small room [no windows] which is his official office, but he prefers the corridor with the table and chairs and the staff tea room opposite as lots of staff come and go by there. His little office is somewhere for him to write and somewhere he can keep cigars and cigarettes and chocolates for the guests and the Queen's personal stationery. The whole area is quite dark even in good daylight. It's actually a wide corridor leading to storerooms, the cellar and a staff t.v. room. It's the nearest place in the house to the stairs that lead into the royal rooms. It's the optimum position for him to station himself in, between attending the Queen and carrying out his other duties as there is no page's room as such, and he doesn't want to miss anything as he is not one for hiding himself away. The staff consider the space to be neither a room nor a corridor. It's considered to be an area. The page's area.

The house is quiet at the moment because most staff are on an afternoon break and all the guests are still out on a picnic lunch apart from the Queen, who has returned and now is writing in her sitting room upstairs. William is usually off in the afternoon, but he's chosen to come on duty; to answer the bell to the Queen or the house telephone or in case any guests happen to drift back to the house and may require something [which they won't].

William can hear Jason walking along the royal floor above. Jason is tracking the lines in the green tartan carpet as he walks down the long corridor on his way to see Sir Alastair in a private sitting room. He's trying to think of the reason Sir Alastair has asked to see him in there as he never goes in there to see him, ever. He only goes into that particular room to deliver trays of coffee for visitors or if a royal person has a tray of food after arriving late at night.

If he wants to see me about something why don't I go to his office? he thinks. Maybe the equerry or lady in waiting is working in there? He could easily have stopped me in the corridor somewhere, or seen me on his way out the back door or when I deliver his post. I wonder what he wants to see me about? I haven't complained or moaned about not having enough footmen for ages. And then Jason realises what it could be.

Sir Alastair and Jason had a mutual friend, of sorts. Jason served a private dinner in Chelsea one night and one of the guests turned out to be an author of cricket books and an old friend of Sir Alastair. He gave Jason a signed copy of his new book to give to him as they had no plans to meet in the near future and so he thought it would be a nice surprise for his old friend.

Oh, I bet he just wants another cricket book, he thinks, as he arrives at the room and knocks on the door, which is unusual. He enters.

Sir Alastair is sitting behind a tiny desk in there. Jason closes the door behind him which feels strange as ground floor doors are usually left open. This is going to be a private meeting for some reason, he thinks. He walks in and Sir Alastair welcomes him with a smile.

"Come in Jason. Thank you for coming to see me, take a seat," he says.

"Thank you," says Jason, as he sits on the chair directly in front of the desk and waits for Sir Alastair to speak. It's not a book he wants then, he thinks.

"So, how is Mister Tallon getting on? Bearing up I hope?"

Jason thinks: who's Mister Tallon? Oh, he means William! Jason wasn't used to people calling him Mister Tallon. Everybody called him William not Mister Tallon and certainly never Billy.

"Yes Sir Alastair he seems fine," he replies.

"Queen Elizabeth is very grateful for the way that everybody has been rallying round and ensuring everything runs smoothly while William has been away. It can't have been easy for him having to arrange everything for Reginald's funeral, but let us hope that things get back to normal as soon as possible."

"Yes we've managed really well. Things have been exactly the same without him."

Jason congratulates himself on being so diplomatic.

The place had run like clockwork while William was away. The steward who covered for him had never worked there before so he let the staff get on with it. Jason had enjoyed the peace without William around but had got to thinking it was becoming a little monotonous and dull without him, even though he could be unbearable at times. There wasn't much fun around. For instance, there was a set of bronze figurines depicting Highland Games in the dining room. William would take the one with the hammer thrower and position it so that the end of the hammer was in the bowl of the glass at the equerry's (usually) seat at the dinner table. [He forbad us to move it] If the equerry happened to be abstaining from alcohol then it was impossible to lift his only glass. This usually would not be a problem until William instigated somebody to make a toast, thus embarrassing the person chosen to host the bronze kilted man. This may sound cruel, but really it was easy to navigate this particular situation as William's jokes could be very childish. He thought the whole thing absolutely hilarious.

"I know it can be difficult at times Jason, but remember that all of us must cushion Queen Elizabeth from any unpleasantness and friction that may occur amongst the staff. Everyone must try to get along with each other otherwise their standard of work suffers, and we don't want that. Now Jason, William seems intent on making up lost time and staying here his usual six weeks but secretly I think he wants to stay until the very end of the trip to keep himself occupied, so just try to keep the routine and everything will be fine."

"Yes sir."

"Let us hope that William can begin to recover

from the tribulation of losing Reginald now that he's up here. The Scottish air will do him good and Doctor Woods is going to keep an eye on him, as I hope you will do too."

"Yes sir I'll do my best." Nothing wrong with that thinks Jason, William hasn't mentioned it yet so there's been no awkward conversations.

"Thank you Jason."

Sir Alastair notices that Jason doesn't move from his seat.

"Is there something else?" he asks.

"Well Sir Alastair, I know there's likely to be a few changes around here now that Reg has passed away. I mean, we've been a footman down for a while now and so I'm doing the job of two people. I pack all the silver and stuff for all the trips and William relies on me a lot and all the other departments are fully staffed. So I wanted to ask if we are going to get another footman?"

"I'm not promising anything, but there may be a lot of restructuring going on now that Reginald has died. People will be in line for promotion. Nothing has been decided yet so if I were you, I'd tread water for a while and see what happens. If I need to see you about anything, I'll send for you, so don't worry."

"But I don't want a promotion Sir Alastair, I like the job I do now. I could just do with another pair of hands, that's all."

"Leave it with me and I'll think about it, but as I say I'm not promising anything. Is there anything else I can help you with?"

"No, Sir Alastair, thank you." Jason stands up.

"Well done!" says Sir Alastair.

Jason leaves the room and makes his way back downstairs. William hears his footsteps again on the ceiling, coming back this time. Jason enters the page's area and William begins to interrogate him as soon as he comes down the steps.

"Where have you just been?"

"Nowhere," replies Jason, as he thinks to himself: here we go again, where have you been and a thousand more questions.

"I heard voices in the study. Were you talking to Sir Alastair?"

"Yes," says Jason, who wasn't prepared to give anything away.

"What did he want?"

"Nothing."

Jason takes off his jacket and wraps it round the back of a chair next to the table.

"You were talking a considerably long time about nothing?"

"He just asked me to give a message to somebody," says Jason. He's not going to give in, is he? he thinks. Why can't he get the message that's it's nothing to do with him and that I want to be left in peace? Then Jason thinks that he could use the cricket book story as a cover. He was a terrible liar but had learned that if you have to tell a lie, it's easier to put as much truth in it as possible in order not to be tripped up.

"Who are you giving the message to?" asks William.

"A mutual friend."

"Mutual friend? You mean you and Sir Alastair have a mutual friend. Who's that?"

"Oh, you don't know him."

"How do you know I don't know him if you won't tell me who it is?"

Oh God, Jason thinks, this must be how it feels to be married.

"He writes books about cricket and Sir Alastair

asked me to get a copy signed for him, as they sold out at the bookshop, that's all."

"Cricket? I didn't know you liked cricket?"

"I don't," sighs Jason, thinking this will never end. He's becoming niggled by this line of enquiry, but he won't give in.

"Then why was he asking you to get a copy of the book then?"

"Because, it's just that we both happen to know this person and Sir Alastair asked me to get a copy of his new book when I see him next that's all, as Sir Alastair won't see him for a while."

"You seem to know a lot of people?"

"Not at all."

"Have I ever met this friend of yours?"

"You have actually. He came to a Trooping day once."

"Oh well, if he was talking about cricket then I wouldn't remember. Now then, would you address these parcels for me please, I can't seem to find my glasses, and could you stamp and bundle those royal letters for London?"

Jason is a little agitated now. After all that, and William wasn't interested in the end. Jason was only trying to avoid this interrogation as there seems to be no privacy working here. William curtailed his line of questioning probably only because once he'd learned he'd already met this friend of Jason's at a Trooping day in the garden once, he wasn't interested who it was. The poor chap in question had obviously not made an impression either way on William to merit any further investigation.

Jason stands at the large work table against the wall and picks up a felt pen and takes up one of the boxes William has wrapped in brown paper and string. It's the size of a six-bottle champagne box. He recognises the size and shape and weight straightaway, he knew it was Veuve Cliquot Champagne in the box. There really wasn't much point in trying to disguise it as an insignificant brown paper parcel. Jason thinks he'll have a little fun now at William's expense after all those silly questions. It's my turn to ask the questions now, he thinks.

"Where are they going?" he asks.

"Address them to the royal cellars Clarence House, would you?"

Jason casts a knowing look then starts to write.

"Royal cellar, Clarence, House," he says as he writes.

He writes on a box then examines another one, which turns out to be similar.

"This is champagne isn't it? Why are you sending champagne down to London? There's plenty in the cellars there already?"

"Don't question me. Just do as I say," replies William angrily.

"All right," says Jason, smiling.

"What, all these four boxes are going?"

"Yes," says William impatiently.

"To the royal cellar?"

"Yes!"

"At Clarence House?"

"Y-e-s!"

"Why don't I just write your address?" says Jason under his breath.

"What did you say?" barks William.

"I said this is turning into a right mess, the pen's leaking, I'll have to get another one."

"Oh forget it! I'll get the boy to do it when he gets back."

"No no it's all right, I've almost done it now. I wouldn't rely on him anyway, he asks a thousand questions before you can get him to do anything for you."

Jason notices a large irregular shaped parcel and holds it up.

"Blimey! What's in this one?"

"Never mind, just write this address on that one and post it, here!" barks William, as he points to a note on the table and taps the table with his finger. Jason writes the address.

"Yes all right," says Jason, as he carries on writing the address.

He decides to stop teasing William about the parcels for the time being. [People know what William gets up to, but they would never dream of challenging him about it. William seems to think he's being very clever and covering his tracks. [All the boxes of booze he sent would be posted or driven south so would be waiting for him on his return to Clarence House and he would transfer them to his little lodge or the flat]

Jason sorts the small pile of official letters and stamps them and the parcel with some special 'ER' and '1' rubber ink-pad stamps and pops a rubber band around them. [William had told me once that you could send anything in the post with those two special official stamps, even a stuffed elephant, as long as it was wrapped in brown paper and string] Jason then sits down at the small table opposite to where William is sitting. There's a small 1980s telephone switchboard on the table [they answer the phone] next to the ubiquitous Letts desk calendar. Also on the table is a glass of whisky. William just has to pop into the little room directly opposite the table to fetch the bottle and some more glasses if he needs to.

"That new tartan carpet is very bright. Is that the right green for Royal Stewart?" asks Jason.

"Well the old one faded badly, only the royals can use that tartan. It's an ancient hunting tartan. When Prince Philip came here to visit I opened the front door to him, it was his first time at the house since the new carpet was laid but he was so taken aback when I opened the door that he didn't come in, he just stood there for a second. He looked at the tartan wallpaper, looked at the floor, looked at the walls, looked at the floor and said,

Goodness me, it's like a bloody biscuit tin!"

They laugh.

Timothy bounces into the area in high spirits. He has settled in really well and the kitchen people seem to like him. He hangs around them a lot and talks to them while they cook and wash-up. That is until the chef in charge shoos him away so they can get on with their work. Timothy is carrying his battledress jacket under his arm. He's also carrying a mug of coffee and has a small burgundy leatherbound menu book wedged under his arm, too.

"William, menus for you from the chef," he says, and places his mug of coffee on the table while he takes the book from under his arm and plonks it down. He then leans against the wall and sips his coffee.

"Why did he give it to you? It's Robert's job to deliver the menu book?"

"I was in the kitchen talking to the girls," replies Timothy. Who is always in the kitchen talking to the girls, it seems.

"Never mind. Now then, what are you going to have to drink?"

"I'm fine thanks I've got some coffee."

Jason and William are sitting down either side of the table. There are only two chairs, so Timothy has to stand.

"Oh," says William, who is very disappointed at Timothy's refusal of a drink.

"Did you see me talking to Prince Charles earlier on? He was really chatty. He was asking me where I come from," says Timothy, apparently thinking they'd be impressed for some reason that one of the people they work for has actually spoken to him.

"Oh, the Prince of Wales asked you where you came from, did he?" says William sarcastically, as he stands up. "How thrilling for you. And what was your enchanting eloquent reply to this question I wonder? That I come from the pantry your majesty!" he says in a strong northern English accent, (mimicking a footman William knew who once said that to the prince).

[There could be a lot of snobbery amongst the staff if you used the incorrect title when referring to a royal person. Only The Queen and Queen Elizabeth were 'Your Majesty'. The Prince of Wales was 'Your Royal Highness', and Princess Margaret was 'The Princess Margaret'. Some people took delight in correcting others. There was no work manual at Clarence House, you had to work things out for yourself and rely on your fellow workers to help you. The first time I served Prince Philip I was so nervous I mistakenly called him 'your majesty'. I knew it was wrong somehow as 'your royal highness' didn't sound eminent enough for The Queen's husband, but I was so nervous it was better than saying nothing and there wasn't a job manual to refer to like at the palace. Nobody told you anything to start with, you had to just get on with it]

Timothy sneers at William and doesn't reply but his eyes convey an evil look of contempt. Then he picks up a folded broadsheet newspaper that's lying on the side and sits down on William's chair and opens it and begins to read.

"That was Lady Clara's newspaper, so it won't all be there as she keeps the crossword. She likes to check the answers the next day," explains William, who now turns to Jason.

"Now Jason, you'll have a drink?"

"Yes please William, I'll have a vodka and diet Coke,

thank you."

Timothy glares at Jason across the table, obviously shocked and horrified at him accepting a drink when he knows he doesn't normally drink and also telling everyone else not to accept drinks from William.

"Splendid," says William, overjoyed at the prospect of having at least one drinking partner for the cocktail hour, which is fast approaching (about an hour or so away).

William pours Jason's drink and tops up his own glass. He then goes into his little office opposite and drags out another (staff) Victorian chair. He places it in the open doorway facing the table and sits down. He reaches over to pick up his glass. Timothy can't be seen as he's hiding behind his newspaper, smouldering slightly.

"Lady Clara said the BBC are showing an episode of Hancock this evening on BBC 2, so we must make sure we record it for the Queen for future use," says William. "Although I'm not sure he's a favourite, but we can't get those old Dad's Army tapes out again, she's seen them all thousands of times before."

William is hoping that Jason will offer to sort it out and record it and Jason is hoping anybody else but himself would do it as he couldn't work the new complicated digital video machine. The old-fashioned one it replaced did the job perfectly well.

"Where's Robert?" asks William, looking round.

"He said he was going to put new stationery on the equerry's desk then going to the laundry room to dry out Major Pemberton's clothes. He fell in the river again," says Jason.

"He'll need drying out with a few sherries tonight then."

"Oh, I meant to tell you William, chef says the

menu's changed, it's not soup tonight. The equerry caught a salmon so they're going to have that for the first course."

Jason only remembered this as William mentioned sherry. He was thinking he'd have to change the sherry glasses for white wine glasses now that the first course was fish. Everything was still done the old-fashioned way around here, (sherry with soup, white wine with fish etc.).

[There was an elderly gentleman guest who was on meagre rations of alcohol due to his medication so, William would slip a good glug of sherry into the chap's soup at dinner, so his wife never knew. It was appreciated. This isn't the same chap who fell into the river. He was a doddery old Major who used to tip in five pound notes — slowly! He would take ages peeling each blue note one by one from his wallet, making a presentation of it. I never got past fifteen pounds, it was too painful; for both of us]

"Yes, I saw him getting out of a Land Rover at the back door when I was coming over from my room. What on earth was he wearing? Lemon coloured corduroys, doesn't he have any breeks?" asks William.

"That's nothing. You should see all Major Botsford's rainbow shades of cords. Makes Leigh Bowery look dull."

"Maybe he's called Wendy at the weekends?"

They both chuckle. Timothy sneers, not because he's never heard of Leigh Bowery but because he hates them both. He's not reading a thing, just listening jealously.

"Some of the police are better dressed than the aristocracy," says William.

"I know," says Jason, "but that's only because they get those tweed suits on expenses so that they can blend in with the countryside."

"Yes," says William, "and in that get-up one of them looks more like Toad of Toad Hall!"

They both laugh again.

"I almost bumped into that boring little detective when

I was walking over."

"Oh yes?" says Jason.

"I'll never forget the day he refused to handle Queen Elizabeth's walking sticks when she gets in the car. It's not my job to do that sort of thing he said. Can you believe it? All the others do it, so what's so special about him?"

"He wouldn't help me by opening the Daimler boot once when I ran out with half a huge Brie and some flowers for a weekend at the Lodge, which I forgot to send until the last minute."

"I know. And he point-blank refused to take out the footstool at the theatre and hand it to a footman, point-blank refused! The little shit!"

"William, I've never heard you swear before!"

"He'll pay for that one day you know, he'll pay."

"Anyway, what would he do when the car reaches its destination and the Queen gets out and asks for her stick? What would he say then?"

"It's like the time that lady in waiting said to Princess Margaret that she was finding it more and more difficult to give a full and low curtsey, and Princess Margaret just said,

Really? Everybody else seems to manage!"

They both laugh.

Timothy grips the pages of the newspaper tighter and grinds his teeth.

"Did you have a nice lunch at Doctor Woods?"

"I did," says William. "You should see the farm they've got it's wonderful. They've got a lovely big Aga. They've got ducks and chickens and everything. They are so happy there. That's his second wife you know. I had to laugh at their little boy he looks just like his father, head full of curls and a big round face. His mother was feeding him and when he asked her for some more pudding, she held the spoon to his lips and said,

(Scottish accent) What's the little magic word that we say? so he said,

NOW!"

They laugh and Timothy puts down the paper and glares at them. He doesn't say a word. He really resents Jason drinking with William like this.

Jason picks up the paper and has a look.

"Where's Robert?" asks William again as he glances at the menu book then to Timothy. "That menu book should have gone up ages ago."

"I'll take it now then," says Timothy, as he jumps up snatching up the book and his jacket and runs off.

William shouts after him as he runs up the steps, "Oh very well, leave it on the landing table for Robert to take through, but don't go into the Queen's rooms."

"I know!" comes the reply from Timothy, who's halfway there already.

Jason opens up the newspaper to read, looking forward to ten minutes of peace.

William looks around. The place is so quiet. He doesn't fancy ten minutes of peace, he fancies telling jokes and having a little drink before the rest of the guests come back filling the house and wanting their afternoon tea then changing it over to the martini jug and nibbles.

"Queen Elizabeth said to me once, How do you know what you will want to eat in three days time?

It must be depressing having to fill in that menu book in advance all the time. I mean, I know it's necessary for the kitchen to organise for a large lunch or dinner party or whatever, but you'd think that she could just ask for an omelette or something at night when she's alone in London without having to stick to the choice she made three days ago. Princess Anne just pops in for cheese and crackers and a coffee, that's her lunch. She doesn't have time for anything else even if she wanted to."

Jason says nothing. William looks around again in despair and disgust that nobody wants to talk to him.

"Oh well if nobody's talking to me."

He folds his arms and sits up in the chair, his back straight, chest out, his nose in the air. [When done in a certain way the folded arms were a sign of defiance and boredom, a prelude to asserting his opinion or registering his disagreement or anger about something, but they could also signal happiness, so it was tricky]

Jason looks out from the newspaper.

"I'm trying to have a quick look at the paper William," and he goes back to it but notices William sitting in silence when he peeks over at him.

"Oh never mind me, if I'm boring you," says William in a surly way.

Jason peers from around the newspaper. He's quite prepared to hold a conversation from behind the pages. He knows that people around here don't take into consideration if you're reading a book or concentrating on the television or writing a letter, someone will come along and start chatting. He thinks of something to keep William occupied. He pretends there's a sale on at one of William's favourite shops.

"There's a sale on at Halcyon Days?" he says.

"I've nearly got more enamel boxes than the Queen."

William relaxes a little now but still folds his arms.

"I designed a lot of the Queen's ones myself."

"Really?" says Jason. He's heard all this a hundred times before but he's fine saying "really" and "oh yes" now and again to keep William happy and to keep him talking so he can look at the paper.

"When I die I'm going to bequeath all my memorabilia to the nation."

(From behind the paper) "Really? What will you do? send it to a museum or something?"

William sniffs and lifts his nose in the air, "I don't know, whatever. Leave it to The Royal Collection, or whatever."

"I'd send it to local museums where people can see it for free if I were you. They should rename it The Personal Collection as The Royal Collection gets bigger and farther away from the people day-by-day. I've seen all the stuff you've got on show in your little house, there's hardly anywhere to sit. Must take you ages to dust all that lot."

"I don't really, I just flick a duster about and blow," and he imitates how he blows, while making a sweeping action with his hand causing his gold bracelet to jangle a little. "You should have seen it when I moved in, the place was full of damp, an old storeroom. I had a battle to get them to decorate it for me. When I did eventually move in Queen Elizabeth came to visit me and I mentioned that I didn't even have a fridge or a cooker and all she said to me was,

Oh don't worry, I'm sure they'll come," as he impersonates a woman patting the back of her hairdo. "I thought she was going to get them for me, but she never did. I suppose anyone of that class and generation didn't have to think about things like that. You'd get married and set up a house and anything you needed would be put on a list."

Jason tries to concentrate on his paper and William folds his arms even tighter. He is hurt that Jason would rather look at the newspaper than face him and have a chat over a drink. He doesn't like being ignored or having no audience to play to and he wants Jason to know it. He tries to encourage him into conversation about his thoughts on Queen Elizabeth as he knows Jason likes to hear about them.

"I don't suppose they'll put anything like that in the biography though. It's too mundane, too real. That's why they always get a safe pair of hands to write these things, someone who won't embarrass them, as they see it."

"How?" asks Jason, who's intrigued at this strange remark.

"By telling it how it really was. By painting a picture of an extraordinary person who is also an ordinary person in-between days. That's why history never changes, as there's usually only one version, written by someone who probably wasn't even there. Even if they were around, they neglect to endeavour to paint the whole picture by asking all witnesses. And when those people die, it's too late! It's sad really to lose that connection with the past, especially with this lady. But historians and biographers are like lawyers in a courtroom, who never ask the witness a question unless they assume that they already know what the answer is going to be. If I were a witness, I would never want to be that predictable."

(From behind the paper) "Well you're definitely not that!"

William stares into space and contemplates his thoughts. "Hitler called her the most dangerous woman in Europe you know."

"I know he did," comes the reply from behind the paper.

"And to think that we serve her tea in her favourite little pink and blue cups. She never renounced her responsibility and she passed that quality on to her daughter. What an amazing legacy to leave the modern world. And yet, people think she's just a little old lady."

Jason says nothing. He's reading an interesting article in the paper.

There's a long silent pause.

William was looking for a reaction from Jason when he mentioned Hitler and Queen Elizabeth, but Jason knows about that from years ago, William told him. They've become too familiar with each other as people tend to do who work together for a long time. William looks over but can't see Jason for the paper, so he sits bolt upright when he realises that he isn't paying him enough attention. He wants to shock him into listening to what he has to say.

"I've organised my funeral arrangements! I've arranged the catering with the restaurant and already paid for the main course so all my friends can go and have lunch on me."

It hasn't worked. Jason is preoccupied and finds the news in the paper more interesting. He doesn't look round from it to answer.

"Really? What's that then?"

"My favourite, Eggs Benedict," declares William, still sitting upright with his arms folded.

"Oh yes, for how many?"

"I don't know do I? as I don't know who's going."

Jason has caught on now. He's never heard William discuss this topic before, so he glances round in order to conduct some preliminary enquires about this strange idea of his.

"Does that mean that anybody can just turn up on the day then?"

"If they want. I won't be there to care, but it's all paid for."

Jason is satisfied that the topic didn't turn out to be that interesting after all, so he lifts the paper again to continue reading.

"You are so lucky to have so many glamourous friends," he says.

"I'm not, and I don't have lots of glamourous friends."

"You have! You are always being invited to parties and being taken to shows or to a posh restaurant, you're always going out somewhere. I don't have lots of rich friends doing that for me."

"I don't have lots of friends," insists William, who

seems to want to make a particular point about this.

Jason lowers the paper to look at him.

"You do, what are you talking about?" he says, thinking that William is trying to appear modest for some unknown reason. "You are always having people for drinks in your little house or going off somewhere to a party or to an opening of something."

William waits before he answers again. He's still sitting upright with his back not touching the back of the chair and his arms folded, looking straight ahead at the wall.

"Friendship at gunpoint," he says, quite simply and calmly.

"What? I don't understand. What do you mean?" asks Jason, who's looking for some more information as he's quite shocked to hear such a statement from William of all people. However, no more information is forthcoming.

William pauses, he seems to be annoyed at having to repeat himself and he's still not looking at Jason but looking straight ahead at the wall opposite.

"What do you think? Friendship at gunpoint!" he says sharply.

Jason sees that William really means what he says but still he can't believe it. He can see it's not William being flippant or playing for a reaction and certainly not playing for laughs. If it's true it would mean that William's legendary partying is nothing more than a travesty. Perhaps it was a reaction to Reg's death, he thinks, but he couldn't work it out. William was being so sincere. Jason knew that people can react in strange ways after a funeral so he decides to try to placate him, if he can.

"Oh William. You don't mean that, that can't be true?"

"It's my life," snaps William, momentarily catching Jason's eye, almost as if he is embarrassed and annoyed to have admitted such a revelation but moreover it was a look as if to say, "how would you know about my life and the way I feel?"

Jason feels really awkward now as he doesn't know what to say for the best. He changes the subject to try to persuade William out of this melancholy mood he is getting into.

"Look," he says, scanning through the pages of the newspaper, "I'm going to set the video for that Hancock thing before they start coming in. I can't find the television pages, I think there's some of this paper missing? Have you seen this article about President George Bush? He's on a secret private holiday in Scotland for a few days. Apparently, he's visiting a distillery in the area and he's popping to Balmoral to have picnic lunch with The Queen by the river. And they say he's keen to get some tips off the Queen Mother, her being an experienced fly fisher."

"I didn't know anything about that did you?" asks William.

"No I didn't."

"Can't be very secret if it's in the papers. Who wrote the article?"

"Doesn't say. It's on the society pages."

"That's odd. I'll have a word with Sir Alastair about it, it may be wrong if it's in the papers. We'll do the President a nice Scottish afternoon tea anyway if he comes, he should like that," says William.

At this moment Timothy returns. He stomps down the steps from the royal floor just above them and enters the page's area. He removes his jacket and flings it around the back of a chair and sits down opposite Jason. He has no clue about what Jason and William have been talking about. He puts Jason in mind of a Springer Spaniel in the way he unceremoniously bursts into a room and flops about. Timothy sips his coffee from the mug he left there earlier, it must be cold by now but that doesn't seem to bother him. Jason glances up from his paper. He's still searching for the t.v. guide to set the video machine. He's determined to keep as upbeat as possible by pretending that there's nothing wrong and trying to lighten the atmosphere caused by William's admission. He turns and searches the pages over and over again still looking for the television section.

"Everything else seems to be about the Prime Minister. He gets around, doesn't he? He's going on holiday again, Italy this time. He certainly makes it look like a nine-to-five job with all the free time he seems to have," he says.

"They say he might not even come up this year to see The Queen. Prime ministers always come up to Balmoral to see The Queen and then come over here to have tea with Queen Elizabeth," says William.

Timothy hears the words prime minister and presumes he's caught the gist of a conversation about the talk of the Prime Minister having an official private jet.

"Have you seen the headlines about him?" as he points to Jason's paper. "Passionate Prime Minister rallies round the country, they say he wants his own private jet to fly around in, that's so cool."

William goes mad, he's in a hypersensitive state so is quick to react. Timothy's remark touches a nerve, so all William's resentment and angst comes flooding out.

"Passionate? Passionate?" he squeals. "He's not passionate! I'll tell you about passionate. I've known Prince Charles and Princess Anne since they were this high," (he holds out his hand to indicate the height of a child) "and I think it wouldn't be disrespectful to say that apart from Queen Elizabeth and The Queen, they are the two most passionate people I know. Passionate about different things admittedly but passionate all the same, as when they say something they mean it. They don't say things in order to be liked or admired, they say them because that's what they feel. If you're not passionate about something you may as well be dead!"

"How do you know I'm not passionate?" asks Timothy indignantly.

"The only thing you're passionate about is yourself. The Princess Royal is travelling all over the country every week doing charity work but you hardly ever see that in the papers. As soon as the Prince of Wales airs his views about something he is shouted down by the Fleet Street hoi polloi, The poor Queen can't say a word. They've got no control of what appears in the papers. That's why you never hear from them, never complain, never explain. People believe whatever is splashed across the headlines. If The Queen so much as sneezes then the whole world knows about it but I bet you couldn't name this country's Employment Secretary? Home Secretary? Agricultural Minister? Head of Defence? There you are then. You can't name any of them and yet I bet all of them get police protection just like The Queen, but you people are always complaining about The Queen. Nearly every single person in the whole world knows who The Queen is, and even more people would recognise Queen Elizabeth as she was the last empress of India for God's sake, and yet these politicians, these dull boring people arrange themselves into this power machine over us, they get the same if not better treatment than the figurehead of our nation, the head of our church!"

The house bell rings.

William instinctively but slowly stands up and reaches for his jacket while still talking and leaning over Timothy keeping eye contact. He is determined to say his piece because he feels so strongly about it and Queen Elizabeth and the bell ringing or anything else isn't going to stop him. He feels that this young ignorant boy is spouting his naive opinions and he deserves to be put in his place and have a few things explained to him by an adult.

"Politicians are the most mundane, conceited, unimaginative people promoted to the most extraordinary positions of power, but somehow still regarded as being mysterious and magical and irreproachable in some way. And not only that but we are lumbered with the privilege of financing their every whim. So don't talk to me about the royal family being a waste of money because if it wasn't for them then this country would be taken over by president bloody Blair!"

He buttons up his jacket but can't quite fix the waist strap through the buckle due to his bad temper, so it's left hanging. He marches up the steps and leaves the room to answer the bell and attend the Queen.

Timothy is slightly shaken by the ferocity of the speech but nonetheless waits for William to leave, then he puts his feet up on a chair and picks up his mug of coffee. He attempts to appear unnerved, but he looks upset and annoyed.

Jason slowly lowers the newspaper, making sure William has definitely gone before he says anything.

"I don't know how you get yourself into these situations?" he says.

"What did I say?" asks Timothy, genuinely confused.

"The wrong thing obviously. I'd make myself scarce if I were you. Why don't you go and lay the duke's kilt and stuff out on the bed, the way that William showed you, remember? Or if you go and make someone's bathroom chair into a wrap-around with the

211

towel, that'll get you a tip; always works for me. Or go and check the tea things and the drinks tray for the drawing room ..."

Jason stops talking and hides behind his paper again as he hears William coming back through the door at the top of the steps. William returns holding an absolutely huge [empty] red crested cream envelope, his waist strap is still hanging down. He was so angry he went in to see Queen Elizabeth without noticing it. He clumps down the steps and stands directly in front of Timothy again and carries on from where he took off.

"And why, do all these so-called world leaders have to film themselves meeting each other all the time? Why can't they get on with the job they are paid to do without us having to act as voyeurs to all their handshaking on the news. And then to add insult to injury, they wheel out their boring wives to show us. They are just another kind of so-called celebrity. They don't run the country. The Civil Service and private business keep this country ticking over not the politicians or the prime minister. They're just people who form careers out of messing things up, while making their fortunes which suits their needs, not ours."

Timothy isn't standing for any more of this, he's off. He stands and pulls his jacket off the back of the chair.

"I'm taking the dogs out," he says.

"No!" William shouts, "I'll take them out for a walk then they might get some decent exercise for a change!"

He throws the envelope onto the desk in temper and storms out.

Timothy flops back down on the chair, with his head bowed, arms folded, fuming mad, playing back the whole argument in his head trying to work out what it was he said to provoke such a visceral attack.

"What does he know about walking the dogs?" he asks, as he glares after William with a disdainful look.

Jason lowers his newspaper now. The place is quiet and the threat has gone, even if the issues are still hanging in the air. Jason feels it's time to explain to Timothy how William fits into this set-up and how Timothy does not.

"Oh nothing Timothy. He's only been doing it since before you were born! Haven't you seen all his photo albums about working here? There are photos of him taken in the nineteen-fifties of him walking the doggies in Green Park with his Brylcreemed hair and Burberry mac? He looks like a young Cliff Richard. Although I think everyone looked like Cliff Richard in those days?"

"What photos? I haven't seen any photos," grunts Timothy, who is angry with himself with the incompetent way he just handled William.

Jason folds up the newspaper and places it down.

"He used to take out about six dogs for a walk in the public parks around Clarence House, but the footmen had to stop taking them there, when our dog bit a member of the public's dog. That's why Robert takes ours over to the palace garden in the afternoon."

Timothy's face screws up with an evil look of disdain and contempt for Jason.

"I don't know how you can sit there and drink with him every night and laugh at his jokes?"

"Because he's funny, that's why! You're not exactly a bundle of laughs yourself are you? And I need some relief from the treadmill being stuck up here for weeks. Anyway, I usually only have one sip of a drink with him to be sociable. There's always somebody around here he can collar and have a drink with, I know what he's like, I'm not stupid."

"Well you could have fooled me."

"Obviously then I did fool you. This should be the

213

best job in the world, in our line of work this should be the best job in the world, but it's spoilt if people are attacking each other. He only gets angry with you Timothy because you show him no respect, and he's just lost his partner for Christ's sake."

"He should go then, retire. He's an old man, a loser!"

Jason can't believe the disrespect and lack of empathy Timothy is showing again.

"There you are you see! Don't you even respect the fact he's been here for fifty years?"

"Why should I?" Timothy's face is still infused with anger and contempt.

"Because he's not just gonna let you waltz in and take over. You're not William. You never will be. He never lets anyone in, we're on the sidelines here so we can never be like William, I mean, have you got the next fifty years to spare? He's done it, he's been here for that fifty years."

"I'm only staying here so I can put this job on my C.V."

This line sounded as if it came from an innocent the first time he said it, but now Jason finds it extremely offensive.

"Oh really? And what's that going to say? That I spent the last twelve months arguing with a sad old fogey loser, and in the process I got on everybody else's nerves?"

"You argue with him as well."

"Only because you wind him up Timothy. You don't know how to read him that's why you can't get on. I've worked with him for years, don't you think I know all of his little tricks by now?"

Jason can't believe the audacity Timothy displayed by saying that. What made him think that he could compare his relationship with William against his? Some young kid who's only been around for a matter of weeks when Jason has had to endure William's ways for years.

"Why are you so interested anyway? It's not as if you're

going to get Reg's job. You've been stuck in the same job for years," says Timothy.

"I don't want Reg's job. I'm quite happy with the one I've got. What makes you young people think that you can have anything you want if you want it badly enough, huh? Where's the skill in that? What's wrong with picking what you need from life and leaving the rest for someone else? Try to find the joy in things for goodness sake. You don't have to rule the world."

"Yeah well, you've had your day."

Jason can't believe it. What a nasty piece of work this Timothy turned out to be. He must have some really warped issues going on in his head, he thinks.

"Haven't you got any respect for anything?"

"Yes. My future career."

"Well that's not going to be here thank goodness, you don't belong! I like working here because I belong but I'm not sure why you chose to come to this place. I don't think you seem to realise that I'm good at my job because I make an effort, and that means sometimes I have to show interest in his same old stories and laugh at his same old jokes when I'd much rather be somewhere else but actually sometimes, he is very good company. Not that you'd notice. If you don't make any kind of effort, all you'll take away from this experience is bad memories and the feeling you've not achieved anything unless you just simply enjoy being here and being with the company you're in."

Timothy stands up, slips on his jacket loosely then pretends to flick some dust off his shoulder, rather too dramatically to say the least. He must think he's in a rapper video or something.

"Why don't you do us all a favour, and just fade away, you sad, pathetic, creepy little weirdo?" and he leaves. Jason is so surprised that he sits there open-mouthed as he watches Timothy go.

"Charming!" he says, then takes a slurp of his drink.

He sits there for a couple of minutes until he hears the sound of William's footsteps approaching. William returns looking rather sheepish. He's obviously calmed down now and he looks about for Timothy before he decides to sit down at the table opposite Jason.

"I thought you were walking the dogs?" says Jason.

"I was, but Queen Elizabeth saw me and came out and took them up the path." William looks around him. "Where's the boy?"

"It's all right, he's gone."

"I shouldn't have flown off the handle like that. I hate swearing. I shouldn't lose control it's bad for my nerves."

William removes his jacket and neatly hangs it on the back of the chair, then sits at the table with Jason.

"The doctor's given me some sleeping tablets but they don't work. I can doze off for a couple of hours then find I'm wide awake at four a.m."

"You should have a nice hot herbal bath before you go to bed, helps me sleep," says Jason, and he takes another sip of his vodka.

"It's nothing, I'm just a little tired I'll be all right. Is everything ready for tonight? You know it's not soup for dinner now?"

"Yes William," Jason rolls his eyes, as having told him this minutes ago.

"Nothing's happened while I've been out has it?"

"No William, everything's fine. You've only been gone five minutes."

"Yes well, get the boy to make sure the fire's stacked up with logs, [even in summer sometimes] give Robert a rest, and make sure there are plenty of tea things left out for the latecomers. There's hardly anyone back yet and I bet Lady Clara is already eyeing up the martini jug."

216

"All right William don't panic there's nothing to worry about. Everything's under control as usual."

"I'm not panicking, I merely asked you a simple question and frankly I could do without you fussing around me all the time."

"Me, fussing? Well pardon me if all my fussing gets things done around here."

"How dare you speak to me like that."

"You know we've kept everything going perfectly fine with you not here. Not one thing has gone wrong, yet I'll be really glad to get away from this place for a few hours tomorrow when we go to Glamis."

"What do you mean go to Glamis? You're not going to Glamis."

"Yes I am! There's a load of us going on a trip, it's been arranged for ages haven't you seen the memo? It's the staff outing. We finally got the chauffeur to agree when you were away and it's been decided we're going to Glamis."

"Yes of course I've read the memo but I'm going out for lunch again tomorrow with Doctor Woods so you'll have to stay here in case the Queen comes back early, and to take care of the fire and do the phone and the post."

Jason stands up in a rage. He feels that William is manipulating the situation again.

"No way! There is absolutely no reason why I should stay here when there are two other people who can do it."

"Well you try telling that to Robert then, because he and the boy are going out tomorrow with the ghillies to try their hand at fly fishing, and before you say anything it was at Queen Elizabeth's suggestion so there! Anyway you've already been to Glamis so I can't imagine why you'd want to go again."

"What are you talking about? I've never been to Glamis."

"What?" says William rather puzzled. "You have! You must have done. You went with me one year don't you remember? The equerry gave us a lift back in his sports car."

"That wasn't me," declares Jason.

"Wasn't it? Who was it then?"

"I don't know and I don't care, but if you didn't get pissed so much you'd remember that kind of information for yourself."

William slams his hand on the table with all his might. He is incandescent with rage.

"Right, that's it! I will no longer have anything to do with you! From now on ours is purely a professional working relationship, I'm washing my hands of you. From now on I will neither help nor hinder your career. That's it, finished!"

"What have you ever done to help my career?"

William stands up.

"You've just gone too far this time. You're on your own!" he yells.

"Huh!" says Jason, "I'm always on my bloody own, it's me who gets everything done on time around here."

"How dare you! You've no right to speak to me that way."

"Oh, get lost! I'll be in the laundry room if anybody wants me," and Jason grabs his drink and storms off towards the laundry where he can cool down away from everything.

Timothy rushes in when he hears the commotion. He's wearing his buttoned-up jacket so he must have made an appearance on the royal floor for some reason.

"What's going on?" he says. "What's all the shouting about? We can hear you from the kitchen."

William is really angry, like a bull to a red flag.

"I've had enough," he says. "The audacity! I will not be spoken to like that. They've no respect for me and no

218

respect for the Queen. I never go out in the day and on the two occasions that the Doctor is good enough to invite me for lunch I end up feeling like this. Doesn't anyone understand what I'm going through, don't they realise how difficult this is for me? I just want ..."

He covers his eyes with his hands. He is very upset.

"It's all right Billy, sit down now, come on."

Timothy is very considerate and helps William to sit down, which takes a few seconds while Timothy guides him towards the chair and then guides him down until he is seated. William is very upset and bows his head.

"I just want to be treated with some respect, nobody cares anymore. Don't they realise what a difficult time this is for me, why don't they treat me with a little more respect."

Timothy hands William a tissue. He speaks in a soft caring voice.

"Calm down, just settle yourself and have a drink. He's gone now, it's all right there's no one around. Look, Billy, I'm sorry if I upset you just now, I didn't know what I was talking about. I big myself up sometimes and try to act cool, but I don't mean it. I'm sorry."

"Yes, well, you should think before you speak out of turn like that."

"Let's have a brandy," suggests Timothy, thinking that that's what people do when they've had a shock or an upset.

"No," says William abruptly, "Scotch. And a little soda perhaps."

Timothy goes into the little office to make the drinks, and he hands one to William, who reaches out for it carefully as if he were about to take a glass of medicine.

"Here you are. Here's to good health and happiness," he says, raising his glass in the air and trying to sound as cheerful as possible. "Cheers!"

"Amen," says William solemnly, and drinks some.

"I know you're upset," says Timothy gently, as he pulls up a chair to sit almost facing William.

"It's understandable after a bereavement and I know what I'm talking about. I felt the same way when my brother died."

William looks completely spaced out and weakened from all the shouting and high emotion. He seems to be operating on automatic pilot as there's a wistful look on his face.

"Oh, your brother. What happened?"

"He was on his motorbike going along a fast stretch of the A12 on his way to Cambridge to see his girlfriend, when he lost control and crashed into the back of a lorry and was killed instantly."

"Oh that's awful," says William. "How old was he?"

"Twenty-one. I was still at school at the time in the middle of my exams. I'm afraid I didn't get very good results so had to think of what I was going to do for a career. I'd always had a Saturday job in the local hotel helping out with the wedding receptions there, so they took me on full-time on a temporary basis. I liked it so much so that's when I decided to go to college and do a hotel management course, but I couldn't get a place. I thought I'd try to get a job at Kensington Palace eventually as I'd always wanted to work there, but I never got anywhere with it."

"Oh dear, that's a shame, I didn't know. You never mentioned any of this at your interview?"

"It's not the sort of thing you talk about at job interviews is it?"

"No, I mean about you applying to work at Kensington Palace."

"Oh that," says Timothy hesitantly. "No, well, I didn't want you to think that Clarence House was second choice for me. To be honest with you I thought there was even less chance of me getting in here. I'd heard that Queen Elizabeth didn't like anyone to retire you see."

"Yes that has certainly been the case for some years now. So are you close to your family then?"

"No not really," Timothy says while looking down at his glass. "My parents split-up after the accident and my father married again and moved to Wales. I don't get to see them much these days."

"That's a shame." William takes another gulp of his whisky.

"I'm used to it now." Timothy changes tempo a little, as if he feels uncomfortable talking about himself and would rather talk about something else. "I do admire you having worked here in the same job for all these years William. You really must write a book about your life with the Queen Mother you know, not to include nasty things I don't mean that, just the funny stories that you tell, they should be written down for posterity."

William falls in line with the questions as he's just grateful to have somebody to talk to.

"Nobody would be interested, who wants to read about loyalty these days."

"Don't be so modest," says Timothy, trying his best to flatter him. "From the point of view of social history alone, you owe the nation that legacy. I've read about you; the time when you were a little boy and you went to visit London with your parents. You stood outside Buckingham Palace gates and promised yourself that one day you would work there. Is that true?"

William is in such a melancholy mood he could be

prompted to talk about anything.

"Yes. I did make a promise to myself. I didn't necessarily think it would come true though, but that was a lifetime ago. It didn't just happen you know, all this. I deserve to be in my position. I've had to work for it, earn it, over the years. I made a promise to myself that I would never waver, I couldn't you see. I kissed me mam, [William said it like that] kissed me dad, and left Coventry behind and went to London. I was just a boy. And suddenly there I was, living and working with the king and queen of my country. My dream had come true, but I was really only at the start of my journey, but I was on my way. It was all I could do, to be someone."

"You'll get a title when this is all over then?" asks Timothy.

"You misunderstand me. I'm not looking for a title, they won't give me a title. Sir Alastair will probably become Lord St. James's or something but I'm just a wee boy from Newcastle, titles aren't for the likes of me. Anyway they've never had to strive to make a living or to feed themselves or keep warm, they can never understand. They've never lived with poverty. They will always be unable to appreciate what I've done with my life. I don't exist because of them but despite them. I've always been myself, I've always been me. So I don't need a medal or title to prove it, because I know what I've achieved. That's more important than any title or medal. That really is something to cherish."

"Why don't you retire and go and live abroad somewhere sunny and write your memoirs?"

William laughs. "Go? Go where? Where would I go? What would I do? No. I mustn't give in, not now, I couldn't justify that. I must keep going. Queen Elizabeth needs me … and I need Queen Elizabeth," he whispers.

"You are very close to Queen Elizabeth aren't you?"

"Do you know, I've worked for this lady for fifty years

now, and I still don't know if she really likes me or not."

"Do you have any regrets?" asks Timothy.

William throws back his head a little as if thinking of where to even start answering this.

"Huh! regrets, oh yes. And mistakes. I made mistakes. Sometimes Queen Elizabeth would be in a mood with me all day. And when it came for me to say goodnight your majesty, she would just slam the bedroom door, but the next day it would all be forgotten and all forgiven. A brand new day can do that. But some nights now, they find me, when I'm in my bed, all those ghosts, they surround me. They steal my sleep. We are gathered all together, in the same room, at the same time. It's absolutely terrifying." William's face takes on a cold look of doom.

"Come on Billy let's have another little top-up."

Timothy pours some more whisky; ironically turning the tables and inducing William to have a drink.

"I often wonder what it would have been like for me if my dream had come true to work for Diana," he says. "Did you know her well?

"You could say that. She used to send me a Christmas card every year you know and a birthday card. It was very gracious of her to think of me in that way."

"That's nice. I bet she sent a card to Reg as well didn't she?"

William looks up at Timothy as if a beam of wonderment has surged through his face. "You are the first person to mention Reg's name since he died."

"Sorry," says Timothy concerned, "I didn't realise."

"It's all right."

"I apologise."

"No, it's just hearing his name, nobody mentions

him anymore, it's as if he was never here. He worked here for all those years, yet nobody talks about him at all."

"That's because people don't want to hurt your feelings William, the instigation, it has to come from you, that's why."

"I suppose so, but I wish they would mention him, it keeps him here you see. I think about him all the time. It must be the only thing that keeps me going."

"You can go back down to London again you know, we can manage here for a few days, well Jason can, the house isn't so full at the moment."

"Bless you, but I'm better off at work, and the house will soon fill up with guests again believe me. Reg used to say this place was so like a hotel, with new guests coming and going all the time, that it should have a revolving door. I go to pick up the phone sometimes to call him then realise he won't be there. There was always a good reason to call him during the day. It was probably mostly silly little things really, but it kept us in touch. I took it for granted. Now I've got no one to call. The week he went into the hospital, I thought he'd have some more Chemotherapy and come straight out again, but he had to stay in there and only a week later, he was gone."

"He always cheered everyone up with his singing and his sense of humour. He was a laugh wasn't he?"

"Yes, I miss that. I don't want to live alone, I'm no good on my own. Reg and I were going to go on holidays together to France or somewhere, we used to talk about it. We never could go on holiday together you see as there was always one of us on duty. The plan was that we were supposed to wait for Queen Elizabeth, then we would both retire at last and go away on holiday together."

William is getting himself quite upset now talking about Reg. Timothy is loving it as William becomes more and more emotional. This is great, he thinks, just what I need.

"It wasn't supposed to be like this," moans William, "it should never have happened like this," William cups his face in his hands, "it should never have happened."

"I know, it's hard for the people left behind, like us. No one can understand the agony we go through. Just think of Diana's family how they must feel. They don't even know why she died."

"That's easy," William says as he wipes his wet nose. "I could tell them that."

"Could you?" Timothy says calmly. He is very careful not to get excited at this point as William could be about to tell him something that turns out to be atomic. He has been longing and yearning to have this particular conversation with William about the death of Princess Diana ever since he befriended him months and months ago at a party, long before he started work here. He could never get him to talk about it, even when he was drunk after a party or a show, and suddenly this glittering opportunity has landed in his lap and so he can hardly contain his excitement. It's vital that nobody walks in on them now. He hopes to God nobody comes in and disturbs them, not at this critical stage as this may be the one and only time William will ever speak about it, so he has to keep him talking.

"Yes."

"Tell them what? Who killed her?"

William is very bleary eyed and is not really fully engaged with the conversation as he's still thinking about Reg, but nods his head solemnly all the same.

"Who was it?"

"The press," William says softly.

"You mean they hired somebody to do it?"

"It was the press," William repeats with a completely fixed, glazed look about him now.

225

"What do you mean, one of the press was hired to drive past the car in the tunnel?"

"No. They hounded and killed the thing they loved," he says in a wistful way.

"Is that what you think?"

"But everyone knows what happened," says William, as he catches Timothy's eye.

"But there was so much speculation of who was responsible."

Timothy is still playing it cool, he doesn't want to push too hard, not at this point, almost there, he thinks.

The spirit returns into William's eyes and he pays more attention as he lifts his head to look at Timothy. "What did you expect me to say?"

"I thought that a particular person was involved."

William turns away again. "Even if I did know such a thing, I wouldn't tell you."

William doesn't seem that concerned with Timothy's questions. He stares into the middle distance seemingly recalling an old dream.

"The press lost their greatest star," he says. "They killed the thing they loved and now all that's left for them is just, chicken feed!"

"But the initial investigations were so badly handled," says Timothy becoming agitated. "And all the speculation since it happened has never been resolved."

"It was an accident!" insists William. "It was an accident you stupid little boy! It should never have happened. It was an accident. I don't want to have this conversation, please go and help Jason do some work."

"I'm sorry Billy I didn't mean to ..."

"Please go," demands William, the anguish rising in his voice. "Leave me alone." He turns his body in so that his knees are just under the table so he can rest his elbows down on the top. "Just go. Please."

William cups his head in his hands with his elbows resting on the table.

"All right Billy, I'm sorry. I'll go and find Jason."

"Thank you."

Timothy stands up and pretends to leave the area. He strides through the doorway and stands just past the threshold, out of sight of William, stamping his feet gently on the vinyl floor trying to imitate the sound of him walking away. He walks on a dozen steps making the sound lighter as he goes. Eventually he stops when he thinks the sounds have become inaudible to William. He sneaks back on his tracks as close to William as he dares. William is still in the same position with his head in his hands. He has no idea Timothy is standing in the shadows, watching.

"Oh Reggie I can't do this. Why don't they leave me alone?"

William's elbow slips and he falls forwards on the table knocking over a glass. He is very emotional, as his body begins to quiver.

"Oh Reggie, why aren't you here? I don't want to be alone, I'm no good on my own what's the point? There's no point anymore Reggie. I don't want to be alone Reggie there's no point. What's the point?"

He becomes desperately upset and bursts into tears. He begins to release so much pent-up emotion that he starts to cry uncontrollably.

He buries his head in his hands in order to stifle the emotion bursting out of his face and to muffle the spasm of breath exploding out his nose as he snorts and blubbers, but it's no use. A gush of tears wells out of his eyes and they flood and burn, he can't control it. He begins to sob, with tears streaming down his cheeks and his eyes become just a blurry red mass as he sobs and sobs. He is slumped forward on the chair, barely resting on the seat but he's curled his ankles around the legs of it in order to cling to something, squeezing against the pain. He tries desperately to suppress this force of erupting anguish seemingly rising from out of the earth then shooting up the chair then surging through his whole body, making his head and shoulders rock to-and-fro. The more it occurs to him to try to take hold of himself the worse it becomes; he can't even get hold of his breath. He's trying to speak through the blubbing, so his crying only stops for a second as he sucks in a quick jerky stutter of air in order to breathe, then he starts over again. There is so much anguish coming out that it causes his whole body to shake with the blubbering and weeping, causing the chair leg to tap and rattle on the floor in time with his trembling body. He keeps repeating the same phrase over and over, "What's the point? What's the point?" and there seems no end to his turmoil as he moans and rocks. He never realised how much hurt he had inside and all of it is coming out at once. He weeps and whimpers, and the tears and pulsating emotion just don't stop erupting and gushing out as he sobs, and he sobs.

Timothy slips out a small camera from his pocket and just manages to take a few pictures. William notices him at last so he leaps up exploding with rage, thrashing his arms about like a crazy animal, and shouting at the top of his voice like a possessed man.

"Come on then! Is this what you want eh? Come on. Come on, take another picture and another! Come on then! Come on, come on, you lousy scumbag Paparazzi! You came all this way for a picture? A lousy picture? Is that all? You'd sacrifice your soul for that? Come on then take it, what are you waiting for? You could have asked me anything about my life working for this family for fifty years but all any of you people can do is to think about that poor girl. And you thought I would just roll over and play your sordid little game did you? Well I'll tell you something: I WILL GO TO

THE GATES OF HELL and I will not betray the ones I love! So take a picture of THAT why don't you, and put that in your newspapers, because, I-AM-NOT-FOR-SALE!"

William tries to grab the camera but Timothy is frozen in shock by his outrage so he's unable to release it.

"Feeding off people's misery you voyeuristic weirdo! Asking me those sick questions and taking your stupid pictures of tables and noticeboards. Stop it stop it! Give me that, that's enough, stop!"

William wrestles with Timothy for the camera and eventually manages to prise it from his grip as he notices two plain-clothes detectives have already surrounded Timothy and are holding him back, but William attempts to stop them.

"Okay now William this is it, we've got him now," says one of them.

"No don't!" shrieks William totally panicked. "Doctor Johnson! Doctor Johnson! Doctor Johnson!" he shouts. "I'm all right. Give me one more minute," he begs. "Please? I just need to finish what I'm saying. One more minute, please? that's all, one more minute?"

The detectives look at each other while they both have hold of Timothy, then one nods to the other indicating their agreement. One of them restrains Timothy for a second by pulling his hands together at his back while the other one removes Timothy's jacket and searches it. The other one then frisks him starting at his head, checking for any weapons, cameras or recording devices. The other detective takes the camera off William and removes the small notepad and the pen from Timothy's jacket pocket and examines the whole garment while her colleague runs his hands around Timothy's collar and head, over his tee-shirt and then over his limbs, the front and back of his torso, around his waste, inside pockets, between his legs and down the legs and around his ankles and even pokes his fingers into each shoe. He then lifts each ankle up in the air like a boxing referee checking a fighter to look at the soles of his shoes. The detectives are satisfied. They nod to each other in agreement.

"Very well William. One minute. We'll step outside," says one of them. "And I am watching you," he says as he wags his finger over Timothy's nose. They both withdraw from the room.

William tries to calm himself down and gather his thoughts. He feels for the table behind him and starts to crawl back into the chair he was sitting in. He grasps the corner of the table and slowly lowers himself back onto the seat, feeling exhausted. He's still catching his breath.

"How long have you know ..."

"Shut up!" shouts William angrily, "shut up! No dialogue from you is necessary you stupid little idiot. Just listen."

He can hardly speak, so he has to take a few breaths before he can say anything. He wipes away some spittle from his chin. He holds his chest and can feel his heart pounding rapidly. His whole face is red and wet with anguish. Timothy is standing directly in front of him.

"That was my, er, code word, for them to er, stand down. Because I want to finish what I'm saying, as, er, as I will never see you again. I don't want to see you ever again," he says.

His shoulders slump down with his head as he tries to catch his breath. He is extremely weary.

"I, er, insisted they not barge in unless you were molesting me." He takes a gulp of air and wipes his nose with his sleeve. "You are not molesting me are you Timothy?" looking up at Timothy for a second. "No, of course not. And I never molested you did I, or tried it on? No. I learned my lesson on that score years ago."

He has to pause now and looks down for a second while he catches his breath before he can speak. He looks up at Timothy although he can hardly see him through his sore, tearful eyes.

"So why couldn't you have been my friend? Why? I did all the right things. I recommended you to Sir Alastair. I took you to the theatre, I introduced you to all my friends. And you repay me by being a reporter?"

Timothy doesn't even attempt to reply. He looks ahead, emotionless. He lets William carry on.

"Why does it never work out? Why do people always do that to me? Why can't they want to know me for me, of who I am, not because of where I work or who I work for? What about me? Isn't that good enough?"

Timothy just stands there and waits passively, not interested at all in what William is saying. He glances at him occasionally not looking the least bit concerned, just checking to see if his lips are still moving as he knows he won't be able to leave until William has finished speaking [and pouring out his heart]. William is unaware of this so carries on with his innermost thoughts.

"Perhaps this is me? I'll just be remembered as a soundbite, or a handle, or a condensed caricature of the Queen Mother's butler. Well guess what?
— I, am REAL!" he shouts.

"And guess what else — SO-ARE-THEY!" he yells, pointing his arm to the floor above, exclaiming this last remark so forcefully that it makes Timothy flinch. He doesn't move though.

William continues.

"And I've got photos you know. Amazing photos,

loads of them. Oh yes. Of me and Reg, and staff and Queen Elizabeth, taken all over the world. My photos are much better than your photos. But I don't think I'll bother now, if nobody is going to be interested, I may as well flog all my collections. And to top it all, somebody's stolen my beautiful little Fabergé egg. Why? Why? That was mine, that was given to me," he cries desperately, while thrusting his forefinger into his chest.

He manages to calm down and pauses for a moment, managing to compose himself a little more, having gathered enough energy to carry on. He looks up at Timothy's eyes.

"Do you know who Doctor Samuel Johnson is Timothy?" he says, in a soft, quiet voice.

Timothy blinks as he realises this question requires an answer. He hasn't moved from the spot since William started to talk, he's been standing there thinking up headlines. "Er, the dictionary guy?"

"A man of words, like you. They tell me you went to university to study English. Well Timothy, there are two men in this room at the moment, you and me. One has merit without riches, the other has wealth without merit. Which one of us is which do you reckon Timothy? Which is which?"

William doesn't expect an answer from Timothy and Timothy doesn't attempt to give one. William only wants him to listen and to tell him that what he is doing is wrong, and maybe pass on some useful advice to the boy in the process. He doesn't give a damn if pleading like this with Timothy makes him look foolish or weak in any way because he's not doing this for his own benefit. He knows it would be more feeble if he said nothing.

"Please stop this. You are still young. Do something else with your life, something worthwhile. Something decent. What you are doing is trading on people's grief. You are stealing their privacy, and dignity. Their lives. You are stealing their lives."

Timothy has stood motionless all this time patiently standing facing William but mostly looking elsewhere, at the walls mainly. William can't understand why there's no reaction from him. Nothing at all. Not even the word sorry. William is exhausted now but still he tries one last attempt to plead and beg with him. He is prepared to get down on his knees and beg if necessary.

"Please don't do it any more," he pleads.

He is completely running out of energy now. He doesn't even have the strength to talk any longer. The tone of his voice rises in intonation even more, before his voice becomes hoarse and he is totally exhausted, and he can say only one more word.

"Please?"

Timothy hears just a pathetic little plea. He stands motionless, and pauses long enough to allow William's words to dissipate in the air so they become nothing.

He rises up in his stance and slightly puffs out his chest, stretching his shoulders and neck, limbering up like a sprinter before the start of a race. He looks down at William to check to make sure he has finished talking.

Thank God this is my turn to speak now, he thinks, so he takes the floor.

He says the words coldly.

And deliberately.

"I did go to university, but I dropped out after a year when I got bored," he says.

"I am sorry William."

But he doesn't mean it.

He turns away and makes towards the doorway but the detectives are already there upon him and snatch their prey. They don't even look at William as they lead Timothy away into the gloom where William cannot see, but one of them will come back in a minute and check on him and look after him.

Sir Alastair has been informed and will probably be already waiting in the office upstairs.

William can't bear to even look up at Timothy now. His eyes are so sore and tearful that he couldn't focus anyhow. He hears somewhere to the left and behind him, the words pumping out of the policeman's mouth: "I am arresting you for theft, you are not obliged to say anything, but anything you do say will be noted down and may be used in evidence ..."

The words petered out in William's head.

Nobody has trespassed on the scene, being too embarrassed to come near or too wary to approach the trouble.

William is alone.

Meanwhile he perches on the chair.

He looks a rather sad and pathetic figure.

Sitting there staring at the floor, slouched over. His limp body slightly twisted on the chair. One elbow resting on the table next to a whisky bottle.

A vacant look in his eyes.

His troubled face.

Unhappy.

Confused.

And hurt.

It was all supposed to be so wonderful, this life.

It is terrible what stress can do to a human being.

The damage it can leave.

He has nobody to talk to, nobody to entertain and no one to make him laugh.

He is in his sixties but that's not old these days.

He is lonely, and alone.

The only thing he can think; is to reach out his hand for the glass in front of him, and to reach out his other hand for the bottle.

Whisky is always a dependable friend.

If not, it will bring him some temporary comfort.

At least.

It will.

THE WRATH OF SIR ALASTAIR

On the floor above, Sir Alastair is seated waiting for Timothy
at a wooden desk. A very neat, splendid wooden desk set out
tidily in a very neat small room he uses as an office in
Birkhall, and which he shares with the equerry and the lady
in waiting. The equerry has his own desk alongside, that is
more or less the same style but not as neat. The desks almost
touch each other as the room is so small, so there is just
about enough room to manoeuvre oneself behind either of
the desks onto one's chair whilst retaining the poise and
elegance of one's official position. The wall behind the desks
is lined with bookshelves and the other wall has another desk
and two large windows looking out onto the garden. There
are a couple of antique church chairs along the wall by the
door under a set of Scottish landscape watercolour paintings.
One of the chairs is covered in maps and papers and a tin of
shortbread, a large bar of chocolate, a squash racquet and a
jacket, (obviously the equerry's). As this is not at an official
residence, this office is only really used in the morning to
answer the post or to use the telephone.

Sir Alastair reads a police report while he waits.

Timothy has been asked if he wished to contact anyone
and he declined, but he did request to visit the lavatory,
which he did accompanied by an officer. He then asked for a
glass of water which he drank and then asked for his jacket
back as he said he was feeling cold wearing only a tee-shirt.
The door to the office has been left fully open and Timothy
appears in the doorway escorted by a plain-clothes police
officer, who indicates for him to enter, which he does but
the officer waits outside leaving the door open. Timothy
marches in and stands in front of the desk looking down at
Sir Alastair defiantly. Sir Alastair looks up, and as soon as his

236

eyes set on Timothy he becomes enraged and shouts at the top of his voice.

"Get out and come back properly dressed!"

"I beg your pardon?" replies Timothy.

"Queen Elizabeth's livery," he snaps. "You don't have the right to be wearing it. Now get out and come back when you are properly dressed."

Sir Alastair is quite correct of course. He is talking about Queen Elizabeth's royal cypher of monogrammed letters. It is embroidered in thick red thread onto the jacket pocket of Timothy's uniform. All the footmen have them. The letters of Queen Elizabeth's monogram differ from that of The Queen as they are rounded in shape after the style of Edward VII, rather than squared like The Queen's are. Also, the jacket has brass buttons with the same cypher. Sir Alastair could not bear to see this imposter marching into his office dressed in a uniform connected with Queen Elizabeth.

Sir Alastair had felt uneasy with the idea of engaging in a sting, as the police had put it. Yet he was eventually persuaded when it was pointed out to him that he had engaged with certain such similar operations in the past that had yielded positive results, so he came around to it in the end. He had made arrangements personally to ensure that Timothy did not interact with Queen Elizabeth on a one to one basis at any time. This had been achieved at least, as several officials and indeed several guests knew what was going on but not Queen Elizabeth, as it may have been too upsetting or distressful for Her Majesty at her noble age. However, there was always the chance that Timothy could be caught or would reveal his purpose at an inappropriate moment [Queen Elizabeth is still outside walking with the dogs].

Timothy can see that he's touched a nerve of 'this old tosspot,' as he thinks, so he intends to try and have some fun with the situation.

"I don't think you should speak to me in that way Sir Alastair" he says smugly, lifting his chin.

"Our readers will be very interested to learn how you treated this matter."

At hearing this, Sir Alastair stands up in a rage pointing towards the door.

"I repeat," he roars, "please leave my office and come back properly dressed!"

Timothy is only marginally fazed at the volume of anger in Sir Alastair's voice. He proceeds to remove his jacket.

"Well, if that's the only way I'm going to get to talk to you, I shall."

He unbuttons his jacket slowly, taking his time releasing each brass button in a deliberate and controlled way, knowing that Sir Alastair will have to wait for him to finish completely removing it before he would speak again. So he takes his time savouring this little performance. Sir Alastair stands in silence for a second or two then sits back down, waiting for this jumped-up reporter in front of him to finish. Timothy tries to catch Sir Alastair's eye, but he can't. The only sound to be heard at the moment is the gentle ticking of a clock and Timothy undoing the jacket as he stands staring at Sir Alastair's bowed head. Timothy takes off the jacket and carefully turns it inside out and folds it in order to hide the cypher and drapes it over his left arm. Only then does he make eye contact with Sir Alastair again.

"Is this good enough?" he says sarcastically, lifting his eyebrows.

Strictly speaking, Sir Alastair does not hold the authority to detain Timothy now he is under arrest, so this private meeting will have to be as brief as possible, a few minutes at the most. That is all he could justify to the police having told them that he wished to speak to Timothy for a minute before he is taken away. He intends to give it to Timothy with both barrels during this interview, but he is worried as the embodiment of this procedure concerned with a gentleman such as himself, would manifest itself merely as a slightly raised voice. And he feels that to initiate it now so early in the conversation would be a mistake, as the timing in these matters is critical. Talking of both barrels and such, it occurs to him that Timothy has the advantage in this particular game by holding the best cards. Sir Alastair has no ammunition whatsoever, apart from an ace card he could play if he could only think of it. He decides to use a trick he learned years ago from his old masters at Eton College. The crux of it was, that the way to affect the best possible outcome in a negotiation, is to deal your ace card into the game when your opponent is least expecting it in order to unnerve them, and so render them more susceptible to accept defeat. It's only very much a case of style over content.

So, by the end of this brief conversation within the next few minutes, he will have to say something to prevent this reporter from publishing and in the process save his own reputation as a private secretary. So he is desperately racking his brain to determine what that ace card will be, because he doesn't have a clue what the hell he is going to say or how he can save the day.

He dismisses Timothy's flippant attitude and answers him in a plain, matter of fact sort of way.

"As you will soon undoubtedly learn, this conversation will remain strictly confidential due to the court order that has already been issued."

That's the legal bit out of the way, he thinks.

The expression on Timothy's face transforms from conceit to bemusement.

"And please be aware," states Sir Alastair, "that the police have only delayed questioning you in order for me to let you know personally of the utter contempt I have for what you have done. I have no desire whatever to speak to the likes of you. You're not a journalist. You are an insufficient hack with depraved, underhand motives. You're a disgrace!"

"I'm a professional journalist working for an international news group on a case of a breach of national security, and I prefer the handle investigative journalist if you don't mind."

"And what's this particular assignment supposed to be," snaps Sir Alastair. "Your own personal Watergate?"

Timothy moves right up to the desk and places his hand on the edge. He is a man who feels passionate about his job and he loves a good political debate with his colleagues, but he is on such an egotistical high at the moment that he is in danger of making a fool of himself. He had promised to deliver the world on a plate to his editor and he feels capable that he is about to be able to fulfil that declaration any minute now.

"I penetrated your security procedures," he says, "and so undermined the whole security network surrounding the royal family and military personnel. You should be thanking me. It's lucky for you I'm not a terrorist, just think of the damage I could have done if I were."

Timothy seems rather pleased with the way he is handling himself in this discussion, so he sits down in the vacant chair making himself at home thinking to himself that this is a doddle. He is completely unable to control the huge grin emerging across his face.

Sir Alastair thinks to himself, that he was going to give this young man a fair hearing, but this self-righteous little tick has been taking liberties and trying his patience, so now he intends to fasten him to a metaphorical missile marked 'professional journalist' then press the fire button, launching the whole bally lot sky-high duly dispatching Timothy Craig into professional journalistic oblivion.

"You broke a position of common decency and trust and managed only to take some photographs of a noticeboard and some tables."

"I only took those pictures to show where I'd been and the places that I had access to. I took pictures of rooms here as well, and I took pictures of the Queen Mother sitting down for lunch in the garden don't forget and of William drunk at the Opera House. I could have had a gun, not a camera."

"Yes well," concedes Sir Alastair, "they both can do the same sort of damage in my opinion."

Sir Alastair feels that he could not surely be in a minority to hold this point of view. You shoot a gun, you shoot a camera: both can result in collateral damage.

"It's your fault!" carries on Timothy.

"It was through your negligence I was employed here with false credentials and without checking my references properly. I could have been anybody. I could have been a terrorist and murdered every person in this house right now. I could have planted a bomb or I could have been gaining intelligence for foreign extremists."

"There was absolutely no possibility of you doing any of those things. We knew exactly who you were from the start. We knew you never had a bomb or a weapon at any time. We thought at one point you may have connections to jewel thieves who operated in this way in the past, so we thought we could possibly recover certain stolen items by engaging with you, but obviously that's not the case."

This remark riles Timothy making him jump to his

feet.

"Oh please! You don't really expect me to believe that rubbish and that you knew what I was doing here, do you? I've upset national security single-handedly and you're trying to play it down and pretend that our country is properly protected from terrorism; when really it's not even protected by basic reference checking for basic jobs."

Timothy does believe this wholeheartedly. He had proved it. He found it astonishing that he managed to get an interview with the royal household never mind being offered a job. After all, it was a joke to begin with, just a laugh with his journalist mates in the pub to see what would happen. It could not have been easier he thinks, as he recalls the first interview he had over the telephone. It was actually on the pub's telephone. He had given the personnel department the pub's telephone number and he happened to be in there when they called. He claimed on the application form that he worked there but they never checked it out. After that, he went to London for an interview. He created a false Curriculum Vitae and some references and realised it may well be possible to pull it off or be able to get inside the palace walls at least. Even that would be a good story for his newspaper. The next thing he knew he was in! It was crazy. Although, at every stage and every day, he thought he would be found out by the next look he got from another member of staff or a guest or when he walked into a room, or sometimes he would flinch when somebody entered the room, he thought his time was up. But it never was. That never happened until just now with William. He had loved doing it. It was the best adventure he had ever had, and it would do wonders for his career he thinks. It did go on a bit too long maybe towards the end. Doing this sort of work is so boring, it's not his cup of tea at all. This lot must be mad to work here in this house, waiting for bells to ring all over the place then go running after them everywhere. Tragic. At one point he was wondering if they were ever going to get around to finding him out, and so he would be a flunky forever. But who cares now, he thinks. Me and my paper have tested how ridiculously easy it is to get a job next to royalty and military personnel. What a coup. He was on top of his game, no, on top of the world!

"We've proved how vulnerable our country's security status really is," he fires out the words tapping his finger on the front of the desk to the same beat.

"We've done the nation a favour!"

"Do you really consider this tabloid sensationalism to be an art form Mister Craig, making art out of misery? Why do journalists think themselves so supreme? I can't recall ever hearing of a stunning feat of engineering or a medical breakthrough that was due to investigative journalism. I can only think of it unravelling the crooked machinations of commerce and politics. So I don't know what you think you're doing here? Can't you think of anything constructive to offer your readers? If you really want to be a hero then do something tangible. Go and work in a hospital or help give out food to the homeless under Blackfriars Bridge. If you really cared about people you would find something worthwhile to do."

"We are not aliens!" Timothy shrieks. He is getting very impatient. "You can talk to us you know and we have other stories. The public deserve the right to know what goes on in this country. You cannot gag the press. Free speech is a fundamental right to the people of a free society!"

"In that case I wish you were dead! You deserve to be dead! I wish I had a gun to your head right now and I'd shoot you dead! How's that for exercising my fundamental right to speak freely, huh? Not very wise, is it? Naturally I do not wish you dead at all, that would be ridiculous, but it does demonstrate how futile your argument is as we cannot become hostage to our passing thoughts and anger. If everything was transparent and we all went around saying and doing whatever we think, the world would be in a state of anarchy."

Suddenly Sir Alastair realises that he betrayed his emotions and not wanting to appear vulnerable in any way, checks himself.

Sir Alastair thinks tabloid newspapers are not worthy of delivering yesterday's news never mind today's. Not even that, as it seems to him, they are not worthy of delivering any kind of information because they cannot be trusted. What they publish is not news. News should be pertinent to society. How can what they do be classified and justified as news? As far as he is concerned it really does fall into the category of lurid sensationalism. Unprogressive unintelligent hype. He wishes he had time to convey to Timothy what he thinks on the subject of press intrusion. People like Timothy and perhaps the public too, don't seem to realise the true impact the media has on real lives. Royals are not cartoon characters on television despite constantly appearing on television, they are real people, and the endless intrusion of privacy of royals and celebrities and non-celebrities causes real hurt. It causes hurt through embarrassment by smashing through decency and blowing up respect, bordering on debauchery with its filth and voyeurism, and the demonic relentless pursuit of Princess Diana was sometimes too ridiculous to be believed. It is terrorism. Terrorism!

"Good try Sir Alastair, but I'm more concerned with public interest, I mean, I'll be absolutely fine as I've still got a job, in fact, this is my job, but yours is looking a little shaky at the moment if I may so. What do you say we move this along towards an arrangement that will benefit everybody? It could turn out well for everyone concerned, including you. My company represents fifteen per cent of the news and media output in the world. We have an extensive range of titles and services with a gross turnover of over one billion. We employ over one hundred thousand people including millionaires, celebrities, professional sportspeople, politicians, financiers and businessmen. We are always looking for new voices. What do you say to that then Sir Alastair? How do you fancy contributing to one of our publications? It shouldn't have to take up any more than an hour or two of your time each week and you don't even have to come into the office, unless you want to of course. And it pays, handsomely."

Sir Alastair pauses for a moment before he answers this and thinks, So this is what Timothy has been angling for is it, a deal? Even though it must be one of the most lousy, derisory deals ever offered. He wasn't expecting this. Shocking to think that Timothy's editor must have briefed him and given him the authority to represent the newspaper and to negotiate, as they usually get their legal departments to do that. Especially after the blatantly amateurish way Timothy attempted to manipulate William, however, it occurred to him that if this young upstart had been foolish enough to agree to take part in such an hare-brained scheme in the first place, then the newspaper must be desperate and deserved to face any consequences.

William had seen straight through Timothy early on apparently, but was too vain and conceited to admit it. False friends have always been a burden on William due to the nature of his job, nothing new there. Only when he told the police and they explained to him that they could use this opportunity for possibly locating stolen jewellery that had been purloined in the same way in the past; did he agree to participate in an entrapment.

All these thoughts flash through Sir Alastair's brain in an instant so he loses no time in deciding that this is the right time to play his ace card, delivering the succession of compounded blows swiftly. He had been frantically racking his brain for it and suddenly it just clocked on and made itself available for work. It had come to him at last and he knew it was his best shot. He knew what he was going to say now, but his speech had to be carefully timed to trigger the series of hits perfectly. So, he commences to say the words clearly, in the most matter of fact way, and with perfect timing.

"I could say that you simply left before your probational period was over to take more suitable alternative employment elsewhere," (counting in his head, "one, two, three").

"Or I could say, that the matter is strictly confidential owing to Mister Craig's mental state, (one, two").

"Or, I could say, that you are being questioned about an incident, as jewel thieves have targeted royal residences via staff in this way in the past and succeeded in stealing a number of valuable items."

"Hold on!" protests Timothy, "that's got nothing to do with me. I don't know anything about that egg. William must have dropped it somewhere, he showed it to everyone whenever we went out anywhere."

"I could say you are a bully. Look at the way you taunted William. It's fortunate that the police stepped in when they did before you had totally annihilated any self-confidence poor Mister Tallon has left at the moment due to his personal life. I can choose to say whatever I like. In fact, I've been practicing my little speeches all afternoon. It's great fun, and yes, I do like the sound of my own voice."

"Don't be such a sanctimonious prick. You don't seem to understand who you're dealing with here."

"Or I could say that you are a terrorist, of sorts. You are certainly classed as an undesirable now, a miscreant, a potential threat."

"How dare you!" Timothy says, somewhat shocked.

"I'm not a terrorist."

"That is what the United States Government will see. They take their national security extremely seriously."

[Indeed they do. A US President came over for a State Visit once, and the footman who was detailed to open the president's car door on arrival inside the quadrangle at Buckingham Palace was told not to touch it at all, the president's security staff were going to be the only ones to open the car door!]

"Don't you understand Timothy? You've compromised your own integrity as a citizen of this country, and the United States, if you will. Who's to say exactly what your intentions were? As far as anybody knows, as far as the American Embassy knows, you may have been planning to harm the ambassador or members of his staff that day he came to lunch."

"Why would I want to harm the American Ambassador? He's got nothing to do with it. If I wanted to harm somebody in America I wouldn't bother with a small fry like him I'd go for the big man at the top, I'd go for the president."

"I wouldn't say that if I were you Timothy. You must be forgetting that the President is coming here for tea soon. Were you planning to harm him when he arrived or poison his food perhaps? That would never have happened of course as we were planning to terminate your activities by tomorrow at the latest."

Timothy panics and becomes flustered.

"No you don't understand I didn't mean to say I would want to harm the President of course I wouldn't, I didn't mean that."

"Oh dear," says Sir Alastair, "you're not coming

over terribly well Timothy, in the circumstances."

"I'm just a reporter I'm not a terrorist or a militant or even political, I'm just an ordinary guy, a nobody. I've got nothing to hide."

"Precisely. We know nothing about you, or rather we don't know enough about you. That's the problem because our American friends like to know everything about you, whether it's good or bad. Having a blank sheet against your name is unfortunate. If that's the case then you will be treated as a potential threat. You will have to go through the same process of examination and interrogation as a known criminal or potential terrorist would do. There are no soft options. No mercy."

(This is where the computer takes over. A database can store an infinite amount of information about the population. The authorities rely on this information but there still have to be procedures to manage the system. The life history and digital traces of an individual cannot be summoned up with a few clicks of a mouse. There has to be a sorting system. On an everyday level it's akin to applying for a credit card for the first time. If you have no credit history then it becomes difficult to borrow a large amount if any amount, at first. It doesn't mean you aren't credit worthy. It's purely a risk assessment set up to protect the lender's interests. But in this case Timothy has more than a polite letter of refusal of credit at stake. His liberty is at stake.)

Timothy realises he is on the threshold of disaster if he can't convince Sir Alastair that he is harmless. He now wishes he hadn't been so cocky.

"You must know who I am by now?" he says. "You must have already checked out my passport and driving licence and employment history with the paper?"

"Undoubtedly," says Sir Alastair rather pompously. "We would have also been checking your name against police and military records but even that takes time. Once your D.N.A. is taken they can check it with our national database relatively quickly but if you don't appear on any of our records then we still won't know who you truly are. All those documents you mentioned could be forgeries like the employment records and references you supplied to us."

"But I'm Timothy Craig, ring my paper now they'll vouch for me," pleads Timothy.

"So, after all your deceit and confusion about your identity you now want me to know who you really are, but now you're asking me to simply take your word for it? It won't do Timothy it's too late. You may go in a minute and telephone anyone you wish, but everything else is out of my hands now. I want to warn you that the Americans will want to satisfy their own protocols by making their own enquiries. Due process will follow. As far as I understand it, they will start by making enquiries from people who claim to know you including family, neighbours and colleagues. They'll use facial recognition systems to trace where you've been, but it takes time. It can take months and even years to do a thorough job of it and I doubt very much in your case it will just be a matter of a couple of interviews at the Embassy. I'm afraid they may want to take you into custody."

"You can't do that to me you can't, I've done nothing wrong," protests Timothy.

"Timothy, you walk in here as cool as a cucumber and then proceed to challenge me and everything I stand for. Before you came in, you'd not even taken the opportunity to make a telephone call to your editor to tell them you'd been arrested. Surely they must have a legal team on standby for this eventuality? So I must assume that you want to do all the negotiating by yourself without any advice from lawyers or anyone, you want to be a lone wolf. Well I'm not taking a chance. For all I know you could be anybody or anything."

"But I've not even threatened America or anyone. All I've done is to apply for a job using false credentials," says Timothy, his voice now becoming hoarse with the shock of everything not going his way.

"Exactly. You've committed fraud but your criminal intentions are still unclear to us. So when they get to hear about you, they will most likely investigate you in order to determine if you are a threat. And you will be seen as a security threat, I mean, that was the whole point of this sordid little exercise. Ironic isn't it. Yet I can't see what it is you were trying to prove? I don't need to say anything young man, you are able, and very likely to in my opinion quite frankly, to put yourself into an American prison all by yourself, by your arrogance and by going public with this story and publishing your photos and reporting what you've stolen. I would rather say nothing in order to protect Queen Elizabeth. It would be too upsetting for Her Majesty if all this got out. So you see Timothy, it's your choice. You must decide how much you value your freedom."

Timothy says nothing. His eyes glaze over and he stands motionless, seemingly unable to move his body apart from tipping his head to one side like a farmyard chicken.

"We don't need to do a thing," continues Sir Alastair. "Apart from letting them know of your existence of course, how ever and whenever we choose. They will monitor you for the rest of your life probably, if you carry on like this. You will be tracked. You won't ever be allowed to visit the United States, they won't let you in. Your name and details will be flagged up whenever you use the internet because your emails will be monitored. Our American friends are good at dealing with the seditious element like you. Don't be a fool Timothy. You've got yourself into a terrible mess. You will have a criminal record now. That will effect any future employment. You've sold out for nothing."

Timothy's knees buckle which causes him to fall backwards until his bottom lands on the seat of the chair. He sits there open-mouthed as the reality and gravity of the situation seeps into his brain.

Sir Alastair continues. "Your employers have used you and taken you for a fool and so through your culpability you will never be trusted again. This story could hold the headlines for a while, but after that it will mostly be forgotten, but the system won't forget you, unless you change your ways. The words potential terrorist appearing next to your name on a surveillance report could mean the American government could have you extradited and whisked off to an undisclosed prison somewhere, hooded, handcuffed, in an orange jumpsuit — in shackles! In solitary confinement to be detained and interrogated interminably. You may never see your family and friends for months and the whole thing liable to reporting restrictions! Is that really what you want?"

Timothy is dumbfounded. How can he have been so stupid, he thinks. He remembers the American Ambassador coming to lunch in the garden but at the time he thought nothing of it. He was too engrossed in his plan about Princess Diana. He desperately searches for something, anything to say to combat the vision of turmoil forming in his head but all he can manage to spit out are a few futile words.

"You insidious little shit!"

"Timothy, the police are waiting to question you. Once you leave this room I can't help you any more. I can only advise you to stop playing this silly game. You are classed as a criminal now. Your file will exist long after I'm gone — that's not a threat, that's a fact. My advice to you would be to confess to making a terrible mistake, and to be as contrite as possible, and hope to God that you are speedily delivered back to a normal life."

The colour drains away from Timothy's face. His voice becomes weak and feeble. He utters his last words to Sir Alastair, if only to demonstrate definitively to himself that he is awake, and this is not a bad dream.

"I don't believe this?"

"It is time to go now Timothy. There's nothing more for me to say. Let's hope our paths never cross like this again."

"Thank you Inspector!" Sir Alastair calls out to the waiting protection officer, directing his request towards the doorway.

To which the detective appears and twitches and nods his head slightly to indicate compliance.

Timothy's body quivers as he edges out of the room sideways in incredulity, looking forwards and backwards as he goes, until he meets the restraining grip of the detective who escorts him away.

Now Sir Alastair is alone.

Sir Alastair's job is done.

WOULD YOU LIKE ICE WITH THAT?

Sandringham is a warm, comfortable house, set in an estate in the lovely quiet countryside of Norfolk.

The main part of the house which is open to the public, is decorated in the typical royal style. The building comprises of thickset walls and stout staircases. The rooms are filled with original Victorian and Edwardian items. There are trophies along the walls and chunky gilded picture frames everywhere. The interior is not stuffy or dour or dark, as it would have probably been at some point in the distant past but quite colourful and bright.

Yet Jason thinks there is something unusual about the place, the main house at least. Apart from the daily newspapers and some magazines and I think there must be a television somewhere, the modern world of the last one hundred years seems never to have been allowed to come in. Almost like a perfect film or stage set. It's as if the place was purposely being kept as a tribute to the past.

He noticed that Sandringham looked exactly the same when it was open to the public as it did when the royal family was in residence. Apart from the removal of some trinkets and the raincoats removed from the hall and taking away the wooden jigsaw from the Saloon and the chocolates off the grand piano, the house was like that all the time. The only differences he could tell were the extra mats put down for the visiting public to walk upon and the velvet rope-barriers. Jason felt that he never wanted to work in a museum, which Sandringham was in a way, to him at least. That's what he didn't like about it. It was stuck in the past.

The Queen Mother usually went to Sandringham twice a year. Once for the annual flower show in July for a week when she hosted a private house party there, and in December for the traditional royal family Christmas when The Queen hosted. Whomever is hosting would bring their own staff to run the house for that period. For the visiting staff there wasn't much chance to get out to see the surrounding countryside of Norfolk as the area is quite remote around Sandringham, so it takes time to see places properly, which is a shame. For Jason though, it was the same job but in a different location as he was getting jaded. William was too, as he was growing older and had outrun so many of his colleagues, so he had less and less in common with the younger ones coming through. William had seen the people he'd worked with for years retire and leave one by one, until he was one of the very few left of the old brigade of staff, in London and Norfolk at least except for some members of the Queen Mother's household of course. He could have retired but he probably thought there was no point in doing so especially at this late hour, as it would look like a dereliction of duty or a betrayal of a promise, even now. Even if that promise was made to himself. All his working life had been taken up by his royal service to Queen Elizabeth. He became a stalwart member of her staff, but these later years became monotonous for him. It's not fair to describe him as a tired and confused old man at this point because he was never tired and confused, he was always as sharp as a pin. He was still more than willing and capable to work, and these days Queen Elizabeth's household routines were so well established they ran like clockwork and William knew his job inside out. So the only way he knew how to emphasise his dedication was to be there and to be available and to remain loyal, which he did. But he also still drank to excess sometimes.

Now, it is seventeen months later in early February

2002.

The royal family have spent Christmas at Sandringham House in Norfolk this year, as usual. All the guests have gone home, and The Queen has just left to return to London. Queen Elizabeth has stayed on longer than planned due to a bug she caught at Christmas. She did not return to Royal Lodge in Windsor this year as usual for the customary service for the late King on February the 6th. At this time, she always returned to the royal chapel in the grounds there for the special service but this year it was held inside Sandringham House. She has not attended any church services at Sandringham in recent weeks either. Also, she had to cancel attending a regular meeting in Norfolk with The Women's Institute on the 23rd of January. She is continuing to recover at Sandringham. The Princess Margaret is not well either unfortunately, and has stayed longer than usual at Sandringham but she has now gone back home to London.

Not that much has changed with the household or with the staff. Jason is still here, and Timothy is long gone thankfully. The routine is the same like most people's lives except that Queen Elizabeth has become more frail and so has The Princess Margaret. William is getting older too. Jason still has his work cut out dealing with William more and more these days whenever they travel. He didn't usually come to Sandringham at Christmas, but a queen's footman had recently been offered a fabulous job so has left. This meant that Jason was asked to cover for a while to give Robert a break.

Jason is running around looking all over for William. He's been looking for a few minutes now and he hasn't turned up to be in the usual places with the usual suspects.

"William? William? Queen Elizabeth's asking for

you." He keeps calling as he walks away from the hall down a corridor. He's learned over time to call as loud as he can because the fabric of such a robust house can take it, and it's necessary to be heard. There have been times in the past when he'd walked straight past the room where William was drinking with some friends. William had said,

"I didn't hear you calling me, why didn't you shout?" So Jason has shouted since then. It happens quite often these days.

"Wi-l-liam! Where are you?" He stops walking for a moment trying to think of the next best place to look. "I'm getting fed up of this, where is the silly old sod now? I was going to take the dogs out for a good walk," he says to himself.

Unfortunately, this can happen with William at Sandringham these days. He holds impromptu drinks parties with the older staff members he's known for years, and anyone else who wants. It could be anywhere at Christmas time because The Queen's staff are running the house, so he has nowhere to base himself because he's not in charge of the drinks store. This means if he wants to hold a gathering of his mates then it has to be in a storeroom or bedroom or a broom cupboard almost. He usually holds court in the wine room next to the page's room when Queen Elizabeth is hosting the week in July, as he has custody of the cellar key then. That's the perfect venue because everything needed is already there, bottles line the shelves on the walls. Even if you went in there to collect some ice from the ice machine, you'd be offered a drink. You were obliged to stay and chat with him and to listen, more importantly. Like all drinkers he wouldn't take no for an answer, which is being the biggest bore in the world for a nondrinker regardless of how many funny jokes they know. There's something resembling a sad clown about a heavy drinker. William always managed to cover his duties admirably in those times, and he'd be off like a shot if he was called for.

At Sandringham there is no dedicated bell for Queen Elizabeth's page, she only has a dresser's bell, so William has to rely on her to relay the call down to him via the telephone before she darts off to the Queen, [one refused].

The first time in the day he saw the Queen was usually mid-morning with a tea tray and some digestive biscuits [which the dogs usually got given] but this was not set at an exact time, so he had to wait for the bell to ring first. Any supplementary requests (out of her solid routine) from Queen Elizabeth could be made in person or via the switchboard and sometimes a handwritten note she knew would be found easily. Lately though they were trying out a pager that William had clipped to his waistband. He didn't know how to set it or to clear calls, he was never technical in that regard. He didn't use a mobile phone either. He and Reg had never even learned to drive.

It's a different set-up here in Sandringham. In Clarence House William is stationed in the page's room which is next door to Queen Elizabeth's private suite of rooms. All easily accessible from there, and so is the rest of the house, and so is the rest of London so to speak. In Sandringham the page's room, or page's vestibule as they call it, is well away from the private rooms and bedrooms, it's near the kitchen and dining room and tucked away around a corner with no arterial corridor. Sensible really, as from there the footmen can base their operation to service the whole house. Dressers and valets can pop down the service stairs from their workrooms to the royal bedrooms to do their duties, so they're sorted. However, this does mean that William is stuck in the vestibule for long periods at a time just waiting for the telephone to ring [as it will go unanswered if no other staff happen to be in there] and getting bored by himself, because he is a vivacious person who likes to be with other people except for when he's not drinking. Then, he is quite happy to potter about by wrapping gifts for Queen Elizabeth or writing letters to his friends.

And so, when he's by himself in the page's vestibule his mind tends to turn to the thought of drinking. It's the only sociable thing available to him away from home. [The hours of William's job spanned all day and night. There was nowhere to go when you were off duty especially in Norfolk and Scotland, apart from the staff bar or your own bedroom, so drinking became a substitute for going out] The danger was that William held the cellar key and ordered the alcohol in Queen Elizabeth's household. And so, when he was sitting waiting for long periods, the way the notions of throwing a little impromptu drinking party tug at his elbow and present themselves is always the same, as he would think to himself,

And what does one need for drinking? Alcohol. Well, that's a given. Other people, yes, I can always find somebody around here. Conversation, some jokes to tell, glasses to put the drinks in and somewhere to throw a party.

There is something William's forgotten. Oh yes, ice! he thinks. William can't see the point of it but some people insist; it's very strange!

Jason has to run now as the house is so big. Not as big as the palace but still an extensive building to cover in the shortest possible time. The blue Range Rover is waiting outside the front door with the driver in it and Queen Elizabeth has asked to speak to her page and he's nowhere to be found.

He doesn't realise it but he's still holding one of Queen Elizabeth's famous blue Grenfell raincoats in his hand. There's more than one, and not all the same make as far as he can tell. He was putting it on the radiator to warm when Queen Elizabeth's car suddenly appeared outside the front door then someone gave him the message William was missing. It took him by surprise, so he went running off with it to look for him.

He hears someone whistling as they're coming down the stairs further down the corridor, so he hurries through the double doors ahead and sees Peter a Buckingham Palace footman, who is carrying an old dog bed that he is throwing out. Jason knew he was going back to London later as they both were booked on the same transport. Luckily for Jason Peter is still in his uniform from seeing The Queen off.

"Peter! Can you do me a favour and wait for Queen Elizabeth when she comes out of her room? I'm trying to find William, have you seen him?"

"No, I haven't seen him since breakfast. Has he gone awol again?"

"Yes, I've tried all the usual places but normally he turns up in the right place at the right time at the last minute. He's like a homing pigeon."

"But not lately eh? He's getting worse, why does he do it?"

"He's got nobody to talk to anymore Pete. Don't you remember when Reg was alive William was on the telephone to him every five minutes about something. He's lonely I suppose."

Jason looks around as if still searching.

"But if he helped me with all my trays he wouldn't have time to be lonely."

"That's your own fault," says Peter unsympathetically. "He's getting worse. I don't know how he gets away with it, he's a law unto himself?"

"Well he's been here for so long."

"Yes, but Jason he can't keep using that as an

excuse. He'll shoot himself in the foot one day if he hasn't done so already and all those years of service will count for nothing."

"I know, but what can I do? I've told him about it, but I can only go so far you know, remember he is my boss."

"Well we wouldn't cover for our boss like that. After all, we've all got a job to do. I don't know how your Queen puts up with it."

"Who could replace William now if he left? It's a classic case of better the devil you know."

Peter doesn't look convinced in the least. He's heard all this before from Jason. The palace staff would never get away with the sort of antics William gets up to. They have a laugh, but they don't go overboard with it. The staff bar is closing down there too. It would seem times are changing, and people make their own arrangements for entertainment these days. Everyone can please themselves.

"I do my best generally," says Jason, his eyes looking all around as he talks to Peter. "But even I've had enough of him lately. I just want this morning over as I leave today then I'm out of here on holiday and Robert is coming back to take over."

"Robert? Why is Robert coming? Aren't you all going back today? I thought you usually went back by now."

"Yes we do Pete, but Queen Elizabeth is staying on until she feels stronger and to try to fend off that cold."

"What's William doing then, isn't he going back with you?"

"No. I think he wants to stay here to look after her."

"Well I can't see what use he'll be. This must be one of the few times Queen Elizabeth truly needs him and he's always tipsy. Tell him he'd better be careful, or he might find himself being sent back to London with his tail between his legs with the way he's behaving lately."

"Our set-up is different to yours Peter. William isn't just

a page like yours. We don't have all different staff like you. We don't even have porters moving furniture and a workers union like you, so if our queen wants something we do it. Your lot wouldn't even bother setting up lunch by the front door here to catch the sun like we do in the summer. That's the difference."

"Our queen wouldn't ask."

"Your queen's too polite to ask."

"Our queen is amazing!"

"I realise that. I'm just saying as far as I'm concerned, if you're looking for the queen of modern times, our queen wrote the book!"

"It's the same family you muppet!"

(Buckingham Palace is different to Queen Elizabeth's house it's true. It's considered a national palace and a symbol of the country, considered to be more so than St. James's Palace or the Palace of Westminster and also, it's a government building run on government lines of business. Clarence House is also a private home for Queen Elizabeth so rules and regulations aren't so strictly adhered to like at the palace.)

[I caused a stir once when I worked an extra night at Windsor Castle at a private royal birthday buffet. I was about to light some candles as I saw the Corgis and The Queen were entering the room, but was stopped by a footman who told me, "That's a porter's job and the union won't like you doing it." So I had to blow out the candles before anyone saw. I couldn't believe it. On reflection it does make sense for such a large workforce to have a union but it's a shame if that takes away the personal touches a person can bring to their occupation]

Jason can't delay any longer as the Queen is waiting, and he needs to bring William to her. He begins to walk away but suddenly remembers something and doubles back to Peter.

"I know what I wanted to ask you Peter. Were you here the week before Christmas when Queen Elizabeth gave William that note at the dinner table?"

"No I wasn't. What's that all about?"

"Well I don't know if it's true because I wasn't here either, but I heard that he was helping to serve dinner one night, when he walked all the way around the table and presented Lord Snaresbrook with a handwritten note from Queen Elizabeth?"

"What did it say?"

"Please leave the room as you've had too much to drink."

"Oh my God! To Lord Snaresbrook? What did he say?"

"I think he looked a bit confused and passed it off as a silly joke or something, unless he realised it was meant for William."

"Was it meant for William though?" asks Peter, who is already working out in his head who he can ask when he gets back to London, and who to tell.

"Well that's what I'm trying to find out even though it's not Queen Elizabeth's style, but I don't really care if it was true or not as either way it makes a terrific story, but I really want it to be true."

Jason squeezes his fists with glee to think it could be true, only because it's such a camp story; no other reason whatsoever.

"If the papers got hold of some of these stories, they'd have a field day," says Peter.

"Tell me."

"Whatever happened to that reporter, what's his name?"

"You mean Timothy Craig." (Jason knew his name well enough.) "Nothing. Nothing happened to him. He's still a reporter as far as I know but who cares? He made us all look stupid."

"True."

"Anyway I must go," says Jason, heading off, "as I've got to keep looking as the Queen wants to see William. I think it's something about seeing the horses. I don't know where he is, and he never answers that bloody pager!"

"Queen Elizabeth's going out to see the horses? In this weather? With a cold?"

"Pete, this is Queen Elizabeth we're talking about here."

"Point taken. If I see William, I'll tell him and I'll go upstairs now and wait for you."

"Thanks."

Jason rushes off down the corridor that leads to the dining room and around the corner to pop his head round the door of the page's vestibule, just in case William is there. He knows he won't be there of course, but he has to look even though there's so much ground to cover in a short time. That's why he has to run. Now that The Queen's staff have left, William and he have it to themselves, so he may be there with some permanent staff. Jason runs into the vestibule but it's empty so William is obviously somewhere else. Sandringham is a long sprawling house with nooks and crannies everywhere.

I'm just going to check down here then that's it, Jason thinks to himself,

I'll go back to the Queen if he's not there. I'm not going up to the staff floors to check; he can forget it!

The staff rooms are on different floors and in a maze of higgledy-piggledy rooms where you could easily get lost. William could be anywhere. [The arrangement of rooms was like something out of Harry Potter]

He is shouting out intermittently as he runs.

"William? William?"

No luck, so he runs on, past a kitchen entrance through a porch on his way outside to the staff bar and hears somebody laughing coming from behind one of the doors. He has to skid to stop and turn around. He goes straight in. He comes across William who is holding court with some fellow drinkers in a sort of workshop storeroom. They are surrounding him like a group of disciples sitting at the feet of their leader, or a bunch of students hanging on to every word of their professor. William is in full swing and it's obvious to Jason he's in the middle of an anecdote; a dogs one.

"That reminds me of the time Her Majesty had two new Corgi puppies," says William, who sees Jason come in but just glances over for a second as he knows he will wait until he's finished the anecdote, and so he continues reciting it without missing a beat.

"She was getting ready to leave for a banquet over the road at Buckingham Palace. The car was waiting at the door and she said,

I'm a little perplexed.

Oh, but I have your fur your majesty I said.

No, no, I don't mean that, she said, I can't find the dorgs!

They were so small she didn't notice them under her crinolines." William shrieks with laughter, obviously finding this story as funny as the first day he told it.

"William?" says Jason angrily, "the Queen wants to see you, I think she wants to go and see the horses. That's the Queen's ice bucket!" he yells, and points in the corner to a china ice bucket on the side that he's also been running around the house trying to find. "I've been looking everywhere for that!" He seizes it from the side and thrusts it under his arm like a crazed warrior would take a trophy from the burning battlefield.

William glances over but still concentrates on his little audience of friends. Jason waits patiently, knowingly, as he's heard it all before so there's no point rushing William. He'll only come when he's ready these days. Jason looks inside the ice bucket while William is finishing his story. (Don't know why. It's a similar thing to lifting a teapot lid in a restaurant when the waiter brings it to your table.)

"Now, have you got a drink?" William asks his friend as he moves into the last leg of his show. "Have you got a drink?" he asks another, checking that everybody in his audience is 'well oiled'. "Very well, I must just tell you this before I go. The switchboard put through a call from a friend of mine recently who said to me,

Now before I start Billy, I want to get something off my chest. I can't stand it any longer.

So I said whatever is the matter? And he said,

I think the operators are listening in to our calls, so I said,

Oh, surely not, and he said,

No, no, I'm convinced! Anyway there was no pacifying him as he was so wound up about it. So we had our conversation and the call ended, and later on the operator put through another call to me. She told me who it was and everything, and before she connected me she said,

By the way William, you can tell your friend that we don't listen in to calls!"

William claps his hands once and shrieks with laughter again, finding this story even funnier than the last time he must have told it, apparently. He gets up from his chair and the people clear the glasses and bottles then disperse quickly and disappear to wherever and to whatever they were doing before. William and Jason start walking back together towards the hall.

"I was going to bring the ice bucket back," says William by way of an apology.

"Where have you been? Why didn't you answer your pager? You didn't click the button back again did you? You said you knew how to do it now, it won't bleep unless you push the button back every time it goes off. They think you're ignoring it. Give it here let me show you how to reset it again."

Jason snatches the electronic pager from William's waistband.

"I thought I did, wretched thing!" says William.

"Look William, you must make sure it's receiving if Queen Elizabeth wants to be able to contact you, so you must learn how it works."

"Oh never mind that now, where is the Queen?"

"There was a time when you used to tell me off for disappearing in this house without saying where I was going. Even popping to the loo in this great country pile is like going on a jungle expedition. It's not C.H. you know!"

"I'm well aware of it. I've been coming here for years. I didn't ask to wear this blasted thing. Why doesn't anyone use the telephone anymore?"

"Well that's the point, they would use the telephone if they knew where you are. This is giving you a false sense of security and I can't keep thinking up excuses to Queen Elizabeth, who is getting fed up with this by the way I'm certain of it."

Jason clicks the pager gadget and hands it back.

"You'd better be careful. I go on holiday today don't forget Robert takes over, he won't cover for you. So when he goes searching for you and he can't find you, he'll probably tell the Queen you're still in bed or lying in a ditch or something."

"Oh surely not, Robert wouldn't ever say that?"

"Hello! Do you really think we like running all over this great big house searching for you and your little drinking parties all the time? I've been coming here for fifteen years and I still get lost in the staff corridors sometimes, and I didn't even know those furniture workshops EXISTED until last Tuesday, when I was passing by and could hear all that cackling seeping out from your little gathering on my way to the staff bar, which, incidentally, they are talking of closing due to all the drinking going on whilst on duty."

"We have always had a staff bar, always. A little drink on duty never hurt anybody," pleads William, who knows that Jason is saying all the right things, and like all heavy drinkers he won't believe a word of it.

"Well if that were the case and you drank in the staff bar that would be easy, as I'd know where to find you and I'd go straight there and collect you from your port and lemon. But you can end up with a bottle of whisky anywhere in this place even outside somewhere. And I'd appreciate it if you didn't use the Queen's ice bucket in future because she thought I'd lost it."

"Well I had to take an ice bucket with me, it was the only one I could find at the time. You can't throw a drinks party without ice, it's unnatural. And I was the one who made them get that ice machine in the first place, so I thought I'd better use it."

"But William, you don't do ice, and anyway, most people fill the glass with ice before they pour the booze, not the other way around!"

"One should always be well prepared, for any eventuality!" William chuckles. He's never far from a laugh wherever it may be. He had no intention of using the ice. He may have taken it along just for a laugh.

"I don't know why I bother?" says Jason who is

totally exasperated with it all now.

"I can look after myself!" snaps William. "Where is Queen Elizabeth at the moment?"

"Probably waiting in the hall for you by now, if she hasn't already left, it's been ages."

"You have got some carrots for the horses?"

"Yes of course!"

"And you did put the raincoat to warm on the radiator?"

Jason thinks for a second then realises the raincoat is in his hand. He glances at William with an apologetic look, but William just tuts.

"Where did you say I was?" asks William.

"Oh, I said that you were trying to seduce the grooms in the stables then going on to have a drinking competition with the soldiers."

William stops in his tracks. He is stunned. He pulls at Jason's elbow to swing him around to face him.

"You didn't say that?"

"No of course not! I said that you were talking to chef about menus."

"Oh well done!" says William totally relieved. They carry on walking.

"But I rather think the first explanation would have been more fun!"

William shrieks with laughter and slaps Jason across the shoulder. Jason clutches his shoulder in pain.

"Ow! Will you stop doing that, that hurts!" he yells, trying to rub his shoulder with the same hand he's carrying the raincoat with.

"Nonsense! I only tapped you."

"Well I'll tap you in a minute then and see how you like it?"

"Oh do shut up!"

"Shut up yourself."

"Do you ever shut up? You're like a London Sparrow."

They keep walking along and William stops at a large wooden chest against the wall in the corridor.

"Have a look in this chest, see if there's a nice rug we can use for Queen Elizabeth's knees in the car." [If they find a nice one then he can use it as an excuse for being absent from his post]

Jason gets a better grip on the ice bucket; he wasn't letting go of it now, and passes the raincoat to William. Then he struggles to open the heavy lid with one hand and takes out a folded woollen rug.

"No! not that one." William yells so sharply that it gives Jason a fright. "You must never use that one!"

"Why not?"

"Because that one was given as a Christmas present to The Queen from Mrs. Blair!"

William seizes the rug and examines it, handing the raincoat back to Jason.

"Oh, but it's good quality," he says, unfolding it and giving it a shake. "Feel that. No rubbish," he says as he rubs it against his cheek to feel the softness of it.

"Ooh, it's gorgeous. No label. Must be hand-made."

He takes a final look over it and declares his verdict,

"Oh, but it's beautiful. Absolutely exquisite. I simply must use it for Queen Elizabeth!"

He bundles up the rug in his arms and sweeps away with it down the corridor leaving Jason flustered while trying to close the chest lid and to follow him. William goes ahead but stops and turns around to call for Jason.

"Well come along, hurry up! Goodness me, how on earth do you ever get anything done? You're like a fart in a box!"

Jason manages to close the lid without dropping anything and trots along to catch up with him. Then they carry on walking together.

"Do you mind?" he says. (Even his timing is terrible never mind his material.)

"Oh shut up."

"No, I won't actually."

Jason has found his voice at last, of sorts anyway, well, it's a start.

"I sometimes wonder what it is I've done to deserve you?" says William, as he holds the swing doors open for Jason to get through.

Ironically Jason is thinking the same thing about William. William hurries off ahead again, and they go to find the Queen.

REQUIESCAT IN PACE, HER ROYAL HIGHNESS THE PRINCESS MARGARET

It is the next day on February the 9th 2002. The Queen is now in London. William has also returned to London. He may have been due to go back there after finishing his scheduled working period at Sandringham on February the 8th when some other members of Queen Elizabeth's staff took over, or he may have wanted to stay on to support Queen Elizabeth but was sent back, this particular point is not clear.

He would have been able to go back to his gate lodge or his Kennington flat, but there was no one else living at either place bar himself. Reg wasn't there anymore. William and Reg had worked together and lived together for years. Reg used to keep his flat in Kennington and William was based in the lodge during the working week. They spent their weekends together in the Kennington flat. The gate lodge went with William's live-in job and Reg had a bedroom at Clarence House that went with his live-in job. The Kennington flat was privately rented by Reg, which he had had for years, since he took it on to look after his elderly ailing father. It was reported once as being a grotty little housing association flat in South London. The fact is that it's not a grotty little flat. And the housing association referred to must be the Duchy of Cornwall because that was the owner and landlord when William retired. It's the kind of flat a young professional couple would aspire to who want to live in the middle of London. A nice little two bedroom ground floor flat. One of the bedrooms Reg turned into a dining room. French doors lead out to a tiny private garden, which is a much sought-after luxury in the middle of London. Such a place would be anyone's own little private oasis, and it was theirs, until Queen Elizabeth died then it was private no more.

The gate lodge where William lived was situated along the garden wall of Clarence House along The Mall. It's a perimeter wall of St. James's Palace and it's where masses of flowers were left when Princess Diana died. Then the majority of tributes were left outside her home Kensington Palace, but the public left flowers and tributes at all royal residences in London as a sign of their respect and their sorrow. It was a sad, humbling, poignant scene to see this on television never mind see it in person. And sadly, these scenes were about to be repeated.

Millions of people who had never met Princess Diana expressed an intense outpouring of emotion when she died. They weren't necessarily grieving for the person as they didn't know her, but perhaps for the human qualities she represented as a person. And of course, for the fact that she was killed with two other people in a terrible car crash while being chased. Everyone knew she was kind and thoughtful. She showed us altruism and compassion. These are qualities we already know but she was in a unique position to broadcast the value of them all over the world. It has been suggested that she was locked forever in a gilded cage, so it was an easy choice for her to take on such a charitable crusade. Not necessarily, as she could have easily chosen to do nothing more than play tennis all day and get photographed coming of fancy restaurants at night like a lot of privileged people do. She was already being photographed whatever she did, so she used her celebrity to put charities and issues in the same spotlight as herself. By doing this she did help, and she did make a difference for the better despite whatever reasons there may have been, she did do it. She was out there. But her fame was also her downfall. I suppose she showed us what we should be doing to help each other by drawing attention to the shortcomings and problems of the world.

The problem ordinary people have with helping the rest of the world is that our governments have different ideas, and business, war and religion get in the way.

Flowers are being left outside Kensington Palace again now but this time for Her Royal Highness, The Princess Margaret who lived there. News bulletins everywhere are broadcasting the sad news that Her Royal Highness, The Princess Margaret has died following a stroke, aged seventy-one. She'd been unwell for a long time and she died peacefully at six-thirty a.m. at the King Edward VII hospital. Her children Lord Linley and Lady Sarah Chatto were with her at the London hospital. Messages of condolence came from all over the world, including many tributes from politicians and the UK Prime Minister Tony Blair, who said that she would be remembered with a lot of affection as she had given a great deal of service to the country. The Archbishop of Canterbury, Doctor George Carey said, "She was a much-loved member of our royal family and a great support to Her Majesty throughout The Queen's reign." Several foreign leaders including Irish Prime Minister Bertie Ahern sent their condolences to The Queen, as did the Pope in a telegram and Don McKinnon, the Secretary-General of the Commonwealth.

People were leaving flowers in memory of The Princess Margaret against the garden wall of Clarence House and St. James's Palace, too, just along from where William lived at gate lodge. It can be imagined that they left them there with the thought of Queen Elizabeth losing her daughter. For a lot of people it brought back sad feelings and thoughts of when they were left there for Princess Diana.

The funeral of The Princess Margaret is to be held on Friday the 15th of February at St. George's Chapel, Windsor Castle in only six days time, but Queen Elizabeth is still considered too frail to make the long car journey from Sandringham. The journey would take three hours by car or one hour by helicopter. Usually Queen Elizabeth would have left Sandringham by now to be at Royal Lodge for the service for the late King in the royal chapel on February the 6th. Her Majesty would have normally been in London and Windsor at this time of year. Another news bulletin was broadcast a few days later;

'The Queen Mother is determined to attend the funeral of her daughter Princess Margaret on Friday, despite her frail health and recently taking a fall and injuring her arm. She is still at Sandringham in Norfolk where she is recovering from a severe cold. A decision won't be taken until the last minute but it is thought that she will make every determined effort to summon the strength to take the hour-long helicopter journey from Norfolk to Windsor, to pay her last respects.'

An hour in a helicopter is a long and intense journey. It's the lesser of two evils to be endured if you are injured and in pain like Queen Elizabeth must have been. It would cut away two hours from the car journey from Sandringham to Windsor but it's not as comfortable as a car can be. For one thing, the passengers in a helicopter should wear headphones to be able to communicate with the pilot and the other passengers as the engine and rotor blades make so much noise. It depends on the type of helicopter. If you don't like flying then being wired up to the thing and looking through large windows feels like you are flying it. It's nothing like an airplane as some airplanes are quieter than going by train, and you can't see out the windows that well on a airplane so it's not as alarming. It is not as comfortable as being driven in the back of a Daimler. No, the best way to experience helicopters is on a short flight over a resort, holding someone's hand; preferably not the pilot's!

Following the news of the death of The Princess Margaret, The Queen is to travel to Windsor. Prince Charles is travelling to Sandringham to support his grandmother and will join Prince Philip who is already there. The funeral will not be a state occasion and a memorial service will be held at a later date. The Princess Margaret's ashes will be laid next to the remains of her beloved father, King George VI, in St George's Chapel. The princess's decision to be cremated is believed to have been influenced by the fact that there is no more room for normal burial in the chapel's royal crypt. It was reported in 'The Scotsman' newspaper that Lady Glenconner, a life-long friend said that the late princess had not wanted to end up at Frogmore in Windsor Great Park, where Queen Victoria and Prince Albert are buried. Instead, she preferred the royal crypt at St. George's Chapel in the grounds of Windsor Castle, where her father King George VI is buried. "She told me that she found Frogmore very gloomy," said Lady Glenconner, a former lady in waiting to the princess. "I think she'd like to be with the late King, which she will now be. There's room I think for her to be with him now. She just said she was going to be cremated. I think she wanted her family and her friends at her funeral. Obviously, later on there will be a memorial service when her charities will be represented, but for her actual funeral she wanted it to be as private as possible."

A cremation is a break with royal tradition, but it is the only way for the princess to be laid to rest in the crypt with her father the King because there is no more allocated space in there.

Her Majesty, Queen Elizabeth did make the hour-long helicopter journey from Norfolk to Windsor, and she attended the funeral of her daughter The Princess Margaret at St. George's Chapel on Friday February the 15th 2002. Her Majesty then went to Royal Lodge.

She fulfilled her usual diary obligations after that in March of a lawn meet and lunch for the Eton Beagles and a party at Royal Lodge for the Grand Military race meeting, but she did not attend Cheltenham Races that year as per usual. Queen Elizabeth was one hundred and one.

REQUIESCAT IN PACE, HER MAJESTY, QUEEN ELIZABETH THE QUEEN MOTHER

On a Saturday afternoon exactly seven weeks after the death of The Princess Margaret, yet another momentous news bulletin was broadcast on television. A presenter's voice said,

"It is Saturday March the thirtieth, two thousand and two. Now on BBC one, a special BBC news, with Peter Sissons." And then a newscaster appeared on the screen and he said,

"Good evening. Her Majesty, Queen Elizabeth The Queen Mother has died in her one hundred and second year. She died at Windsor at three fifteen this afternoon. Buckingham Palace said the end was peaceful and The Queen was at her side. Members of the royal family are arriving at Windsor tonight. Prince Charles, who says he's devastated, and the Princes William and Harry will return from their skiing holiday in Switzerland tomorrow. The Prime Minister has led the nation's tributes. She was, he said, admired by all people of all ages and backgrounds. Revered within our borders and beyond. She symbolised Britain's decency and courage."

This news was not expected by the public, (or by us). Only three weeks ago Her Majesty had hosted the usual Eton Beagles lawn meet and lunch at Royal Lodge. That weekend, at the Grand Military race party The Queen was going to step in for her, but she made an appearance at the last minute. She made the effort to stand up periodically to greet her very many guests as they were presented to her one by one, and I saw that the line of people trailed out of the saloon to the hall. This was what usually happened every year at Royal

Lodge, so there was no reason for anyone to believe things would change.

William could not have been listening to the radio or watching television when the news was being broadcast because he didn't know about it. Someone from the press telephoned to his home seconds after the news broke wanting a reaction from him, and that was the first he heard about it. He was entertaining a friend at the time so she and he were understandably shocked. The second person to telephone him just after that was me, when I saw the television news. Nobody from the royal household called him.

William had not been on duty to serve Queen Elizabeth since he left Sandringham as she didn't return to Clarence House in London, she went straight to Royal Lodge in Windsor Great Park, where she stayed. William didn't work there as it was fully staffed, so he had been kicking his heels all that time.

Sometime later William is walking along The Mall footpath outside the garden wall going towards gate lodge. He may have been looking at the floral tributes or he may have been on his way back from the flat or the shops as he's wearing casual clothes and he's carrying a small bag. He is waylaid by a camera crew who happen to be filming the scene. A reporter is doing a piece to camera when a colleague alerts his attention to William approaching, about to walk past through the shot.

"Mister Tallon," says the reporter approaching him as he walks past, "your reaction please, how will you remember Queen Elizabeth?" And William stops, and the reporter positions the microphone in front of him. William is caught unawares, but the reporter is polite and did not chase him because he was walking by, so he gives a quick response but it's obvious it's only going to be a brief reply as he wants to get away. He appears to hesitate at the start of his sentence.

Perhaps he was trying to be guarded in what he said but he appears sincere on the film, if a little subdued, which is understandable in the circumstances.

"Most of wonderful employer," he says, a little breathlessly and emotionally, "very compassionate. Incredibly kind. Very understanding. And I loved her. So sorry, thank you. Very much." And he strides off and rushes away towards the gate lodge. He can't get away quick enough, but you can tell he doesn't want to be rude. That was the only interview ever captured of William properly talking about Queen Elizabeth.

On Tuesday the 2nd of April the Queen Mother's coffin was driven from Windsor to the Queen's Chapel at St. James's Palace, where her family, friends and household were able to pay their respects in private.

On Friday the 5th of April it was placed on a horse-drawn gun carriage to be carried to lie-in-state in Westminster Hall. It was draped in her personal standard and on it lay her diamond encrusted crown from her Coronation in 1937 with its infamous Koh-i-noor diamond set in the Maltese Cross at the front. The coffin was carried from the chapel in procession along The Mall and across Horse Guards Parade and then on towards Westminster Hall with members of the royal family walking immediately behind, followed by some members of the Queen Mother's personal staff including William.

At Westminster Hall it was placed high on a purple-draped catafalque on the same spot where King George VI lay-in-state in February 1952, and was guarded round-the-clock.

Her Majesty would lie-in-state from Friday until Monday. The funeral was on Tuesday at Westminster Abbey.

Thousands of people queued outside in the cold

for up to seven hours so they could pay their respects. Large crowds were expected to file past the coffin but the officials at Westminster Hall anticipated closing the doors on the first day at 6pm. Also, it was rumoured that 10 Downing Street was worried that not many people would turn out on a cold April day but the numbers that did turn out over the next few days was unprecedented. It transpired that an official at Westminster Hall took the decision to keep the doors open all through the night in order to keep the flow of people moving.

People came from all over. Some missed work, some travelled from all over the country and from abroad. They came because it was important to them. It was the end of an era. A woman in the queue said it was the only thing that anyone could do and it was such a small thing to do but it meant so much.

Perhaps they were saying farewell to Queen Elizabeth as well as saying goodbye to a bygone age that she represented to them. An age where people had peace to enjoy their lives away from the relentless forces of modern life. A modern life where we have to pay to stop, pay to go and pay to stand still. And people wonder why the British don't smile that much?

The Queen broadcast a personal message on the television thanking everyone who had waited to pay their respect and sent their condolences and comforting words and messages.

I can truly say that during this period I must have been in a sort of limbo, if not shock. It was unexpected and surreal. I wanted to suggest we staff go along the queues of people waiting to go through Westminster Hall throughout the night, handing out hot drinks and chocolate, whatever, but I never did regretfully. It would have been a good thing to do, a good memory.

William wore a large sprig of rosemary as a sign of

remembrance beside his medals at the funeral. Clarence House staff travelled to Westminster Abbey on two coaches under police motorcycle escort through the closed-off streets around Buckingham Palace and Birdcage Walk. There were people standing behind barriers everywhere. The staff made their way straight off the coaches into the Abbey having to walk past hundreds of the public crammed behind barriers near the entrance.

Arriving in the midst of all those onlookers like that was a weird unpleasant feeling, having all those eyes trained on you. A stifling feeling, like being closed in, albeit being on display, as though one's life was being controlled by an unseen hand and one's liberty was taken away. A tiny insight of how it feels to be royal perhaps?

After the Queen died William kept a low profile. His voice was hardly ever heard in the house. It did go quiet for a time. He would come into Clarence House but he was very reserved and seemed to make no demands on anyone for anything apart from getting a few shirts washed and ironed as a favour, or for lunch or to collect some sandwiches from the kitchen. He didn't seem concerned or interested with anything else that was going on, he was very subdued. Almost as if living day-to-day, like us all at that time.

When the Queen had gone, we were practically left to our own devices and the whole scene became disjointed. The feeling can be likened to a train stoppage or a massive luggage system breakdown at a major airport where no announcements are made, and the information display boards only ever show 'delayed'. No reassurance or useful information is forthcoming. Some staff members left straightaway and some went around in a daze not knowing what to do for the best.

Generally all this time raced by in a blur of pageantry and a sporadic stream of black mourning letterheads and memos. It started from when The Princess Margaret died.

Some duties in the house still had to be completed as some household members and officials had to be served and accommodated occasionally while carrying out their duties. It was a strange feeling of limbo. It seemed very odd to be laying up a table or a room in the same way we always had done. There seemed little point to it without Queen Elizabeth being there. A Memorial Service for The Princess Margaret was held at Westminster Abbey on April the 19th.

Queen Elizabeth's homes and staff were instructed to wind-down in the intervening weeks but not a lot could be done, as Clarence House and Royal Lodge were in dire need of updating and refurbishing after years of postponing the work, because Queen Elizabeth was not expected to live to a great age.

So, they would have to be emptied and then the buildings stripped back and redone.

All of us were made redundant and nearly all of us were given notice to quit our accommodation, including William of course. Later on, a few staff would take up jobs at Buckingham Palace, but it was difficult for some to adjust from the moderate, unique private set-up of Queen Elizabeth to the larger, more impersonal, expansive corporate set-up of the palace. Eventually, Clarence House staff all went our separate ways, although it took a while for some of us to secure another position and somewhere else to live.

Meanwhile, a letter was sent to the staff of Clarence House and at the end of it was an invitation to a farewell party at the house on Thursday the 2nd of May at 6.30pm, which lifted our spirits a little. After a day or so, no news or details of a catering company was forthcoming about the party so a few of us enquired, to find out that nothing of that sort had been booked and no other arrangements were discussed.

The person who invited everyone must have given no thought as to who was going to do the work and set up this farewell party. He must have thought it would appear as if by magic. Well, in this particular case the only people who were able to set it up were us. And it couldn't have been a breakdown in communication because nothing was mentioned about preparations in the individually named two paged letters he sent out. So in effect we were invited to a party that we had to organise ourselves!

This person didn't work at Clarence House. He appeared from the high echelons of the hierarchy in the palace system. The initial compliment of being invited to a party soon gave way to disappointment for the housemaids and kitchen staff and footmen at Clarence House who had to do it all as invited guests. They did it for everyone else really as it felt pointless otherwise, but with the house on wind-down they had very limited resources available, so it wasn't a very good show. William didn't attend.

Things don't happen by magic. They happen by work and people should not be taken for granted like that. Having faith in people is a much better idea and value than having blind faith in a bureaucratic system — whoever you are.

THE 50TH JUBILEE FLYPAST

The Annus Horribilis of 1992 must have cast its shadow on 2002 for The Queen for the sad reasons that Her Majesty lost her sister and her mother within the space of seven weeks. This year was also the fiftieth anniversary of The Queen's accession to the throne. It was The Queen's Golden Jubilee, just eight weeks on from the funeral of Queen Elizabeth.

Preparations for such a historic occasion were planned well in advance and so the details of the catalogue of events were already in place. The 50th Jubilee celebrations were to go ahead regardless. Nothing could be allowed to disrupt them. There were official Jubilee visits planned for The Queen to visit Jamaica, Australia and New Zealand for a period starting from the 18th of February, just three days after the funeral of The Princess Margaret.

The Queen's diary is so extensive that dates have to be organised months in advance and even years in advance, there is no changing plans or rescheduling where international plans are concerned. We all know Her Majesty never declines to attend anything for personal reasons, except illness of course. It's not like an ordinary person being able to get out of an obligation if they feel they shouldn't do it for whatever reason. That's not to say that ordinary people have easier lives because of course they do not. Life is hard for many people in the UK, many of them the working poor despite this nation being called a rich country. (Rich in oppressive market forces perhaps, yes.) Life goes on for them all whether or not they have the means or the mind to cope, unfortunately. Pageantry and the royal family are not to everyone's liking. The point is that The Queen is committed to duty and we can't expect any more commitment from our Queen. We all know this.

Her Majesty flew abroad and carried out the Jubilee visits to Jamaica, Australia and New Zealand. When she was abroad she telephoned her mother Queen Elizabeth every day at Royal Lodge. The Queen returned on March the 3rd and went straight from the airport to Royal Lodge to see her.

The whole of the UK was celebrating in some way and The Queen had a packed diary of commitments that took Her Majesty and Prince Philip all over the country meeting people and visiting places. The weekend from Saturday the 1st of June was the culmination of the 50th Jubilee Celebrations, with a classical concert in the garden of Buckingham Palace on Saturday, Jubilee Church services throughout the UK on Sunday, a pop concert in the garden again on Monday and beacons being lit throughout the UK and Commonwealth. On Tuesday the 4th of June the pinnacle of the celebrations happened. There was a procession in the Gold State Coach to St. Paul's Cathedral for a National Service of Thanksgiving. A luncheon at Guildhall, and the Golden Jubilee Festival in The Mall in the afternoon. The finale was a flypast that included twenty-seven aircraft from the Royal Air Force and a Concorde from British Airways that flew down The Mall then over Buckingham Palace at a height of 1,500ft and at a speed of 280 Knots. It was headed by a C-17 Globemaster, then a TriStar with two Tornado GA4s, a Nimrod with two Canberras, and others. A Concorde and the Red Arrows were the last to appear.

Some Clarence House staff went on the roof to watch and listen and experience the aircraft flying over as they would be flying directly overhead. Seeing the flypast and seeing a Concorde in formation with the

Red Arrows and their famous red white and blue vapour trails as they all flew over the horizon was a thrilling and noisy experience. For some of us, it was quite a poignant experience being in the middle of all that celebration and not knowing what the future held for us, with the prospect of being jobless and homeless. William wasn't prominent in the crowd if indeed he was there at all, I didn't notice him there but, he probably wouldn't have gone on the roof as it was a bit tricky to access it. He may have been entertaining some friends at his gate lodge as it's a perfect position on The Mall to see a flypast, especially if he popped into Clarence House garden to watch it.

Some people may think they will never meet The Queen as to them she is only another type of celebrity or dream figure they see on television and in the press. This is a shame because they stand a good chance of seeing her if they take a timely trip to the capital city. For a lot of people she is such a distant figure that she's not real to them and will not become real until they see her with their own eyes. For so many of the population she has been a constant presence on the landscape of our lives as we all grew up with her being there. The Queen has been constant herself too. Constantly reliable and constantly dutiful but probably unknowingly constant in another way. If you ever meet The Queen, and she looks at you, and she gives you one of her special smiles. I guarantee it will lift your heart, and it will stay with you always. So if you ever happen to overhear somebody in a café or on the tube say, "The Queen smiled at me today." Don't dismiss it out of hand at all, thinking they are being condescending because they're not. They are simply describing a unique experience. And now you'll know what they're talking about: The Queen has the most amazing smile.

BBC Television reporter Jennie Bond summed up the day's celebrations beautifully in her description of it:

"A spectacular flypast and the sound of a million people

joining a patriotic singalong have brought the final days of the Golden Jubilee celebrations to a close on this glorious June day in London. The Queen and senior members of the royal family watched from a balcony at Buckingham Palace as twenty-seven planes, ending with Concorde accompanied by the Red Arrows, flew above The Mall. It was a sight to behold, and everyone's eyes were skyward. So they went across, straight over the palace. It was a major tribute, and a unique tribute to The Queen and to all the royal family, who were standing on the balcony and watching this amazing tribute. It was a sight. Up into the sky it went. And no one could say a word while it was going overhead, the sound was absolutely piercing. And The Queen, really enjoyed it."

THE LITTLE HOUSE ON THE MALL

William moved out of gate lodge in 2002 when Queen Elizabeth died, like the other staff had to vacate their rooms or flats or cottages as the accommodation went with the job. He then moved into his Kennington flat permanently.

It is now 2007, five years later.

William pays his respects and says goodbye to the Prince after they have taken tea together at Clarence House. He has been thinking about visiting his old gate lodge all afternoon. He intends to get the driver to let him out the car for a minute on the way home. Nobody would see on a overcast autumn afternoon like this. He won't tell the driver until he gets in the car though, as it's best to spring these things onto people, rather than pre-warn them of one's intentions, he thinks. Otherwise it gives people a chance to think up excuses.

He has been thinking about the gate lodge a lot lately. He's never noticed a light on in there whenever he's been driven past in a taxi or a friend's car. Perhaps the occupier was always out? he thinks. He wondered if somebody was living there now, a gardener or gatekeeper perhaps? Or maybe it was being used as a ticket office for the Clarence House tour. They'd said that was the reason they needed it back after all.

Clarence House was refurbished and then opened for public viewing when the royals are away, just like Buckingham Palace and other royal residences. Proceeds go to 'Royal Collection Trust'. Tickets for these tours are usually sold from a central ticket office, which, at the time of William's departure from his house included a wooden 'demountable' cabin erected outside Buckingham Palace on the edge of Green Park. And then it was taken down again at the end of the season.

I can't remember if they put up that ticket booth anymore now, do they? Maybe my little house might even be rented out privately, he thinks. If there was somebody living there, then he was definitely going to knock on the door and introduce himself and hopefully he would be shown around.

He thought about that funny little house that had been his home for so many years, when he'd eventually moved out of Clarence House where most of the other staff lived. It's been said, that when the Queen Mother came to inspect it when he first moved in, she glanced into the bathroom and declared,

"What fun, isn't it marvellous to be able to take a bath in The Mall. Do you know, I've always wanted to."

The bathroom was in line with the front door so it's lucky there was no letterbox! Passing tourists had no idea there was somebody living there but that didn't stop them knocking on the door. William was used to it.

It was totally open to the street then, anyone could walk up to it. Not now though so much, as a chain barrier can bar access to it. A set of gates has been installed at the north end of Stable Yard too.

He stared at it in the afternoon gloom. He remembered how he did so much entertaining in that little house, all his famous friends went there. Anyone he knew went there if they wanted a drink and a laugh.

On top of the normal quota of furniture anyone would have, the place was crammed full of his collections of gifts he'd been given by the royals and others, and the art he liked to collect, and a surprisingly extensive collection of royal programmes and tickets to royal gatherings and formal services etc.

Over the years William made it known that he liked the possible idea of his royal memorabilia collections going to The Royal Collection when he died. Only the possibility, he wasn't fixed on it. Amongst the hundreds of handwritten notes and letters from royals, and gifts and mementoes, he must have had an item to mark every royal occasion ever since he started in their service. In fact, it would be before that because he collected royal papers and magazines as a boy. In his collections was everything from a chair from the prince of wales investiture ceremony designed by Lord Snowdon, to Royal Opera House ballet programmes from the 1970s, to a silver and gold presentation box inscribed by Queen Elizabeth. Who knows what else he had, that could have been given completely privately?

There may have been conversations at some point between William and The Royal Collection about the possibility of making arrangements to take in his possessions. Perhaps they refused the offer, if there was an offer. Obviously this would have been upsetting for William, if this actually happened. Perhaps the curators felt that William's collections would sit incongruously with The 'Royal' Collection, as William was not royal, he was employed by a royal, so they may have felt showing William's collections alongside theirs would compromise its integrity. It would have to be considered how his collections would be presented, and more importantly how they would be represented and justified? They may have thought his link too tenuous and therefore not so relevant to the collection's ethos to be included in their archives, regardless of the longevity of his association with the royal family. I don't know about this, I can only speculate like anyone else.

William's old little house was a gate lodge, so it was situated right outside Clarence House on the pavement along The Mall, on the same piece of ground running along the side of Clarence House where everyone congregated to greet Queen Elizabeth on her birthday.

He wanted to walk out of Clarence House after tea with

the Prince and straight through one of the big black metal carriage gates leading out onto The Mall like he always did when he was Steward. There was a time he unlocked the gate himself with his own personal key and let himself in and out whenever he wished. A huge old key it was. Unfortunately, the police officer he asked told him that wasn't possible as it's only opened for royals or officials these days, and he didn't fancy walking through the pedestrian gate they made available to him, as that just wouldn't be the same. He remembered the looks he used to get from the public and tourists when he went through those big gates, and sometimes looks from the police. He could see they never expected him to let himself in, especially with that huge key and dressed in his full uniform garb. Sometimes he would skulk in like a fox and other times he would parade like a peacock, depending on his mood and the weather, and who was around. Other times he would come and go unnoticed without any fuss or concern, dressed in his everyday clothes.

He wishes it was like that now. He can't go anywhere these days without somebody making a fuss or making a lewd comment, he thinks.

The car drives him away from the front doors of Clarence House onto Stable Yard, and instead of going through the gates onto The Mall, it turns away from them going in the opposite direction. It then drives around the buildings, and eventually appears on The Mall for a short way, until it reaches near the front of William's old home.

"Pull up anywhere here please," says William to the driver.

"I can't stop here Mister Tallon. No vehicles allowed to stop along The Mall I'm afraid."

"Oh yes, I forgot," says William.

The driver thinks he just wants a quick glance at the lodge for a second or two before continuing straight on home to Kennington over the river. The car draws up off the main highway, on to the wide drive in front of the large metal gates. This is still on St. James's Park but the police have just seen the vehicle on their cameras drive around the block, so they know who it is. William thinks that only a minute ago he was on the other side of those gates. He looks up to Clarence House and thinks about all the times he spent in there over the years. It appears so different now, so quiet.

The driver unclips his seat belt, but before he can get out and open the rear passenger door William has already got out. He bows to the driver in appreciation and ambles towards the lodge. It's assumed that he wants to be alone, so the driver hangs about the car. A lurking policeman keeps a beady eye on them both.

William approaches his old lodge, surprised to see how dark it was sitting there under the plane trees of The Mall. They spanned both sides of the street like two neat lines of soldiers and provided shelter that seemed to give the lodge some privacy. It occurred to him that this particular scene would have looked the same a hundred years ago as the only thing to have changed would be the lamp posts changing from gas to electric. He thought it made his tenure of a couple of decades look paltry and he wondered if its previous residents over the years had loved it so much as he did. Maybe no one else had lived in it permanently he thinks, maybe it was just used as a place of work.

The lodge is a single storey rectangular shape built of brick. Nothing special at all. The west elevation has the entrance door and a stone window frame and a sealed off door. The south elevation facing The Mall and St. James's Park has three stone framed windows. It has a flat roof. Looking at it now, William thinks of how much of his heart he invested in it over the years. How he loved coming back to it and being in it with his friends, but looking at it today it looked, well, like any other building of its type. That's what I was trying to think about Clarence House earlier, he thinks, as he puts his finger on it, it's someone else's home now, it's just a building to me now, but still, he has to take a look, he thinks.

It looks dark and unoccupied. He goes up to the window next to the front door. He can't see in so he wipes the window with his glove and presses his face against the glass and peers in. The building is obviously empty and has been so for a long time. He can't believe it! This is the last thing he wanted to see. After all they had said!

"It's still empty!" he shrieks out loud involuntarily. "My little gate lodge. They haven't used it! So it hasn't been used since they asked me to leave?"

The sound of William's anguished cries brings his young chauffeur over to investigate.

"Is everything all right Mister Tallon?" he asks.

"Oh Paul I'm so sorry, I didn't know you were there, I'm just coming I won't be a moment. I'm so sorry, I don't want to get you into trouble."

"It's all right I've parked the car. The police are watching it for me. Are you looking at the place you used to live?"

"Yes. I hope you're not going to get into trouble for letting me out the car for a second. Did you tell them you work for the prince?"

"No no, it's fine, really, they know me, absolutely no problem whatsoever."

"Oh good, I thought you may be getting impatient with me."

"It's a bit dark in there. You won't be able to see anything. Would you like to borrow my torch?" asks Paul.

"No, thank you, I'd rather look at it from here."

"They say you should never go back?"

"I know but I couldn't resist taking a peek. I've been so intrigued all this time you see. This may be my one and only chance."

"Why don't you come back and see it in the daylight?"

"Oh I couldn't do that."

Paul is intrigued by this remark. Why couldn't he come back in daylight, he thinks. Was this the grand 'Backstairs Billy' he had heard of, thinking he was too good to mingle with the proles, perhaps?

"Have you ever thought of asking for a proper look inside, you know, officially?"

'No of course not."

"Why not?"

"Because if it got out I had an appointment to be shown around this place again it would cause a riot. There'd be photographers driving up and down The Mall on motorbikes and scooters day and night hoping to catch a glimpse of it."

"Really" Paul says laughing. He thought there was a joke coming up, he was waiting for the punchline.

"Yes. It would become a circus, can you imagine?"

Paul thinks it was William who was imagining. Perhaps the rumours were true and this Billy Tallon character thought he was more famous than the royal family.

"Really, is it really that bad?" asks Paul. "I never realised. Why?"

"Well you know what they're like. As soon as I step out of the door of my flat in Kennington I could be pounced upon by reporters and photographers, ever since Queen Elizabeth died. They follow me relentlessly along the streets, bombarding me with questions, they pursue me anywhere day and night taking photos of me putting out the rubbish or anything."

"Really, I didn't know that." Paul had never heard about this before.

"It's worse than that. They even sort through my rubbish at night while I'm asleep. What on earth are they expecting to find? It's a form of persecution. I went to the police, but they said they could do nothing as the reporters and photographers are just doing their jobs. So that includes humiliating me does it, I said to them. Me? An old man who just wants to remain loyal and peaceful and left alone. So you're telling me that harassment isn't harassment when it's being done by someone who works for a publication? Is that what you're saying? But they couldn't answer that properly, they wouldn't help."

"I see," says Paul, who understood now. William wasn't being paranoid after all. "So this is the only chance you've had to have a look is it, on your way home from tea with the prince?"

"The Prince has been so kind to me. I simply couldn't miss this opportunity of seeing my little house again, as no one knows I'm here you see. Even now they can poke their long lenses into my face. I never know when they may pop up. I feel violated. But I won't give in, especially not now, I'm determined. I just wanted to see this little place one more time."

Paul thinks it best to humour the old boy, as he seems a nice chap.

"Couldn't you have carried on living here then, when Queen Elizabeth died?"

"I thought about being a guide perhaps, but no. They discarded me like an old unwanted shoe. They said it was needed as a ticket office and gift shop for the Clarence House visitor centre. Everything is branded these days. Not me though, I'm not for sale. Then they said it couldn't be used after all, due to health and safety issues that would have to be addressed, whatever that's supposed to mean? So the real reason for it could be anything in that case?"

"I've never known it to be used for anything while I've been here," says Paul.

"That's a shame, as it would have made a wonderful ticket office, or I could have moved back in couldn't I?" says William, cheering up at the thought.

He likes Paul, this young chauffeur. Probably because Paul doesn't really have a clue who he is and only knows him vaguely through rumours and gossip. William likes this because it means they can meet on equal terms. It's nice to be able to walk along the street and not be stared at or prejudged. He also thinks he may be up for a laugh as he seems to have a sense of humour. He would like to see him laugh again, so he gives it a go.

"I say Paul, imagine if I had stayed here, I could have been one of those photo opportunities like you get at the end of the roller coaster rides in theme parks couldn't I? People could have had their photo taken with me as crowds of them were spewing out the gates at the end of the tour?"

Paul chuckles. He likes that. Reg would have laughed too, he thinks.

"Oh my God!" realises William, clasping both hands over his mouth in self-mockery.

"Perhaps that's what they were afraid of? Perhaps that's the reason they didn't want me to stay on?"

Paul chuckles again, he likes this guy. This is the first time they've met. Paul remembers seeing William on the television with Queen Elizabeth years ago. Shame they hadn't met before as he would have been fun to work with, he thinks.

"Well they missed a trick didn't they?" says William, becoming more serious. "As it seems to be all about money with them, it's not about people. I just wanted to end my days there, in that little house, but they didn't want me, so they got rid. Their loss. They wanted to remind me of who I am I suppose, the suits."

"Suits?"

"We called them the suits. The collection of faceless bureaucrats. The pen pushers. The movers and shakers. Da management."

"Oh, I know what you mean."

"Well, I already know who I am. I, am little Billy Tallon. I'm little Billy Tallon of The Mall, London, England," William says proudly.

Paul laughs again.

"It's true I am!" insists William, and he is being quite serious about it.

"So you belong here then."

"Well, do you know Paul, I think I do. Isn't it lovely to belong somewhere."

Paul says he agrees.

"So that's why I had to come back and have another look so I don't forget. I was here you see. All those years, I was here. But I'm a nobody now."

"Sorry, what do you mean?"

"I became a nobody when Queen Elizabeth died. That's what it says in the papers about me. It says I started life as a nobody, I got a job at Buckingham Palace and I pretended to be a somebody and now I'm back to being a proper nobody again. So why do they want to hound me and print pictures of a nobody?"

"Because you were associated with a famous person I suppose."

"But according to them I'm ordinary."

"Well Mister Tallon, you know what the papers are like. It's their job, it's what they do. They are just supplying a service as far as I can see."

"We can go to the zoo if we want to be entertained

by animals."

"Are you saying you never bought a newspaper?"

"Of course I have, for the news, but giving us a choice in what we read is part of their job responsibility surely. I want the news to read not a celebrity circus. The clue's in the name surely, newspaper?"

"Well you've got the choice not to read it."

"That's not the kind of choice I mean Paul. That's being pedantic. I want them to offer me a choice of interesting things to read, not some rubbish that they want me to read. There's a big difference."

"Well I don't see there's a lot you can do about it."

"I do."

"What's that then?"

"I want fifty percent."

"Fifty percent of what?"

"Of the money the photographers make selling pictures of me that appear in the press and on television."

"Why would they give you fifty percent?"

"Because they're using my identity to make money."

"Your identity?"

"Yes!"

"How?" asks Paul, puzzled.

"Our face is our identity. Our face is how humans present to the world, it's always been like that. Even now in this technological age in almost every country all over the world we still use an image of our faces on passports to identify each other, as it's the easiest and best way there is. Well, they want to take pictures of my face to sell on, so I want a cut, I want a percentage of the profit. If they are using my identity as a commodity to make money then I want them to pay me for it. My identity's a commodity just like anything else is these days, so when they sell my image it's business, money changing hands."

"So you want to be paid every time a picture of you is

published?"

"Yes."

Paul thinks that he's found a right old character here.

"How would that work then?"

"Very simple. When pictures of me are published I get paid, just like a model does. Without me there's no sale is there?"

"I can't see any editor agreeing to that?"

"Nobody's forcing them. They don't have to publish pictures of me. They can use something else."

"If that's what people want to see, they are going to print stories and pictures about daily life aren't they? It's public interest."

"Huh! modern term for witch-hunt you mean, like the Middle Ages."

"It's not like that," Paul laughs.

"Really? Well, if you make up a catchy expression, it's just another way of selling something. It's known as branding and marketing Paul. There's a whole billion-dollar industry built on it."

"I'm sure it's not like that Mister Tallon."

"Well forgive me Paul, but you would say that until it happens to you. It's scandalous the way these photographs are sold just for profit, so I want a percentage. That should stop them by putting a hole in their pockets. It's playing them at their own game, it's the first rule of business you see. If a product is worth something to someone, they'll pay to have it. Now, a photograph of me is worth something to these people, so when the owner sells it, they make money."

"So you want some of that money, you mean?" says Paul.

"Precisely."

"They'd get around that easily, by paying nothing

or a nominal fee for the pictures and paying the photographer a decent amount for doing something else, completely unconnected. That's what most big companies do now anyway."

"Well in that case I would want a flat fee publishing rate."

"A what?"

"The publication knows how many copies it sells in the shops, so I want a cut of that, because they're still using my image."

"Okay," Paul says, sniggering. "But people may not have bought the magazine to see you, it will have other pictures in it too."

"Then I would want a flat fee appearance fee. I've thought it all out Paul there's no way of getting around it. I'm going to beat them at their own game. Why should they use me and be allowed to get away scot-free, why?"

"Isn't that a rather simplistic view of the situation Mister Tallon?"

"There's no way getting around it for them. Everything is branded now. Nothing is free in this country absolutely nothing, and nothing is sacred, especially if it can be sold. Money is the new religion, it's the new God! Everything has been sold off while I was working for Queen Elizabeth. The fabric of this country is owned offshore these days. Everything has a value potentially, so everything is potentially for sale. Even natural things like water and gas are sold as a commodity."

"Yes, but those are things that are processed Mister Tallon."

"Yes, and that is exactly what they are doing with my identity when they take photos of me, because my image can be digitalised and emailed around the world. Because we have an electronic identity these days not a paper one, a digital one! Every single one of us has our own unique identity consisting of our date of birth, name, our National Insurance number, our credit rating, reference numbers on government documents and our D.N.A. And the world of newspapers and magazines only uses digital photographic images these days, digital. It's all been explained to me. A digital identity. Therefore, we all have our own unique personal digital commodity but our face is the key."

"But it only becomes a commodity if somebody else wants to use it. It's not something you could go out and try to flog in the marketplace," says Paul.

"Yes, I understand that but my point goes on from that. The point I'm making is that I still have a right to my privacy in the digital world now that technology is moving on. But because it has moved so much and so quickly, then that right of privacy should now be redefined and clarified in law," replies William.

"But if you start paying fifty percent for publishing pictures, what would happen when you publish a photo of a bank or a factory or a football ground or something?"

"I'm talking about humans! not a brick or a piece of metal. You can't hurt a building by taking a picture of it but you can hurt a human being, by chasing and hounding them while taking the photograph and humiliating them by publishing it! I know Paul because it's happening to me. That's why I'm proposing that if a photo of me or an image that alludes to me is published, that was taken in my private time, then that's using my private I.D. and so I want fifty percent of the sale or a fee."

"Well who gets the money for all these celebrity pictures taken at the moment?"

"I'm not talking about celebrity pictures as they are publicity shots, those people want to be photographed to promote a television show or a pop record, or promote themselves. I'm specifically talking about people who'd rather not have their image published, ordinary private citizens, which is what I'm supposed to be according to the papers, a nobody."

"So what's the situation at the moment then?" Paul enquires.

"Well, whoever owns the copyright of a photograph can sell it for whatever price they can get. The person who took the photograph legally owns the copyright, or if they were employed to take it by somebody. And do you know what Paul, if a photograph of me or The Queen or a celebrity or whomever gets sold, then we don't get a penny. Ever. Because we don't own the copyright even though it's our face on the picture."

"Right!" says Paul. "So, you're just talking about private time pictures not official pictures."

"Yes," says William. "Now we get to celebrity photos, they are a cut above the rest because they can change hands for serious money. Think of Princess Diana. Well, I'm proposing that any pictures taken in private could not be published without the subject's permission or without paying them a fee."

"But nobody could police that. There must be hundreds of pictures of you with the royals."

"I'm not talking about those, I'm talking about the ones of me off duty in my own private time. I'm talking about the one of me putting my rubbish bags out wearing my dressing gown. And one of me eating fish and chips on a bench. And one of me dropping my washing off at the launderette. The one of me nipping to the corner shop for milk before I've had a shave or combed my hair. The picture of me lying drunk in the street."

"I saw that one in the papers!" exclaims Paul. "Nice shirt you were wearing by the way. And you must admit

Mister Tallon, lying drunk in the street could be classed under the banner of committing a crime," he says.

William glares at him with a look that says, "How very dare you," crossed with "what the hell are you talking about?"

"Of being drunk and disorderly I mean?" Paul explains, feeling a little chastised from William's stare.

"It's still in my own time!" shrieks William. "If these pictures are so interesting, then why don't they take the same pictures of other ordinary people doing ordinary things? Somebody from Stirling or Swansea or Southampton?"

"Because that doesn't sell."

"Why not Paul? Let's say, there's a man who goes into a pub in Stirling or Swansea or Southampton and he comes out and falls down in the street. Why don't we see a photo of that plastered across the country?"

"Because the public aren't interested in that."

"So why are they interested when it's me in the picture?"

"Because you are notorious."

"For what Paul?"

Paul feels like he may be drifting out of his depth.

"For being who you are."

"They don't know who I am. I'm nobody according to the press, a lowly flunky. So why are they paying for pictures of a nobody lying in the street?"

"Because of who you worked for," says Paul.

"Exactly! Thank you! my point exactly, I've proved the point, we've come full circle, despite the fact that nobody wanted to concede that my identity belongs to me. The reason they take pictures of me doing everyday things is because my identity sells, thank you! So it is a commodity, just like I said. Anyway, talking about criminals for a second, why do we think we have the

303

right to literally own a person once they've done a crime and to not respect their privacy. Isn't that what the human rights act is for?"

"I don't really think so no."

William disregards Paul's opinion, he's on a roll. He's had a hundred conversations on this topic over the years since the Queen Mother died and had begun to think he was going insane with it, as no one seemed to sympathise or understand, or even care. They don't seem to realise the injury caused that has to be nursed for the rest of your life.

Paul comes across to William as an intelligent young man, and he wants to confide in him.

"And I'm retired now. I've never spoken to the press, never divulged any private details, regardless if I knew any or not and I've never given an interview. I made it clear I never intended to do so in the future either. Ever. I've been true to my word, so why can't they leave me alone? Why don't they believe what I say? Why do they think I'd want to talk to them for money just because other people have?"

"Because they think if they pressure you, then you'll change your mind."

"Aah, you mean if they hang on long enough I will snap and tell them everything, and they'll pay me a fortune. But most importantly and most chillingly, they will have made a larger fortune."

"I suppose so."

"Well they know I won't comment I keep saying it, so why won't they believe me?"

"Well, I suppose Mister Tallon, if you never talk to them they are going to piece together whatever sketchy material they have about you, and if the result isn't quite the truth then well, you can't blame them for that. It's public interest. They want to be entertained I suppose, it's the media."

"And I suppose the public wants this do they? This

so-called public interest, that only seems to exist for one purpose alone, to justify press intrusion and harassment into people's lives?"

"I guess?"

"No I'm sorry Paul, you've got that wrong like everybody else. They say it's public interest when they really mean it's IN the public interest, which is a completely different thing that sounds the same, but it's not that at all. They've got their wires crossed. Like saying the words health and safety and then that's the beginning and end of the conversation. The public interest does not necessarily mean what the public may be interested in, no. It means what's for the common good of the public as a whole. For the good of the public. In the public interest, you see. But some of the press use the misquoted slogan as an excuse to pry into people's lives. There's a law to protect the public interest, but how can there be a law stating that anything the public are interested in about somebody's private life must be freely published in the papers and on television, because that's unreasonable and quite absurd? Yet that's what's happening in effect today because people don't understand and misquote the phrase. People are getting the two expressions mixed up by aping what's written in the headlines. They keep saying the press are doing it for the public interest when they should say, the press are doing it IN the public interest, and so they think the law allows them to publish whatever the public wants. The word interest is confusing the issue. They should use the word good instead, and say the press are doing it for the public good."

"Okay," says Paul.

"And the papers should forget about sensational stories and pictures. That's what all the soap operas on television do with their stupid crazy weird plot lines with bodies under the patio every week, and everyone knows that's not real. So why does the press try to muscle in on their patch?"

"Sorry, I don't know what you're trying to say."

"I'm saying, indiscreet pictures that appear in the press of private citizens causes real misery and pain because it's happening to real people. Not to an actor or a model on television. It's real life."

"Yes but the public can tell the difference between what's real and what's make believe."

"That makes it worse! That means they must enjoy seeing pictures of people in the papers in embarrassing and compromising positions, even people suffering, because they keep buying the papers to see it. That's voyeurism, that's depravity, that's inhumane and sick. That's all apart from the disgusting images readily available to everyone on the internet, which has no restrictions whatsoever in this country even a child can access it all. And digital television is not much better either. The world's gone crazy. Mary Whitehouse gave us the nine o'clock watershed and without that this country would be totally sunk. Why must we be spoon-fed all this filth? It's porn for the masses! The only reason it's so available is because it sells advertising and makes money, that's why! If the press make boring claims about people and celebrities then nobody would buy their publications. The media has to sensationalise stories to entice you to buy their papers and magazines, because if you don't buy them you won't see any of the advertising inside or be exposed to the editor's or owner's opinions, and most of all they won't make any money which is the reason they exist. Nobody cares about me and people like me who they chase for a story, we are their raw materials I know that, I'm not stupid. But that doesn't stop us getting hurt. My life may not matter to anyone else but it matters to me and my loved ones, that's the point, so I am not prepared to be used by them at the expense of that. People are stupid if they believe everything they read in the papers."

"It's just the way it is today," says Paul, "it's just the culture. I don't think people are entertained just by seeing pictures in the papers. It's just something to go along with the words and it's entertaining, celebrities and everything."

"You know what it is Paul don't you?" William answers his own question: "It's envy!"

"Oh, Mister Tallon, how can it be envy?"

"Because this country has changed. People don't want leaders any more, even though no one person can have all the answers. People want to please themselves, but most people are only able to do that by inadvertently becoming a consumer clone. Now it's dog-eat-dog, a case of you've got something I'd like, I want it, or I don't want you to have it. Otherwise why won't they let me be? Why do people judge each other all the time and get jealous about what others are doing? Why don't we all get on with our own lives?"

Paul shakes his head and shrugs his shoulders as if to say, "I dunno?"

"It seems to me," continues William, "that the majority of people in this country look at their fellow man through a telescope. Most people don't even know who lives next door. They seem to only want what they envy. Things they can buy but can't afford but they buy them anyway. Makes me wonder where all this self-entitlement comes from? They don't know or care what privacy is anymore. The concept of privacy has been dropped in favour of narcissism, and there it crops up again; envy!"

"It must be the same the world over these days I think."

"Really? Do you think so? I don't think so Paul. I don't think it's this bad in France. I know somebody who's got a house there. Most people have a clear notion of what privacy is but it seems unregarded in this country. And they would not want their private business exposed solely for the entertainment of others because that's what it boils down to."

"I don't think people think like that."

"Really? You try telling that to the people parked outside my front door then when you drive me home, because I guarantee there will be somebody there and they are not waiting for an autograph I assure you."

William pauses and contemplates for a second. "You know, I have a very clever friend and we met at a party the other day. We were talking about this and he said, that it seems to him our social values are melting away under the searing glare of uncontrolled commercialism. And I tend to agree with him," he says with a sigh.

Paul offers no response to this idea.

"You should go and see the world Paul. Take every opportunity you can to see it in your job. It's not like here."

Paul nods and smiles, thinking it would be nice to travel with the Prince if possible.

"Oh sod it," snaps William.

"Pardon?" says Paul sniggering.

"I'm going to have the last laugh."

"What are you talking about?"

But William isn't listening. He is too engrossed with a plan unfurling in his head.

"Sod it, sod it, sod it, sod it, sod it, sod it, sod it, sod it, sod it!" he yells, and immediately clamps both hands over his mouth, embarrassed for having swore, like little children do as if it would make the words turn around and they could push them back in.

"Wha ... what's the matter?" giggles Paul.

Suddenly a vision in black silently appears from the side like a hulking ship emerging from the fog. A slim tall policeman at least six foot four. He casts a formidable presence.

"Good evening gentlemen," he says in a confident manner. "Does anything seem be the matter?" Which William took as a euphemism for: 'What are you clowns up to? don't you know I'm responsible for the security of this place and I've got better things to do than waste my time with you two quite frankly?"

The suddenness of the policeman's appearance startles Paul and William so much that they freeze on the spot. William still clamps both hands over his mouth so the only visible indicative facial expression are his eyes darting about surveying the scene. They stand there on the pavement like two little boys caught red-handed attempting to climb over a private wall.

"Good evening officer," says Paul eventually. "My name's Paul Murphy and I work at Clarence House. I'm a driver," as he shows his security pass. He thought this was going to be a mundane ten minute drive of a journey taking Mister Tallon home but it was turning out to be an experience. "I'm driving Mister Tallon, who's just having a look at where his used to live at this gate lodge."

All this time William covers his mouth to suppress his giggles.

"I think you may have to move your car in the next few minutes Paul as they want to open the gate," says the policeman.

"That's my fault officer I'm so sorry," says William. "We'll be gone in a minute. I'm just having a last look."

"Very good sir," says the policeman. And he was gone.

William suddenly becomes very quiet. He says

nothing but just closes up his winter coat collar around his scarf and over his chin. He stands silently gazing into the early evening dusk across The Mall as the taxis and cars shuttle past. There's not much traffic tonight unusually.

"Paul? Can I ask you a question?"

Paul answers instinctively saying,

"Yes of course."

"How much money do you think they'd pay me if I told them everything? I mean, tell them the whole lot?"

"I've no idea. Why?"

"I'm going to tell them everything."

Paul is alerted to a threat now. William's behaviour triggers a horror in the back of his mind.

"Do you think that's wise Mister Tallon, we should really be going now," he says.

"Mister Tallon? Call me William!"

"William," echoes Paul.

"Two million? One million? We don't want to be greedy. Five hundred thousand? That's still a lot of money."

Paul says nothing. He doesn't understand what William is talking about. He seems to be having the conversation with himself anyway.

"I should do it here shouldn't I, on the pavement outside my little house?"

Paul wonders if he should wave his hands to the security cameras so the police can see he needs help. But then again, he thinks, help with what exactly? William is still mumbling away.

"This is where I would have lived if I had stayed on so I would have come out my front door and stood about here I suppose, to make my speech."

He seems to be positioning himself whilst imagining how he would arrange and conduct a news conference outside the gate lodge.

"Is that enough or shall we go for the two million?"

"William," says Paul, very concerned now, "we should go now, come on, I'll take you home."

"Oh I don't want to go there. Why would I want to go there? I much prefer it here and anyway, I'm about to give a speech! The press are on their way."

"No they're not William come on, this is a bad idea, come on now get in the car."

"But I'm going to ask for two million!"

Paul tries to lead him away back towards the car. He thinks William must have mixed his pills or something.

"But I'm doing this for you," says William.

"Me, why?"

"So that you can have the money silly. You can tell them if you want, you can tell them what I've said and you can collect the money when I'm gone."

"But I don't want the money," says Paul. "Come on now please." He places both his hands on William's arm to try to gently lead him away.

William shrieks with laughter when he sees Paul's genuine concern. "Ha ha ha, oh goodness me, you didn't think I was being serious did you? I'm only pretending, I haven't gone mad quite yet!" and he shrieks and giggles uncontrollably.

Paul is considerably relieved but moreover, incredibly intrigued now. What is this guy all about? he thinks.

William stops laughing and calms down and wipes the tears from his eyes.

"Oh dear," he says, "I'm so sorry I thought you realised. I must explain. I was just imagining of how it would be if I told the press everything. I would have got them here and done it in front of my old house to achieve the best impact. I'm not actually going to call them."

"Oh, I see," says Paul, even more relieved now.

"But I'm still going to say I want two million," says William.

Paul looks horrified. He's not sure if he even wants to hear this. This could jeopardise his job, he thinks, if he gets involved in anything like this even as an innocent witness. He panics as he thinks William is serious after all. It crosses his mind that it may just be William being decidedly camp, as he overheard someone describe him as recently. He wasn't sure how to deal with such a situation. He wonders if he shouldn't just bundle him away in the car before anybody sees him make a fool of himself, but he is a guest of the Prince of Wales. He can't go around taking decisions to push people around and manhandle them like that, that's ridiculous. What should he do? he thinks, I hope the police are watching this on their cameras, in case I have to testify to a psychiatrist about it or something. He keeps watching.

"Serious face!" William says, pointing his finger towards Paul.

Paul's shoulders relax and drop when he realises William is still joking and playing about.

"You mustn't take me seriously dear boy. Nobody else does."

By having this conversation William has just tested Paul about going to the press for money and he has passed with flying colours without realising a thing. William has been looking for someone like Paul for a long time. It's not true that everyone will sell out to the press. William has found someone he can trust to help him out with his plan. He begins to dance his ballet swirls that he is so fond of doing. The ones like he did in the hall of Clarence House while waiting for Queen Elizabeth to come down in the lift for lunch. This time there is no music playing on the garden room record player, but it doesn't matter as he carries on perfectly well without any. He kicks a heel up here and swirls

312

his arms and hands through the air there, twisting and turning, entranced in a dream.

He tames his movements slightly whilst asking Paul something.

"Are you married Paul?"

"Married? he replies laughing, "yes I am married."

"Of course you are. Stupid question." And William carries on for a second then starts to accompany himself by humming the music.

Is this unusual or is he like this all the time? Paul thinks. Or is he mad, or is he just bonkers and a load of fun and a good laugh? Maybe that's why the Queen Mother liked him? Maybe he's all these things? Paul is chuckling his head off at William's performance now. He thinks that he may have missed his vocation of being a travelling one-man-band street entertainer.

William eventually comes to a halt.

"I do wish there were some reporters with long lenses here now though. Guess what I'd tell them Paul?"

"Well I can guess, but you don't come across as being that rude."

"No, silly," says William flapping his hands and enjoying the banter. "I don't mean that. Now, come on, I'm being serious. Now, do you know what I would tell all those marvellous journalistic people who you so admire?"

"No, go on, tell me William. What would you tell them?"

"Well, I would contact the news agencies all over the globe, and invite thousands of reporters and photographers and there would be at least a hundred news vans parked all down The Mall and in the royal parks, and news helicopters flying everywhere just like when it was one of Queen Elizabeth's birthdays."

Paul raises his eyebrows and grins.

"Well, we didn't get helicopters fair enough, I grant you, but I would have helicopters, because you know what I would tell everyone?"

"No," says Paul shaking his head, laughing.

"I would stand here with my arms out like this," William opens his arms out like the Pope embracing a massed congregation, "and I would invite each and every one of them with open arms to listen to what I have to say. Hold on, wait a second."

He breaks off from his train of thought as he's just remembered something. He rummages in his overcoat pockets and takes out a mobile phone.

"Look Paul, I borrowed a mobile phone. Well you probably know already of course but, as well as being a phone and everything, it's also a camera which I think is amazing don't you?"

He shows it to Paul, who doesn't look much impressed by it.

"Yeah, it's not the best model is it?" says Paul.

"It's my friend Nadia's, she's a nurse, well it's her daughter's phone actually. They live over the road from me on the top floor. Anyway, what I'm trying to say is that Nadia has filmed these people rifling through my bins at night and generally hanging around waiting for me. She got their faces and their car registration numbers and everything."

"Yeah, and so?" asks Paul, who can't see the significance of this yet.

"And so, I have evidence of their crime and a record of their identity as insurance for the future, just in case. And all I had to do to thank her was to give her some expensive perfume out of one of my party goody bags, but she can have as many goody bags as she wants now of course. Now hold on a second while I do this."

William switches on the phone and sets it up to take a picture. He seems quite comfortable and conversant with it, as Nadia's daughter has demonstrated how to work it. He hands the phone over to Paul.

"It's all ready, so just point it at me because I'm going to say my bit to the press now."

"Say-what?" asks Paul, who looks bewildered.

"Now come along Paul concentrate, you must pay attention to what I'm going to say. Come on, humour me?"

If Jason happened to be here to hear that remark, he would faint on the spot. It would probably also be the very first and last time he ever heard that particular expression from William because he would probably die from shock. William only ever played to a captive audience.

(Or is this just being cruel?

Er, no, I don't think so.)

"William, what's going on, what are you doing?" asks Paul who seems totally confused.

"Now Paul, take some shots of me standing here in front of my little house but get as much background in as you can. I want it to look obvious I'm standing here next to my little lodge in front of Clarence House."

Paul does this. He can't decide which way up to frame the picture, as he turns the camera from portrait to landscape aspect. He takes a few pictures of William.

Then William takes back the phone. He then rummages in his overcoat pockets again and takes out a Sony handycam video camera, a tubular shaped device no larger than a can of Coke. It is all ready to go, as he has inserted a brand new memory card and clicked-in a fully-charged battery the way Nadia showed him. He flips open the viewing screen from the side, turns it on

315

and adjusts the zoom in order to frame the shot to his liking.

"What are you doing, what's that for?" asks Paul.

"I'm recording a message for perpetuity, for the digital age. It will be my legacy. Come on, point the camera, I've set it up, just film me now."

Paul does as he's told and takes the handycam and points it towards William, holding it securely with two hands.

William turns away from Paul to gather his thoughts. He looks like an actor embracing his lines before he goes on stage. He stands for a second taking a suitably theatrical pause and a deep breath. He then turns his head to check on Paul behind him.

"You are filming aren't you? Don't worry, just keep filming 'til I say stop."

He turns around to face Paul and the camera, and begins his speech. He seems perfectly relaxed and at ease with the situation as he's been planning to do this for some time. It was important he did it outside the gate lodge and with somebody he trusted, and he met that person today in Paul. William makes the speech as if he was a professional actor filming a commercial on location and has been saying the same words over and over in retakes for the eleventh time. He acts so business-like, as though it was his everyday job. The words simply trip off his tongue and are delivered with the utmost confidence. He begins his speech to camera.

"Now, people of the press," he says, "you all know me I'm William Tallon. I want you to know that I would have told you everything, but you didn't offer me enough money. I would have signed a contract with you to tell you everything I know. To answer any questions and all the questions you asked me. To answer fully and to not leave out a single detail. All the secrets I've been keeping, everything anybody ever wanted to know, I would have told you everything. But I would have insisted on drawing up watertight contracts in advance to protect me from any

316

interference from anyone or anything after my revelations, and not a penny returned. No refunds available. The most important thing for me was to be left alone for the few years I had left to live my life. You would have payed me two million pounds, clearing in the bank first, and you would buy a house for me outright, in France, as I would have had to leave the country afterwards and stay there until I died. That would be the deal. I would have signed all the story rights over to you. I would have done photo shoots and publicity for you for a week before I told you anything, all my expenses and lavish entertainment paid for by you. I would have insisted on wearing a nice designer shirt for the book cover and had my hair styled at Vidal Sassoon." William is agitated with Paul for not keeping the camera steady, so he breaks off from his speech for a moment.

"Do concentrate please Paul, I won't be much longer now."

Paul is finding this experience quite moving. He's never met anyone like William before let alone being involved in such a revelation as this. He feels nervous now as he's not sure if this is genuine or not. It certainly feels genuine. The knowledge that the police are keeping an eye on them through the security cameras was reassuring a few minutes ago but that idea has entirely cleared from his head now. It's just himself and William making this film. William isn't nervous at all, he seems to be enjoying his speech. He appears totally in control and the master director of this little epic they are producing on Nadia's daughter's handycam. Paul spreads his feet farther apart now to get a better stance for standing still while holding the camera in the right position. His heart is racing with excitement and his hands are shaking so he tries his best to keep it steady.

William continues.

"What I'm trying to say to you is that you could have taken publicity shots of me dressed up in a sequinned jockstrap and spurs dancing on roller skates on top of a grand piano if you wanted to, as long as I was wearing some ballet tights as I have good legs for my age you know. Anyway, you'll probably realise by now I'm having the last laugh on you. Because, there are no secrets, I have no secrets to divulge. I have nothing to report. Nothing outrageous anyway, so move along now please as there's nothing to see here. And so you would have wasted your money. I don't know what outrageous atrocities you were hoping me to reveal, as there can be nothing worse than the damage and embarrassment you've already done to the royal family in the past. I take it you were expecting me to produce something heinous and sensational in order to top your running record and ratings? Goodness knows what that could be. I could have done this without blame, but I chose not to, even though it would have harmed no one. If it had happened, then there could have been no repercussions as I didn't trick anyone. You asked me what I knew and I told you, that was the deal. I did nothing illegal, I was innocent. I told the truth because you payed me to tell the truth. It's not my fault if it wasn't the truth you'd hoped for, but then you never asked about the good things, you only ever wanted to know the bad things. That was your mistake. I would have given the money to charity and my estate would have given you back the house on my death, as that's all I wanted, to live in peace in my retirement. But you took that away from me. I would have only taken from you what you took away from me.

And now I would like to add a postscript. Version two of my digital epitaph.

Everything I just said was a complete lie! A complete fabrication. I happen to know things worth much more than two million pounds. I know things that would make your hair curl. How could I work for this family all those years and not know anything, but it's too late now because I'm dead. And you'll never know either way, will you? So how does that make you feel that you missed out? I meant what I said. I am not for sale. Now you can choose which one of these speeches is the truth; not that you're interested or even capable of recognising the truth. All you're interested in is peddling a version of the truth to make you money. Either way I kept my word, I didn't sell out. I am not sold. In the end you got nothing. You chased me for nothing. You hounded Diana for nothing, well, you may have sold more advertising space and got a few sports cars and private schools out of it, but if that's all you wanted, well, good luck in the next world. The point is I said nothing. I kept my word. You might say that I lost, but you'll never know because I could be lying either way. I may still have a treasure trove of secrets to divulge and that must make you sick because you only ever did anything for money! Either way you lost in the end because I kept my word."

He finishes his speech and walks over to Paul, who's a little shell-shocked.

"Right Paul, I'll give the camera back to Nadia and she'll get her daughter to put it through their computer and transfer it to a DVD and give me back the memory card as well, and that will be my contribution to the digital age, for perpetuity."

Paul is in mild shock. His mouth is half open. He can't quite believe what he just witnessed and indeed what he was just involved in. A look of admiration and awe has come over his face as he looks at William who's taking the camera from him.

"That was bloody amazing!"

"Well sometimes Paul, you've just got to show

319

them how it's done. There are still people in this world who actually mean what they say. Oh no!"

He suddenly realises something.

"We've got one more to do Paul, one more!" and he hands back the camera and takes up his position again. "Press record again Paul, would you mind? Press record dear boy, thank you so much. Now this one is for me."

He walks back to the same spot and he gets straight back into actor mode, it's like he was born to it. He readies himself. Paul just goes with the flow.

Paul holds the camera steady again while recording William standing there. William closes his eyes and bows his head for a few seconds collecting his thoughts. He raises it again to reveal a very solemn look on his face, and commences his speech in a very sincere manner looking straight into camera.

"This is what I always wanted to say, and all I was ever going to say, if anyone had ever asked me properly. This is not a confession, or an obituary or an epitaph. It's just a declaration in the simplest terms, regardless of where I was born or where I moved to, whether it was Newcastle or Coventry. I'm a simple man, despite appearances. I like to make people laugh and be happy, and I like a bit of glamour and style. Who doesn't? The most important thing in the world to me are the people I absolutely love the most. My mother, my father, and my Reg. They made me who I am. I'm glad I'm me. I'm just little Billy Tallon. I'm just being honest, I'm being who I am. Didn't somebody say once, you should be yourself as there's no other expert in that field? Well this is me. I came to live on this London street fifty years ago, and I stayed here all that time apart from going to do my National Service. But I came straight back. I've been here since, all through my working life and all through most of my natural life. And this has been my home, I loved it, it was wonderful! I just wanted to see my little house and this street again one more time, so I don't forget. I was here you see, I was here. All that time. Nobody can change it, and nothing can take that away from me despite whatever happens now. I was here. And I won't forget. And I am so grateful, I really am. So there it is."

It seems William has finished his speech but he carries on.

"But I have to say, it's all been amazing, working for Queen Elizabeth all those years."

He closes his eyes as the tears well up and begin to fall down his cheeks. He is so happy and relieved to be saying these words out loud at last and he hopes one day the whole world will be able to hear them, because they are the only words that mean anything to him. The only words that explain everything. The only words to express the joy in his heart for the life he has had, and he wished the world was able to hear so he says the words again.

"It was absolutely amazing. Working and living here with Queen Elizabeth, ab-solute-ly amazing. I'm so grateful. I have no other way of expressing it more clearly, other than to say the words, it, was, am-a-zing!" (He glances up at Paul at this point as if to reiterate the expression just for him.) "My dear, I can't tell you? Absolutely amazing."

He looks up to the sky and smiles. He elongates these last few words as though he wants to make them last forever:

"It, was, ab-solute-ly, am-a-zing!"

He clasps his hands together as if in prayer and draws them to his chest. The tears are running down his cheeks. He bows his head until his chin touches his fingertips. He shuts his eyes and a huge smile beams across his face through the salty taste of his tears.

He doesn't open them again until Paul approaches

him to wrap the scarf back around his neck that has become loose. The same bright red scarf that has become a sort of unfortunate trademark look of his these days, as it makes him look a bit like Rupert the Bear. Not that there's anything wrong with Rupert, he's lovely. But William is a man in his sixties. Paul pulls William's coat together at the front as the temperature is getting lower.

"Come along William sir, it's getting cold."

Paul raises a protective shielding arm about William's shoulders and escorts him back to the car.

"Will you drive me home now please Paul? I need to get changed quickly and go to a party, but I want to be one of the first to arrive."

"Why?" asks Paul.

"Why do you think? Because if I don't like the look of it, I can leave and go to another one."

They continue walking back towards the car. Paul is staring at William, trying to work him out.

"Don't look at me like that!" says William. "I don't feel sorry for myself! Well, I did, but not any more. Why should I? Why should any of us feel sorry for ourselves. What's life all about if we can't have a laugh?"

Paul says nothing. William said it all. They continue walking.

"I had a few bottles of champagne saved up but we drank it all. And the whisky ran out. I think I had something to do with that. It doesn't grow on trees you know."

They reach the car and Paul opens the rear passenger door for William to get in but he gets in the front instead as he doesn't want to be chauffeured alone in the back. They drive to William's flat in Kennington and the car pulls up near the front door. Nadia sees them arrive as she's looking out from her window. Paul plays back the films on the camera while they are sitting in the car and they watch them together then Paul hands it back. Paul escorts William to his door and they say their goodbyes. When William is about to close his street door, and knowing it would probably be the last time he would ever see Paul he says,

"It was amazing Paul. It truly was!"

And then he closes the door and Paul drives away.

He gets changed quickly and takes a taxi to the party, well, the first party of the night, probably, who knows?

Jason is trying to dodge across the busy road through the noisy traffic at the top of St. James's Street in Piccadilly. He's heading towards the cheese shop in Jermyn Street for the last call on his little shopping spree in London. He remembers what Reg said once about this job giving you expensive tastes, and Reg was right, he thinks. He has his quality bath oil, his chocolates, his food from Selfridge's and some clothes, all packaged up in big posh paper bags he is carrying. He can buy all these items online these days, but he likes the experience of going into a traditional shop, especially in London. Above the hum and drone of the taxis going by, he hears a familiar voice.

"Taxi! Taxi!" calls Sir Alastair, waving his arm in the air at the passing taxis, trying in vain to find an available one. He is smartly dressed and carrying a small leather overnight suitcase.

Jason looks down the hill a little way and sees Sir Alastair having difficulty hailing a cab. He is wearing a grey suit, black tie, a stiff white collar over a blue and white narrow striped shirt, and black shiny shoes. He looks as smart and crisp as ever he did. In fact, he's still wearing the same outfit he was wearing earlier in the day when he attended William's funeral at the Queen's Chapel, Marlborough Road, St. James's which is just around the corner from where they are now. Jason went to the funeral also, that's why he's in London now shopping, getting in some treats before he catches the train back to the West Country. He too, is wearing his same outfit of course, as the funeral was only hours ago. Jason has taken the opportunity of doing some shopping in a few posh shops he likes, as he hardly ever comes to London any more. He lives in the country these days. He walks down the road a little way and approaches Sir Alastair.

"Hello Sir Alastair?" he says.

"Hello there Jason!" replies Sir Alastair, turning around to speak. He puts down the suitcase on the pavement to shake hands, "I'm glad we bumped into each other again. I'm sorry I didn't have time to talk to you properly at the funeral. There were so many people to see, the day has flown by."

"That's all right sir. I know you must have been busy," says Jason, who's glad to have bumped into him again as they hardly spoke to each other earlier on and Jason wants a word.

"I came up from the country today but I'm staying at my daughter's this evening so I'm on my way to Paddington to catch a train. Wasn't it a lovely service?"

"Yes, it was," says Jason, as he thinks about the coincidence that he too, is catching his train from Paddington, but not until later tonight.

"I didn't know William knew so many different people," says Sir Alastair.

"Yes, it was good to see some old faces again and some famous ones," says Jason, meaning William's actor friends. Lord Snowdon was there too. There were a lot of people attending, the chapel was full.

"Yes, it's amazing how they fitted everybody into the chapel. Wasn't it interesting music and the singing was beautiful, the opera singer had such a lovely voice."

"Yes she did, and the readings were good. I especially liked the way Derek Jacobi did his. He got William off to a tee didn't he?" says Jason.

[It was as though William was in the room at times. Very spooky]

"I know. Did you go to the restaurant after the service with the others?"

325

(William was true to his word and a group of mourners headed off to Joe Allen for a meal.)

"Yes sir, there was a whole bunch of us. Apparently William left some wishes of how the service should be, he planned a lot of it himself."

"Yes, the whole thing was very well organised I thought, it was all done beautifully. William would have loved the whole thing. Very William!"

Jason is surprised at the way he said 'William' as if said with great admiration. This was totally unexpected from Sir Alastair, so threw him for a second. Sir Alastair must have admired William after all, he thinks, and Jason racked his brain to think of a time when Sir Alastair had ever praised William apart from saying 'well done'. That didn't mean that he never praised him, just because Jason didn't hear it for himself, but he was trying to think anyway.

"Er yes, yes it was, wasn't it?" Jason thinks he must be coming across a bit dim the way he is stuttering but he is still thinking about that comment.

Sir Alastair looks at the shopping bags.

"You've taken the opportunity of doing some London shopping I see?"

"Yes, and some things for work that I can't get where we are. It's funny being back in London as some of the shops change hands so quickly that I hardly recognise some places."

"Ah! but St. James's doesn't alter that much! At least we can rely on that," says Sir Alastair. "So where did you say you are working now?"

"In a country house in Devon, not far from Exeter. I work for a financier and his family."

"Not that far away from me then, a lovely part of the country? So, do you not come up to London much?"

"Not really no, only to get certain things from Liberty or Selfridges or somewhere, or to see a show occasionally."

"So did you see much of William since you left Clarence House?"

"No," says Jason. "I wrote to him a couple of times but he didn't reply. He sent his regards through a mutual actor friend though. The last time I saw him was at one of those Golden Jubilee concerts at Buckingham Palace. I was chatting to him quite happily with some others having a drink, and suddenly he got fed up and turned on me and said that I'd have to move on now as I was blocking the queue for the toilets."

"Oh. And were you?"

"No Sir. We were standing in the middle of the lawn. It was just a euphemism."

"Oh I see. How sad!"

"I think it's quite funny actually, it makes me laugh. Well it does now, when you see it for what it is. That was the last thing he ever said to me. Of all the things he could have said, but that was William for you. William would have liked that. That would make him laugh."

[When someone you know dies it's only natural to think of the last thing they said to you. The last time I ever met William I had walked away from him at that concert thinking I didn't have to put with all that nonsense any more thankfully, because we didn't work together any longer because Queen Elizabeth had gone. I was a bit miffed when I came to think of his last comment to me but then realised it was quite funny really. And you can't hate somebody who makes you laugh, (unless you happen to be an ogre or something,) especially when they make you laugh when they're dead]

"Yes, I rather think it would. I felt so sorry for him after Queen Elizabeth died. He seemed to go completely off the rails at times, got into some dreadful scrapes."

"I know. I heard about it. And all because of drink," Jason says, and he knows what he is talking about.

"Yes. I don't think he quite knew what to do with himself once he left Clarence House. He seemed quite lost. Working there must have been his whole world! It's as if he didn't hold any expectations for anything else in life?"

Jason thinks Sir Alastair can't realise that working there was William's whole life and his dream. It was everything to him. He thinks Sir Alastair can't see this because William's line of work was something Sir Alastair would never choose for himself, or rather, would never have to choose for himself because Sir Alastair had been given vast choices in his life through his circumstances and education. His career prospects were more easily laid out for him and they would never have included anything that was remotely considered to be menial work such as William did. Not everyone has the same choices or chances in life, but they can still progress and excel beyond their circumstances despite that if they want, and are able.

"Oh, but I think he made the most of what he had you know," says Jason. "And he must have exceeded his expectations in life, beyond belief, but I think it must have broken his heart not to have been there at the last, as I think he expected to be."

"Oh, I don't want to rake up all that again Jason, it's all over now. I'm afraid William was a victim of being William as well you know. Anyhow, it just wasn't appropriate for him to be at Royal Lodge as there were already enough people there taking care of Her Majesty. It was the same old story, he was his own worst enemy. All of us get it wrong at some point Jason so we must remember the good things he did. Everything is forgiven in death. He had a good life making his own little kingdom on The Mall, looking after Queen Elizabeth for all those years. We must remember him for that."

"I suppose so," says Jason reluctantly, but he isn't convinced. He doesn't want to argue with Sir Alastair about it now anyway. There's no point, it's too late, so he thinks he'd better reconcile the matter in his head by agreeing to disagree.

"He probably wanted it to go on forever," he says. "I think I did too. I wished someone would have told him to get on with life though, maybe he should have gone to France? You can't keep yourself to yourself, life's for sharing. You must admit he certainly had a good time, and so did we, sometimes, he made us laugh. Not always, but, you know?"

"Yes indeed," says Sir Alastair, who knew what he meant.

(It was reported William cut up his uniforms and threw them in the bin when Queen Elizabeth died, out of the indignity of being banished, snubbed and rejected by the royal family. We may be speculating too far. He did cut up and throw away his battledress uniforms it's true [I saw them in the bin] but there are no reports and no evidence of him destroying his dress uniforms. The papers just mentioned his uniforms they didn't specify which ones, so one could only assume it meant them all. So if he was so indignant why didn't he destroy his dress uniforms and his medals too, as they represented the same occupation? He may have cut up his battledress because he hated the sight of them so much, having had to wear the same unflattering uniform for fifty years and much preferred his black tailcoat uniform with starched shirt and wing collar. There was no evidence of him disposing of them. The battledress was smart and practical but the dress tailcoat uniform was elegant, dressy and certainly more impressive. It was more appropriate for the image of a royal page. Whatever the reasons were, it was his own private

329

business. In the end his personal property was disposed of in line with his wishes. So that should be respected unreservedly.

When William died, the majority of his collections went to auction, including his medals. He may have preferred the value of his medals and collections to be transformed into cash for somebody he knew, which would benefit them more than the items being stuck in a museum, where people would undoubtedly have to pay to see them if they were ever exhibited. They were his private property after all.)

"I hear you're writing a book about Queen Elizabeth?" asks Sir Alastair, expertly changing the subject.

"No sir, it's about William."

"Really? That's interesting. Am I in it?"

"No, but there is a character in it with remarkable similarities to yourself, which is purely coincidental of course!" says Jason.

"Of course! Whatever gave you the idea of doing something like that?"

"I don't know really. To prevent the hype from people who weren't even there I suppose. I wanted it to end with a flourish and not the sudden jolt that we had. It deserved a better ending in my view, so I've given it one."

"And what do you think you will do with the book?"

"I don't know Sir Alastair as I haven't finished it yet, as it's proving quite difficult to cram everything in and to remember everything."

"I must say I never expected anything like this from you."

"You mean because I'm not very bright and I don't have much initiative?"

"I'm sure you could do absolutely anything that you put your mind to Jason."

"No Sir Alastair, you don't understand. Those were the very words you used to describe me, when you gave a verbal

330

reference to a job agency when I was leaving Clarence House. You said that I wasn't the sparkiest employee nor the dullest either, amongst other things."

Jason quoted back Sir Alastair's reference to him word for word, something about not having much initiative but following orders obediently. Jason thought it made him sound like a pet dog. He'd seen a transcription of it left in the office of the house where he worked as a butler. It was Jason's employment file from the agency

"Oh Jason I must have given dozens of references back then as you can imagine, so I must have streamlined my answers somewhat. And of course, it's always wise to underplay your hand in these situations so that your prospective employers don't expect too much, and will be terribly impressed when they come to realise how capable and efficient you turn out to be."

"That's the kind of answer I expect from a politician on the television. It doesn't matter anyway, because if there's only one thing I've learned, it's that even if people don't expect me to do anything worthwhile with my life, that shouldn't mean to say that I never will. I know that now."

Sir Alastair feels a bit awkward now as this is the only conversation they've ever had on level terms because they are not employee and supervisor any longer, so Jason can say what he likes. It must also be the longest conversation they've had without any complaining going on, especially from Jason's side.

"Quite, quite! Well it all sounds very interesting your book and I wish you all the best, well done!" says Sir Alastair, who should get a move on now if he wants to catch his train.

"Oh, here's a taxi now."

Sir Alastair hails it down.

"I must be off I'm afraid," he says as he picks up

his suitcase and then shakes Jason's hand. "Good to see you again Jason. I must say you look very smart!"

"Thank you Sir Alastair." Jason thinks this a great compliment coming from Sir A. and hopes he means it.

Jason had always liked Sir Alastair from the first day he met him for his interview, even though he thought he was a bit snooty at first, but over the years Jason got to know that Sir Alastair's job was quite a juggling act having to please everyone he was responsible for. Sir Alastair had always been the perfect gentleman as far as Jason was concerned.

"It was good to see you again too," says Jason.

Sir Alastair waves and then puts his overnight suitcase into the back of the taxi and gets in.

"Goodbye, take care of yourself," he says, then closes the door. The taxi pulls away joining the traffic. Jason waves and walks towards Jermyn Street as the taxi passes him going up the hill towards Piccadilly. It comes to a halt in traffic not far ahead and Sir Alastair leans out and shouts from the open window.

"Oh Jason, by the way. I hope that this book character of yours who's like me coincidentally, is going to be a decent cricketer? In a purely coincidental way of course?"

"Oh, don't worry Sir Alastair. I think; that he already is," shouts back Jason.

"I'm jolly glad to hear it," shouts Sir Alastair with a smile. "Cheerio!"

"Goodbye!" calls Jason and he waves as the taxi starts to move again up the road. He can see Sir Alastair looking out at him with his arm raised in salute. The taxi falls into a gap in a line of traffic leading around the corner, past The Ritz and along Piccadilly on its way towards Paddington Station. Jason never mentioned to Sir Alastair that he was also catching a train from Paddington, as he knew he'd be offered a lift, and he didn't want that. He wanted to stay in London a while longer before going back to home and work. He'll catch a late train. He tries to visit London when he can, which is very rarely these days. Even so, the pull of the bright lights and the big city, the same ones that William knew, with all the promises those illusions present, will not let him go.

The End.

Epilogue

The explosive Daily Mirror story in 2003 by undercover reporter Ryan Parry who secured a footman job at Buckingham Palace using false credentials, certainly did the country a service by revealing the shameful security lapse concerning job applications to the royal household. However, he did make some people look foolish. They trusted him and befriended him in good faith. After the event, people he worked with said there was something odd about him; but that could be said about anyone. The fact remains that Ryan was able to easily secure a job within palace walls regardless of the embarrassment he caused to fellow workers. Perhaps though, he should have stopped before taking and publishing photographs of The Queen's breakfast table, because that was morphing embarrassment into bad taste.

WILLIAM TALLON

Even when it was over, it wasn't really over for William because they wouldn't let him be. They wanted something from him and thought they could pay him for it or buy him out at any price. But what for exactly? What for? To sell more advertising? Is the human spirit so disposable it can be used for that purpose?

Everybody has their price, so they say. No they don't. It doesn't take a genius to know that. It doesn't take a great scientist to prove it to us, or a stately inspirational political leader to tell us in a great speech, or a superhuman athlete, or a great warrior. Not even a celebrity. It takes an ordinary man from Coventry. Someone who didn't sell out. Who kept his word. Who proved it. William proved it.

Queen Elizabeth had many staff who stayed for life, this was not remarkable. William was an ordinary man with big ideas and he went after the job he longed for and he got it. He worked for one of the most famous people in the world, in a unique situation. William took on an unusual job that had a plain profile, and Queen Elizabeth afforded him the freedom to embellish it with his sense of flair and style making it his own. All things considered he did well for himself, nevertheless he had to work for it.

It must be difficult for somebody to know when their loyalty starts to become detrimental to the person they serve. In William's case it must have been impossible to work out if ever he made that mistake.

For a start, trying to define what loyalty means is a tricky business. It means different things to people because all domestic service jobs are basically similar in their nature, but every one of them will have individual requirements that make it quite different compared to the next job. No two of them can be exactly the same or taken for granted.

You could say that loyalty is putting your employer's needs and interest first at the expense of your own life. Or you could measure loyalty by the amount of years in the job. In William's case it was both.

In William's case it would have been difficult to decide to adapt or change what he did for Queen Elizabeth because he had worked for her for so long. Perhaps such a thought never crossed his mind. William had worked fifty years for Queen Elizabeth, but he was not with her for the last few weeks of her life. Towards the end, at Sandringham, he may have let his sense of timing slip, or he may have missed a message on his pager. He may have misjudged the situation somehow by deciding there was no need to change. Or perhaps he didn't show up one time when he was needed, and that was the one time it counted, and the last straw; who knows? Maybe the course of events that transpired happened naturally and so it made absolutely no difference what he did or didn't do?

In any case he must have known he couldn't blame anyone other than himself for his playful antics, but hopefully he also knew his capability for mischief and laughter and the notoriety surrounding him could never be erased, and from the adulation to the agony, he would probably love to do the whole thing all over again! I think.

Would I love to do it again? Perhaps, for the laughs, if we knew what to except next time. And it was a great experience, and he could make us laugh. And what would life be without that?

By Royal Appointment

Range Rovers, Land Rovers, Rolls-Royces, Sports cars, and cars in general. Rifles, guns. Barbour waxed jackets. Gentlemen's shoes from Jermyn Street. Saddles, horse tack, leather goods, riding clothes. Silver goods, jewellery, medals, locks, safes and vaults. Enamels. Fine carpets and fine wooden floors. Metal objects in general. Fine china for palaces all over the world, fine glass, too; still being used today. Even in Georgian times there were, shoe buckles, fancy buttons, jewellery, snuff boxes, Japanning goods, specialist locks etc.

All these quality items are favoured and loved by royalty and discerning people all over the world.

Range Rovers from Solihull. Land Rovers from Coventry. Rolls-Royces from Derby. Aston Martins from Warwick. Cars and components from Coventry. Rifles, guns, silver, jewellery, medals and insignia from Birmingham. Shoes from Northampton. Saddles, horse tack and leather goods from Walsall. Riding clothes from Market Harborough. Locks from Willenhall. Safes from Wolverhampton. Enamels from Bilston. Pens from Lichfield. Fine carpets from Kidderminster. Fine wooden floors from Norwell. Fine china from Stoke on Trent. Fine glass from Stourbridge, and so many other products and skills in engineering and manufacturing spread all over the same region. And the gates of Buckingham Palace were made in Bromsgrove.

They were all made or are still made in small towns in The Midlands including Coventry. So many other Warrant Holders and companies exist. This part of the country is a rich vein of manufacturing and engineering and creativity. Output declined in the 1980s but that's another story (or is it this one essentially?). So I never understood the way the press and media attempted to disparage somebody because they came from Coventry? Oh, and The Queen's handbags are made in Walsall, too, and Barbour waxed jackets are made in South Shields next to Newcastle, where William was born.

PRIVACY

It is interesting to delve into the possible reasons how we regard privacy today.

Privacy is a value of human dignity and self-respect. Taking into account variations in Western and Eastern culture, everyone in the world would want to be treated with privacy and respect and not humiliated. There is also privacy related to our private business, our money and family life etc. If we lose our comprehension of what privacy means, then how can we protect ourselves in the future in the next phase of the new digital world?

The situation is becoming worse as we are seeing the rise of anonymity and the decline and the degrading of personal privacy. Personal privacy is vital for our wellbeing and too precious to lose, but at the moment it seems to be obscured by the overwhelming desire to consume as much as possible.

Our privacy in relation to the state is gone for good due to the digital age. There's no retrieving it. 'The future is now' was such a prophetic notion that it now belongs to the past. However, we are still in a position to manage our privacy on a day-to-day level in how we interact with each other going about our daily lives, but the law needs to catch up. Only recently a new law was created against 'Revenge Porn', which nobody could have imagined in the past, so who knows what may happen in the future if we carry on the way we are?

We can not ask for privacy to be reinstated to us because we never owned it, as it was always a respect given to us from others. It was based on trust. However, we can give ourselves the right to request or even demand that respect in the future. We should not pander to peer pressure or a prevalent opinion to surrender our identities to powerful corporations anymore. They can still operate their services through the use of advertisers. They don't necessarily need to process extensive information about their customers. The requests for personal data bases to be accessed and used in perpetuum should stop now. It's not like giving away sweets. We are talking about unique confidential parts of our identities as human beings on this planet!

PRIVACY AND THE PRESS AND THE MEDIA

Anyone who appears in the headlines is there for your entertainment as far as I'm concerned. This is the way things have gone. Their identity is affected or soiled for life after it. They may not deserve that. If you want to live in a society where you demand the right to invade someone's privacy, then you have to agree to possibly sacrificing your own. If you consider this to be no big deal, then think of the millions over the world who wish to remain anonymous on social media, including in the UK and especially including the internet trolls and even contributors to restaurant review websites. People on the internet like to hide behind a username. Privacy must be of great value to them, or rather, anonymity must be of great value to them. Privacy is not the same thing as anonymity. Privacy has more nuance to it. It is far more sophisticated than anonymity.

Stalking became a crime in the UK in 2012. Stalking may be reasonably regarded as an intention to cause sexual or physical abuse. However, on the UK Government's CPS website (November 2017) it lists 'Stalking' and 'Harassment' together.

It says;
'Although harassment is not specifically defined in section 7(2) of the PHA, it can include repeated attempts to impose unwanted communications and contact upon a victim in a manner that could be expected to cause distress or fear in any reasonable person.'

It goes on to say,
'There must be evidence to prove the conduct was targeted at an individual, was calculated to alarm or cause him/her distress, and was oppressive and unreasonable.'

And,
'Harassment of an individual can also occur when a person is harassing others connected with the individual, knowing that this behaviour will affect their victim as well as the other people that the person appears to be targeting their actions towards. This is known as 'stalking by proxy'. Family members, friends and employees of the victim may be subjected to this.'

Now there is no suggestion that the people working in the press and in the media are purposely setting out to cause any kind of harassment or distress. But I think it should be recognised that sometimes their overzealous enthusiasm may run away with them, so it may appear to be the case. It may be the case that they inadvertently cause distress in the wake of their attempts to take a photo or ask questions.

Well, nobody can claim to be unaware of people's feelings because being responsible adults, they can tell if they're not wanted, or they should know if they're doing wrong, because their intelligence should tell them that. And responsible investigators should take into account that what 'the public are interested in' (confusing it with public interest) should not be used as an excuse for a catalyst for uncivilised behaviour to be able to victimise people in order to obtain some copy or a picture.

Who set up these publications to be the arbiters of our morals anyway? Any Jonny or Jenny can pick up a camera and call themselves a photojournalist and work for the tabloids, and the opinion polls and forecasters in the UK have got it so very wrong of late.

There seems to be a confusion here about the difference between what 'the public are interested in' and 'the public interest' because the latter can be interpreted as for the common good of the people or society whereas the other one is attempting to satisfy an apparent insatiable appetite for consumerism or anything outrageous or salacious or sleazy that can be splashed across the headlines, generating interest and revenue to publishers. Anything, it seems is acceptable to counteract the everyday news, with some publications.

Well, news is the business they are in so they should focus on it. And a perpetual supply of consumer and salacious material is available to anyone, man, woman or child with access to an internet connection, if that's what the public 'wants'.

The press can't create jobs for the masses unfortunately, but it can operate here freely and use its privileged position to do something useful and relevant and positive to life. And if they feel the need to entertain us then they should do so with some imagination but not with their calling card of shocking vulgarity that some of them seem to favour.

That is if they really do see themselves as a guardian of the nation's morals. Or is this a fantasy? Anyway, this is what the press should be doing in my opinion, as well as genuine investigations of course, but not witch-hunts or feeding frenzies or salaciousness. Not just always gnawing on the same piece of tabloid chewing gum all the time and causing unnecessary embarrassment, alarm and distress to innocent private individuals and off duty artistes and royals who are all entitled to a private life.

THE PRESS AND THE MEDIA

All over the country now there are local papers given away to commuters at railway and bus stations and in supermarkets. They usually have a couple of headlines in them and some advertising, but they mainly contain a property section advertising property for sale for estate agents and developers. People pick them up because they are free and glance at them during their journey but throw them in the rubbish once skimmed through. It seems pointless to produce them and pointless to create all that unnecessary recycling and landfill. There is no doubt that people like to pick up a newspaper. It has a material, tangible feel to it. It can be good company, informative, entertaining, but only if it contains quality copy.

In the UK we are lucky in that we have some television news programmes and newspapers who excel in investigative journalism. This is what you would expect from a free society with a free press. However, some of them do tend to feed off each other and follow one another like sheep concentrating on the same stories and just repeat what's on the other channels. And sometimes they follow an incredible story for days, then completely drop it suddenly but don't go back to inform us what's happening with it. The story is still happening, but we don't get to learn what happens next unless we research it ourselves on foreign websites. The same few programmes can not cover every story of course, so why don't they share things out so we get more depth and content?

So, if the press is to continue to be a regular visitor into our daily lives then it would be rather impolite of some of them to keep arriving rather empty handed. The reporting of news is almost instantaneous now because the process is digital, so they've lost the monopoly of it and become somewhat redundant in that respect. The impact of a news release hardly registers these days due to the ubiquitous 24hr feeds on digital media, therefore the expectancy of a morning scoop has vanished. The monopoly of being first with the news may have gone, but the need for accurate original journalism remains.

When businesses come under threat of closure or being forced out the market, they have to diversify in order to survive. When they do, it elevates the expectations of their customers and their market. Yet as far as I can see, most of the press don't specialise in anything representing the duty of a free press. They are trying to be either sensational or elitist, which turns out to make them appear tacky or supercilious.

I don't think that all the press are engaging enough with pertinent useful objectives that could impact and enhance ordinary people's lives. I know that a traditional newspaper has to generate revenue in order to survive and I realise they have to juggle their act to provide news and another attraction these days, and some local newspapers do very well as they serve a great purpose in their communities. But why don't the big nationals consolidate their position by broadening their horizons and focus more on constructive pursuits for the public. Surely a free press should be dynamic and inspirational? They are perfectly placed in a position to become this country's main campaigners and lobbyists as well as continuing with professional investigative journalism, but they seem to want to entertain more than inform us. It seems that they are all so entrenched in their opinions, too, so that no single one of them has their finger on the pulse of the population and vital issues of this country.

They could launch numerous campaigns such as; to encourage everyone in this country to vote every time and discover what that's all about? Because some people who voted in the EU Referendum in 2016 had never voted before and probably won't ever vote again. It is probable that their lack of interest only reflects the lack of due diligence and abstinence of the government to keep its country's housekeeping duties in order.

And another campaign to modernise the voting system by bringing it into the digital world; not relying on paper voting cards to unverified identities. It should include MP voting in the voting lobbies after all, they should be there to represent the interests of their constituents (who got them there) and the country, nobody else. Bringing these procedures up to date will save time.

How about a new design and purpose for the whimsical Victorian building of the Houses of Parliament before it returns from an exorbitantly expensive five, or seven year overhaul? A circular design for the debate chamber would be a good start instead of the opposition pits we have at the moment, with MPs unceremoniously shouting down each other and wasting valuable time. This worked in Winston Churchill's time, but this style is so naff now, boring, even crass, so let it go for goodness sake.

And one to create laws to invoke parental control at least on internet connections, and one preventing the appearance of any violence or knives or guns on television trailers before the Broadcasting Watershed?

Or a serious genuine definitive campaign to rationalise packaging to reduce landfill and pollution and the need for recycling?

And a campaign to organise and modernise councils to co-operate with the Civil Service, and streamline procurement and operations in order to save money and reduce Council Tax. And to repair society by bringing back desperately needed social housing, that should be protected under covenants perhaps, but never sold off again?

Or, how to properly tax large companies that trade in the UK?

What about bringing in a brand new form of National Service, creating an opportunity and a second chance for young people who don't go to university and people in danger of street crime and drugs? It could also work for other young people by broadening their horizons and expectations of life. It could result in an achievement for them to show potential employers. It could also save some of the money that's pumped into dealing with social problems today.

How about campaigning for regular knife and gun

amnesties?

How about investigating why there are no routine sniffer dog checks for illicit substances on private aircraft and in diplomatic baggage?

These are just a few suggestions, and they may not be the most attractive subjects, yet they are all part of our society and they need urgent attention.

Ultimately the fundamental idea of a free press is of course a good idea, in my opinion, but they won't deserve much respect if they are selling out to advertisers and politicians and celebrity.

I don't want clickbait or fake news, and I don't want to be told what WILL be the news tomorrow in a pre-packaged published product. I don't want distorted information or a biased view reported to me, I want professional responsible journalism.

<u>HYPE</u>

Since the 1980s the surge of designer labels and brands have coincided with the media and the press and politicians pushing forward a consumer lifestyle, in a combined force of hype. This has transformed the culture in this country. It's no surprise then, that today some people in the UK find it puzzling how to demonstrate their patriotism, but are more predisposed to demonstrate their loyalty to a brand, which is made so easy due to the advertising exposure and hype in the media and press, and to some extent, to politicians.

We all look to the media and press and politics for guidance in life, but unfortunately the media and press and politics in this country is so tribal and competitive, pugnacious even, in the pursuit of money that this bad influence on us seems to have ruined our respect for each other as a nation. Politicians especially, seem to like to espouse the idea that you can judge your success in life by what you own, and judge your quality of life by how much you spend. Well, we can't all be millionaires. Most people find it difficult to acquire a decent job and affordable housing. There are people who will slog their guts out for years and will never succeed in the sense that they will never become wealthy. Hard work is no guarantee of success, so the rhetoric spouted from certain politicians in the UK is ignorant rubbish, and the fast buck era seems to have been driven all the way over the years by politicians and the press and the media. The press playing second fiddle to politics, and the media watching on, giggling.

You don't necessarily have to judge quality of life by how much money you have, and you don't have to be exactly the same as some others to be considered successful as being the same doesn't make you a better or lesser person. There's a lot to be said for making an honest living with assurance and contentment, but there needs to be a space for it to reside in society again, and in our heads, away from all the advertisements.

A DIGITAL MARKETPLACE

People say don't worry about it as our personal information is already out there, we don't own it so what's the difference?

The interpretation of ownership of identity in that point of view is very telling. It infers that personal information is a commodity but also not that important. Yet the same indifference doesn't apply to parts of our body, as just by touching somebody can be classed as assault (in the UK). Our identity amounts to a bunch of information it's true, and if you laid out in a line all the composite pieces of information about someone it wouldn't amount to that person, because they are made of flesh and blood and their own life history, and they are also unique. So in that respect it's not that important. It only becomes so when an identity is compromised, misappropriated, defrauded, sold on, blackmailed or destroyed. All these are possible through a digital marketplace, and we can't get another I.D. as a replacement in normal circumstances.

The point is, that privacy is the most important issue in this whole argument. It's a human concern, regardless of who has the right to sell something in a digital marketplace. Still, it's like turning us from humans into machines if we are expected to pool our identity details. We seem to have become so obsessed with making money that we are losing our sense of respect.

It seems we have all duped ourselves with an overwhelming appetite for digital electronic devices, and privacy got lost somewhere on the way. We are already in danger of losing a reasonable point of view about privacy and natural respect for each other, so now, we should step back from the onslaught of digital technology and try to control our fascination with it.

What we need to do now is to separate the privacy we need from the data we can release. It looks like the future generation may have to have an official government I.D. they are born with also a public one, and to respect each others' privacy as much as they can.

Above all, the issue of privacy today needs to be defined in law, or rather, to define the privacy that we are allowed to have. We certainly need to protect ourselves if we are to salvage the last vestiges of privacy available to us, otherwise there will be no privacy left at all. It will cease to exist.

It's a shame we had to learn the hard way, but perhaps in the future people will come to realise that privacy for everyone is something to cherish, after all.

Maybe we won't need a law or any regulation for that to happen, maybe we'll make the adjustment for ourselves? Perhaps we'll manage to forge a code of privacy and respect using social media!

I'm sure there will be new fun apps and wonderful new social media inventions in the future that are fresh and useful, that won't insist on full disclosure of our cache of personal details or attempt to try to exploit or manipulate us. I have faith in people everywhere, so I hope so.

QUEEN ELIZABETH

In portraying Queen Elizabeth in the way they did, the papers and media must have forgotten who she was. Her life spanned across decades, across the whole century in fact. An unusual accomplishment in itself. It spanned through wars and subsequent world changes of national borders being redrawn, regime changes, including a radical social change in the UK with the creation of the National Health Service and Nationalisation. It spanned across changing times, reoccurring shifts of style and changing facets of fashion all through the decades. All this time she was in the public eye.

It could be said then, that the press and media saw her as being from another era, so they misunderstood who she was. This is most likely the case because tastes and styles always clash. It starts with fashion. The tastes and cultures of past times clash against new hyped up styles of emerging tastes of the young, so the impact is distorted out of true proportion.

The young, with their new waves of style and humour seem to resent the virtue of the past for being outdated or of its time. Yet the new wave only exists as a contrast to the past. The young generation never knows this, and the bright young things always disregard the past with prejudice. That's why people always fail to learn much from the past. That could be why they misunderstood who she was, only because she was unfamiliar and they didn't know her, but ironically, she had always been there.

<u>William's Privacy</u>

William was treated as a commodity. He was hounded for money, not for his amusing anecdotes or interesting stories. Of course, there have been others like him too. I don't think that 'we are the product', but merely part of the rapacious process to sell us stuff. The trading of our personal details is small fry compared to the purchases we make as the buying public. All of it comes down to money in the end, but as mentioned before, profit like this comes with collateral damage to someone's life.

It's time now that the idea of regarding people as a commodity on a spreadsheet needs to be dismantled somewhat.

FOOTNOTE

QUEEN ELIZABETH MEMORIAL

There is a bronze statue of Queen Elizabeth by
Philip Jackson along The Mall.

It is situated in a lovely secluded spot between The Mall and
Carlton Gardens in central London. It stands next to the
statue of George VI.
The architectural setting was redesigned by co-architects
Donald Buttress and Donald Insall. The reconfigured
memorial includes remodelling of the walls, steps and
terraces designed in 1954 as a setting for William McMillan's
bronze memorial statue of King George VI. The bronze
reliefs by Paul Day show the royal family in London, during
World War II and episodes from the life of the Queen
Mother.

It was unveiled by The Queen in 2009.

REGRET

It's weird how our emotions live in the same house. In our heads.
The ones I'm thinking of here are regret, anger, kindness, laughter and love.

Regret or anger must be the worst emotions we can feel, as they can cut all ways and they are strong and sharp.
Regret for something that we said or did to somebody, or for not helping them when we could.
Regret that somebody did something to us.
Regret for the way we live our life and not say sorry.

Kindness, laughter and love must be the best.
Kindness and laughter can be shared contiguously; they are great.

Love, in the way it manifests itself in a myriad of ways, and still survives despite everything, must be the most important.
Especially love, love must be the best; if you are lucky enough to find it or experience it.

Please don't waste another minute of your life thinking of anger and regret.
Concentrate on the others and you'll be doing all right.

Made in the USA
Las Vegas, NV
15 May 2021

23091949R00215